Understanding MySQL Internals

Other resources from O'Reilly

Related titles
The Art of SQL
Database in Depth
High Performance MySQL
Learning MySQL
Learning SQL
MySQL Cookbook™
MySQL Stored Procedure
   Programming

Optimizing Oracle
   Performance
The Relational Database
   Dictionary
SQL Cookbook™
SQL Tuning
Understanding the Linux
   Kernel

oreilly.com
oreilly.com is more than a complete catalog of O'Reilly books. You'll also find links to news, events, articles, weblogs, sample chapters, and code examples.

oreillynet.com is the essential portal for developers interested in open and emerging technologies, including new platforms, programming languages, and operating systems.

Conferences
O'Reilly brings diverse innovators together to nurture the ideas that spark revolutionary industries. We specialize in documenting the latest tools and systems, translating the innovator's knowledge into useful skills for those in the trenches. Visit *conferences.oreilly.com* for our upcoming events.

Safari Bookshelf (*safari.oreilly.com*) is the premier online reference library for programmers and IT professionals. Conduct searches across more than 1,000 books. Subscribers can zero in on answers to time-critical questions in a matter of seconds. Read the books on your Bookshelf from cover to cover or simply flip to the page you need. Try it today for free.

Understanding MySQL
Internals

Sasha Pachev

O'REILLY®

Beijing · Cambridge · Farnham · Köln · Paris · Sebastopol · Taipei · Tokyo

Understanding MySQL Internals
by Sasha Pachev

Copyright © 2007 O'Reilly Media, Inc. All rights reserved.
Printed in the United States of America.

Published by O'Reilly Media, Inc., 1005 Gravenstein Highway North, Sebastopol, CA 95472.

O'Reilly books may be purchased for educational, business, or sales promotional use. Online editions are also available for most titles (*safari.oreilly.com*). For more information, contact our corporate/institutional sales department: (800) 998-9938 or *corporate@oreilly.com*.

Editor: Andy Oram
Production Editor: Rachel Monaghan
Copyeditor: Derek Di Matteo
Proofreader: Rachel Monaghan

Indexer: Johnna VanHoose Dinse
Cover Designer: Karen Montgomery
Interior Designer: David Futato
Illustrators: Robert Romano and Jessamyn Read

Printing History:

April 2007:   First Edition.

 This book uses RepKover™, a durable and flexible lay-flat binding.

ISBN-10: 0-596-00957-7
ISBN-13: 978-0-596-00957-1
[C]

This book is dedicated to my wife, Sarah, and my children Benjamin, Jennifer, Julia, Joseph, and Jacob.

Table of Contents

Preface

In the summer of 2003, somebody on the MySQL mailing list proposed a book about MySQL internals. As I read the email, I realized that I had the background to write such a book, but I had just finished writing my first book and was not looking forward to writing another. I tried to talk myself out of the responsibility, saying to myself nobody would ever publish a book so technical and specialized. There simply would not be enough of an audience for it.

Then I thought of *Understanding the Linux Kernel* and *Linux Device Drivers* by O'Reilly. That took away my excuse. I realized the door was open and I was standing in the doorway, but my inertia was keeping something good from happening. I thought about a passage in the Book of Mormon that says "a natural man is an enemy to God," and the principle behind it. If you drift along, seeking only the pleasure of the moment and staying safely within your natural comfort zone, you do not accomplish much. Good things happen when you push yourself outside of your comfort zone, doing what is difficult but what you know deep inside is the right thing to do. I wrote an email with a proposal to O'Reilly.

Interestingly enough, my editor happened to be Andy Oram, who also participated in the publication of *Understanding the Linux Kernel* and *Linux Device Drivers*. He and I worked together on this book, and I appreciate his help very much. I felt that his strengths very well compensated for my weaknesses.

The book presented a number of challenges. Writing about the internals of an application means approaching it as a developer rather than just a user or an administrator. It requires a deeper level of understanding. Although I had worked on the MySQL source code extensively, I found myself doing a lot of research to figure out the gory details of algorithms, the purposes of functions and classes, the reasons for certain decisions, and other matters relevant to this book. In addition, as I was writing the book, MySQL developers were writing new code. It was not easy to keep up. And while the book was being written, I had to do other work to feed my growing family. Fortunately, a good portion of that work involved projects that dealt with MySQL internals, allowing me to stay on top of the game.

Nevertheless, the challenges were worth it. Growth comes through challenges, and I feel it did for me in this process. Now that I have finished the book, I have a better view of the design of MySQL as a whole, and a better knowledge of its dark and not so dark parts. It is my hope that the reader will experience a similar growth.

How This Book Is Organized

Chapter 1, *MySQL History and Architecture*
Introduces the major modules in the source code and their purpose.

Chapter 2, *Nuts and Bolts of Working with the MySQL Source Code*
Tells you how to download the source code and build a server from scratch.

Chapter 3, *Core Classes, Structures, Variables, and APIs*
Lists the basic data structures, functions, and macros you need for later reference.

Chapter 4, *Client/Server Communication*
Lays out the formats of the data sent between client and server, and the main functions that perform the communication.

Chapter 5, *Configuration Variables*
Discusses how MySQL handles configuration in general, as well as the effects of many particular configuration variables, and shows you a framework for adding a new configuration variable.

Chapter 6, *Thread-Based Request Handling*
Explains MySQL's reasons for using threads and the main variables, such as locks, related to threads.

Chapter 7, *The Storage Engine Interface*
Describes the relation of individual storage engines (formerly known as table types) to the MySQL core, and shows you a framework for adding a new storage engine.

Chapter 8, *Concurrent Access and Locking*
Explains the different types of locks available in MySQL, and how each storage engine uses locks.

Chapter 9, *Parser and Optimizer*
Explains the major activities that go into optimizing queries.

Chapter 10, *Storage Engines*
Briefly describes the most important MySQL storage engines and some of the tree structures and other data structures they employ.

Chapter 11, *Transactions*
Lists the main issues required to support transactions, and uses InnoDB to illustrate the typical architecture used to provide that support.

Chapter 12, *Replication*
Gives on overview of replication with an emphasis on issues of implementation.

Who This Book Is For

This book can be useful for a number of readers: a developer trying to extend MySQL in some way; a DBA or database application programmer interested in how exactly MySQL runs his queries; a computer science student learning about database kernel development; a developer looking for ideas while working on a product that requires extensive database functionality that he must implement himself; a closed-source database developer wondering how in the world MySQL runs its queries so fast; a random, curious computer geek who has used MySQL some and wonders what is inside; and, of course, anybody who wants to look smart by having a book on MySQL internals displayed on his shelf.

Although MySQL source is open in the sense of being publicly available, it is in essence closed to you if you do not understand it. It may be intimidating to look at several hundred thousand lines of code written by gifted programmers that elegantly and efficiently solves difficult problems one line at a time. To understand the code, you will need a measure of the inspiration and perspiration of those who created it. Hopefully, this book can provide enough guidance to remove those barriers and to open the source of MySQL for you.

I do not believe it is possible to understand and appreciate MySQL strictly through a conceptual discussion. On a high conceptual level MySQL is very simple. It does not implement many revolutionary ideas. It sticks to the basics. Why is it so popular then? Why do we know enough about it for O'Reilly to be willing to publish a book on its internals?

The reason, in my opinion, is that what makes a good database is not so much the concepts behind it, but how well they are implemented. It is important to be conceptually sound on a basic level, but a good portion of the genius is in implementing those concepts in a way that provides a reasonable combination of good performance and the ease of maintenance. In other words, the devil is in the details, and MySQL developers have done a great job of taking that devil by the horns and twisting his head off.

Thus, in order to appreciate the inner workings of MySQL, you need to get close to the places where that devil is being subdued. Somewhere in the dark depths of the optimizer or inside the B-tree, there is music to be heard as you study the code. It will take some work to hear that music, but once you do, you can feel its beauty. And to hear the music you must not be afraid to compile the code, add a few debugging messages to help you understand the flow, and perhaps even change a few things to appreciate what will make the server crash (and how) if you fail to handle something that turns out to be important after all.

The first chapter provides a brief introduction of how different components of MySQL work together. Immediately afterward you will find a chapter about downloading and building MySQL from the source. You will have a much more meaningful experience studying MySQL internals if you follow the steps in it to get set up with a working, compilable copy of the code that you can change and test at your pleasure.

When approaching a new code base, I find it very useful to look at class/structure definitions and API call prototypes. I have a confession to make: I first look at the code, then read the comments, and I never look at block diagrams unless somebody asks me to. Chapter 3 is for the developers whose heads are wired like mine; it talks about the core server classes, structures, and API.

In Chapter 4 I talk about the communication protocol between the client and the server. Afterward, I hope you will say: "I am thankful for the MySQL API, and I even have a clue of how to fix it up if I had to!"

Chapter 5 discusses server configuration variables. Configuration variables are the controls of the server. Every one of them tells you about some special server capability or perhaps a problem some DBA had to solve at some point. It would not be too much of an exaggeration to say that if you understand the variables, you understand the server. Toward the end you will find a tutorial on how to add your own configuration variables.

Every server has to deal with the issue of how to handle multiple clients concurrently. MySQL does it using threads. Understanding threads and how they are used in MySQL is critical to being effective in working with MySQL source. Thus, Chapter 6 discusses thread-based request handling.

One of the distinct features of the MySQL architecture is its ability to integrate third-party storage engines. Chapter 7 focuses on the storage engine interface and provides a functional example of a simple storage engine.

Although at the moment MySQL supports a number of page and row-level locking storage engines, the core architecture has a strong MyISAM heritage. Part of that heritage is the mechanism to acquire a table lock. The table lock awareness, even when it is in essence a token lock, is important for an aspiring MySQL developer. Thus, Chapter 8 focuses on the table lock manager.

Chapter 9 focuses on the parser and optimizer. This is the chapter I would recommend to a DBA trying to improve the performance of MySQL. The key to optimizing MySQL queries and tables is to learn to think like the optimizer. This chapter also provides an overview of the source code for the brave developers preparing to immerse themselves into the optimizer's dark depths.

Chapter 10 is a cursory overview of MySQL storage engines. It may be helpful to a developer trying to create or integrate her own. A curious reader looking for what is out there may also find it of interest.

Chapter 11 is mostly for developers working on integrating a transactional storage engine into MySQL, while Chapter 12 focuses on the internals of replication.

By no means is this book a comprehensive guide to MySQL internals. The subject is so deep that I do not believe it is humanly possible to scratch the surface even if you had 10,000 pages and the time to create them. To make matters more complicated, MySQL developers are adding new code daily. Fortunately, most of the core code tends to remain intact, so the book has a shot at not becoming obsolete before it is published. Nevertheless, do not be surprised when you look at the current MySQL code and find that some things are not quite like what you see in the book. You are likely to see new classes and calls in the API. On occasion, you may find that an old API call has a new argument. But hopefully the book can always serve as a guide to teach you enough basics about the code to bring you to a level of proficiency that will enable you to accomplish your goals.

Conventions Used in This Book

The following typographical conventions are used in this book:

Italic
> Indicates filenames, directories, and file extensions, new terms, URLs, commands and command-line options, usernames, hostnames, email addresses, and emphasized text.

`Constant width`
> Indicates parts of code (such as variables, class names, methods, and macros), elements of SQL statements, contents of files, and output from commands.

`Constant width italic`
> Indicates text that should be replaced with user-supplied values.

`Constant width bold`
> Indicates user input in examples.

> This icon signifies a tip, suggestion, or general note.

> This icon indicates a warning or caution.

Using Code Examples

This book is here to help you get your job done. In general, you may use the code in this book in your programs and documentation. The longer examples can be downloaded from the book's web site at *http://www.oreilly.com/catalog/9780596009571*. You do not need to contact us for permission unless you're reproducing a significant portion of the code. For example, writing a program that uses several chunks of code from this book does not require permission. Selling or distributing a CD-ROM of examples from O'Reilly books *does* require permission. Answering a question by citing this book and quoting example code does not require permission. Incorporating a significant amount of example code from this book into your product's documentation *does* require permission.

We appreciate, but do not require, attribution. An attribution usually includes the title, author, publisher, and ISBN. For example: *Understanding MySQL Internals* by Sasha Pachev. Copyright 2007 O'Reilly Media, Inc., 978-0-596-00957-1."

If you feel your use of code examples falls outside fair use or the permission given above, feel free to contact us at *permissions@oreilly.com*.

Comments and Questions

Please address comments and questions concerning this book to the publisher:

O'Reilly Media, Inc.
1005 Gravenstein Highway North
Sebastopol, CA 95472
800-998-9938 (in the United States or Canada)
707-829-0515 (international or local)
707-829-0104 (fax)

We have a web page for this book, where we list errata, examples, and any additional information. You can access this page at:

http://www.oreilly.com/catalog/9780596009571

To comment or ask technical questions about this book, send email to:

bookquestions@oreilly.com

For more information about our books, conferences, Resource Centers, and the O'Reilly Network, see our web site at:

http://www.oreilly.com

Safari® Enabled

 When you see a Safari® Enabled icon on the cover of your favorite technology book, that means the book is available online through the O'Reilly Network Safari Bookshelf.

Safari offers a solution that's better than e-books. It's a virtual library that lets you easily search thousands of top tech books, cut and paste code samples, download chapters, and find quick answers when you need the most accurate, current information. Try it for free at *http://safari.oreilly.com*.

Acknowledgments

I would like to express special thanks to Andy Oram for his continual guidance and encouragement as we worked together on this book. I am particularly grateful to the MySQL development team for their cooperation and active participation in the review. The input I received from Sergei Golubchik was invaluable. His knowledge and vision of the MySQL code and architecture is amazing, as well as his ability to pay attention to detail. At times, as I read his reviews, I would wonder if he possibly got tired of the loads of technical detail and would speed-read past some inaccuracies or errors. The next moment I saw a note in red about some little but nevertheless important detail.

Special thanks also go to Brian Aker, Martin "MC" Brown, and Paul Kinzelman for their reviews and suggestions. And last, but not least—special thanks to my wife Sarah and my children Benjamin, Jennifer, Julia, Joseph, and Jacob for their patience and support, as I spent many Saturdays in the office working on the book.

Acknowledgments

## CHAPTER 1

MySQL History and Architecture

MySQL architecture is best understood in the context of its history. Thus, the two are discussed in the same chapter.

MySQL History

MySQL history goes back to 1979 when Monty Widenius, working for a small company called TcX, created a reporting tool written in BASIC that ran on a 4 Mhz computer with 16 KB RAM. Over time, the tool was rewritten in C and ported to run on Unix. It was still just a low-level storage engine with a reporting front end. The tool was known by the name of Unireg.

Working under the adverse conditions of little computational resources, and perhaps building on his God-given talent, Monty developed a habit and ability to write very efficient code naturally. He also developed, or perhaps was gifted from the start, with an unusually acute vision of what needed to be done to the code to make it useful in future development—without knowing in advance much detail about what that future development would be.

In addition to the above, with TcX being a very small company and Monty being one of the owners, he had a lot of say in what happened to his code. While there are perhaps a good number of programmers out there with Monty's talent and ability, for a number of reasons, few get to carry their code around for more than 20 years. Monty did.

Monty's work, talents, and ownership of the code provided a foundation upon which the Miracle of MySQL could be built.

Some time in the 1990s, TcX customers began to push for an SQL interface to their data. Several possibilities were considered. One was to load it into a commercial database. Monty was not satisfied with the speed. He tried borrowing mSQL code for the SQL part and integrating it with his low-level storage engine. That did not work well, either. Then came the classic move of a talented, driven programmer: "I've had enough of those tools that somebody else wrote that don't work! I'm writing my own!"

Thus in May of 1996 MySQL version 1.0 was released to a limited group, followed by a public release in October 1996 of version 3.11.1. The initial public release provided only a binary distribution for Solaris. A month later, the source and the Linux binary were released.

In the next two years, MySQL was ported to a number of other operating systems as the feature set gradually increased. MySQL was originally released under a special license that allowed commercial use to those who were not redistributing it with their software. Special licenses were available for sale to those who wanted to bundle it with their product. Additionally, commercial support was also being sold. This provided TcX with some revenue to justify the further development of MySQL, although the purpose of its original creation had already been fulfilled.

During this period MySQL progressed to version 3.22. It supported a decent subset of the SQL language, had an optimizer a lot more sophisticated than one would expect could possibly be written by one person, was extremely fast, and was very stable. Numerous APIs were contributed, so one could write a client in pretty much any existing programming language. However, it still lacked support for transactions, subqueries, foreign keys, stored procedures, and views. The locking happened only at a table level, which in some cases could slow it down to a grinding halt. Some programmers unable to get around its limitations still considered it a toy, while others were more than happy to dump their Oracle or SQL Server in favor of MySQL, and deal with the limitations in their code in exchange for improvement in performance and licensing cost savings.

Around 1999–2000 a separate company named MySQL AB was established. It hired several developers and established a partnership with Sleepycat to provide an SQL interface for the Berkeley DB data files. Since Berkeley DB had transaction capabilities, this would give MySQL support for transactions, which it previously lacked. After some changes in the code in preparation for integrating Berkeley DB, version 3.23 was released.

Although the MySQL developers could never work out all the quirks of the Berkeley DB interface and the Berkeley DB tables were never stable, the effort was not wasted. As a result, MySQL source became equipped with hooks to add any type of storage engine, including a transactional one.

By April of 2000, with some encouragement and sponsorship from Slashdot, master-slave replication capability was added. The old nontransactional storage engine, ISAM, was reworked and released as MyISAM. Among a number of improvements, full-text search capabilities were now supported. A short-lived partnership with NuSphere to add Gemini, a transactional engine with row-level locking, ended in a lawsuit toward the end of 2001. However, around the same time, Heikki Tuuri approached MySQL AB with a proposal to integrate his own storage engine, InnoDB, which was also capable of transactions and row-level locking.

Heikki's contribution integrated much more smoothly with the new table handler interface already polished off by the Berkeley DB integration efforts. The MySQL/InnoDB combination became version 4.0, and was released as alpha in October of 2001. By early 2002 the MySQL/InnoDB combo was stable and instantly took MySQL to another level. Version 4.0 was finally declared production stable in March 2003.

It might be worthy of mention that the version number change was not caused by the addition of InnoDB. MySQL developers have always viewed InnoDB as an important addition, but by no means something that they completely depend on for success. Back then, and even now, the addition of a new storage engine is not likely to be celebrated with a version number change. In fact, compared to previous versions, not much was added in version 4.0. Perhaps the most significant addition was the query cache, which greatly improved performance of a large number of applications. Replication code on the slave was rewritten to use two threads: one for network I/O from the master, and the other to process the updates. Some improvements were added to the optimizer. The client/server protocol became SSL-capable.

Version 4.1 was released as alpha in April of 2003, and was declared beta in June of 2004. Unlike version 4.0, it added a number of significant improvements. Perhaps the most significant was subqueries, a feature long-awaited by many users. Spatial indexing support was added to the MyISAM storage engine. Unicode support was implemented. The client/server protocol saw a number of changes. It was made more secure against attacks, and supported prepared statements.

In parallel with the alpha version of 4.1, work progressed on yet another development branch: version 5.0, which would add stored procedures, server-side cursors, triggers, views, XA transactions, significant improvements in the query optimizer, and a number of other features. The decision to create a separate development branch was made because MySQL developers felt that it would take a long time to stabilize 4.1 if, on top of all the new features that they were adding to it, they had to deal with the stored procedures. Version 5.0 was finally released as alpha in December 2003. For a while this created quite a bit of confusion—there were two branches in the alpha stage. Eventually 4.1 stabilized (October 2004), and the confusion was resolved.

Version 5.0 stabilized a year later, in October of 2005.

The first alpha release of 5.1 followed in November 2005, which added a number of improvements, some of which are table data partitioning, row-based replication, event scheduler, and a standardized plug-in API that facilitates the integration of new storage engines and other plug-ins.

At this point, MySQL is being actively developed. 5.0 is currently the stable version, while 5.1 is in beta and should soon become stable. New features at this point go into version 5.2.

MySQL Architecture

For the large part, MySQL architecture defies a formal definition or specification. When most of the code was originally written, it was not done to be a part of some great system in the future, but rather to solve some very specific problems. However, it was written so well and with enough insight that it reached the point where there were enough quality pieces to assemble a database server.

Core Modules

I make an attempt in this section to identify the core modules in the system. However, let me add a disclaimer that this is only an attempt to formalize what exists. MySQL developers rarely think in those terms. Rather, they tend to think of files, directories, classes, structures, and functions. It is much more common to hear "This happens in mi_open( )" than to hear "This happens on the MyISAM storage engine level." MySQL developers know the code so well that they are able to think conceptually on the level of functions, structures, and classes. They will probably find the abstractions in this section rather useless. However, it would be helpful to a person used to thinking in terms of modules and managers.

With regard to MySQL, I use the term "module" rather loosely. Unlike what one would typically call a module, in many cases it is not something you can easily pull out and replace with another implementation. The code from one module might be spread across several files, and you often find the code from several different modules in the same file. This is particularly true of the older code. The newer code tends to fit into the pattern of modules better. So in our definition, a *module* is a piece of code that logically belongs together in some way, and performs a certain critical function in the server.

One can identify the following modules in the server:

- Server Initialization Module
- Connection Manager
- Thread Manager
- Connection Thread
- User Authentication Module
- Access Control Module
- Parser
- Command Dispatcher
- Query Cache Module
- Optimizer
- Table Manager

- Table Modification Modules
- Table Maintenance Module
- Status Reporting Module
- Abstracted Storage Engine Interface (Table Handler)
- Storage Engine Implementations (MyISAM, InnoDB, MEMORY, Berkeley DB)
- Logging Module
- Replication Master Module
- Replication Slave Module
- Client/Server Protocol API
- Low-Level Network I/O API
- Core API

Interaction of the Core Modules

When the server is started on the command line, the Initialization Module takes control. It parses the configuration file and the command-line arguments, allocates global memory buffers, initializes global variables and structures, loads the access control tables, and performs a number of other initialization tasks. Once the initialization job is complete, the Initialization Module passes control to the Connection Manager, which starts listening for connections from clients in a loop.

When a client connects to the database server, the Connection Manager performs a number of low-level network protocol tasks and then passes control to the Thread Manager, which in turn supplies a thread to handle the connection (which from now on will be referred to as the Connection Thread). The Connection Thread might be created anew, or retrieved from the thread cache and called to active duty. Once the Connection Thread receives control, it first invokes the User Authentication Module. The credentials of the connecting user are verified, and the client may now issue requests.

The Connection Thread passes the request data to the Command Dispatcher. Some requests, known in the MySQL code terminology as *commands*, can be accommodated by the Command Dispatcher directly, while more complex ones need to be redirected to another module. A typical command may request the server to run a query, change the active database, report the status, send a continuous dump of the replication updates, close the connection, or perform some other operation.

In MySQL server terminology, there are two types of client requests: a query and a command. A *query* is anything that has to go through the parser. A *command* is a request that can be executed without the need to invoke the parser. We will use the term query in the context of MySQL internals. Thus, not only a SELECT but also a DELETE or INSERT in our terminology would be called a query. What we would call a query is sometimes called an SQL statement.

If full query logging is enabled, the Command Dispatcher will ask the Logging Module to log the query or the command to the plain-text log prior to the dispatch. Thus in the full logging configuration all queries will be logged, even the ones that are not syntactically correct and will never be executed, immediately returning an error.

The Command Dispatcher forwards queries to the Parser through the Query Cache Module. The Query Cache Module checks whether the query is of the type that can be cached, and if there exists a previously computed cached result that is still valid. In the case of a hit, the execution is short-circuited at this point, the cached result is returned to the user, and the Connection Thread receives control and is now ready to process another command. If the Query Cache Module reports a miss, the query goes to the Parser, which will make a decision on how to transfer control based on the query type.

One can identify the following modules that could continue from that point: the Optimizer, the Table Modification Module, the Table Maintenance Module, the Replication Module, and the Status Reporting Module. Select queries are forwarded to the Optimizer; updates, inserts, deletes, and table-creation and schema-altering queries go to the respective Table Modification Modules; queries that check, repair, update key statistics, or defragment the table go to the Table Maintenance module; queries related to replication go to the Replication Module; and status requests go to the Status Reporting Module. There also exist a number of Table Modification Modules: Delete Module, Create Module, Update Module, Insert Module, and Alter Module.

At this point, each of the modules that will receive control from the Parser passes the list of tables involved in the query to the Access Control Module and then, upon success, to the Table Manager, which opens the tables and acquires the necessary locks. Now the table operation module is ready to proceed with its specific task and will issue a number of requests to the Abstracted Storage Engine Module for low-level operations such as inserting or updating a record, retrieving the records based on a key value, or performing an operation on the table level, such as repairing it or updating the index statistics.

The Abstracted Storage Engine Module will automatically translate the calls to the corresponding methods of the specific Storage Engine Module via object polymorphism. In other words, when dealing with a Storage Engine object, the caller thinks it is dealing with an abstracted one, when in fact the object is of a more specific type: it is the Storage Engine object corresponding to the given table type. The interface methods are virtual, which creates the effect of transparency. The correct method will be called, and the caller does not need to be aware of the exact object type of the Storage Engine object.

As the query or command is being processed, the corresponding module may send parts of the result set to the client as they become available. It may also send warnings or an error message. If an error message is issued, both the client and the server will understand that the query or command has failed and take the appropriate measures. The client will not accept any more result set, warning, or error message data for the given query, while the server will always transfer control to the Connection Thread after issuing an error. Note that since MySQL does not use exceptions for reasons of implementation stability and portability, all calls on all levels must be checked for errors with the appropriate transfer of control in the case of failure.

If the low-level module has made a modification to the data in some way and if the binary update logging is enabled, the module will be responsible for asking the Logging Module to log the update event to the binary update log, sometimes known as the replication log, or, among MySQL developers and power users, the *binlog*.

Once the task is completed, the execution flow returns to the Connection Thread, which performs the necessary clean-up and waits for another query or command from the client. The session continues until the client issues the *Quit* command.

In addition to interacting with regular clients, a server may receive a command from a replication slave to continuously read its binary update log. This command will be handled by the Replication Master Module.

If the server is configured as a replication slave, the Initialization Module will call the Replication Slave Module, which in turn will start two threads, called the SQL Thread and the I/O thread. They take care of propagating updates that happened on the master to the slave. It is possible for the same server to be configured as both a master and a slave.

Network communication with a client goes through the Client/Server Protocol Module, which is responsible for packaging the data in the proper format, and depending on the connection settings, compressing it. The Client/Server Protocol Module in turn uses the Low-Level Network I/O module, which is responsible for sending and receiving the data on the socket level in a cross-platform portable way. It is also responsible for encrypting the data using the OpenSSL library calls if the connection options are set appropriately.

As they perform their respective tasks, the core components of the server heavily rely on the Core API. The Core API provides a rich functionality set, which includes file I/O, memory management, string manipulation, implementations of various data structures and algorithms, and many other useful capabilities. MySQL developers are encouraged to avoid direct *libc* calls, and use the Core API to facilitate ports to new platforms and code optimization in the future.

Figure 1-1 illustrates the core modules and their interaction.

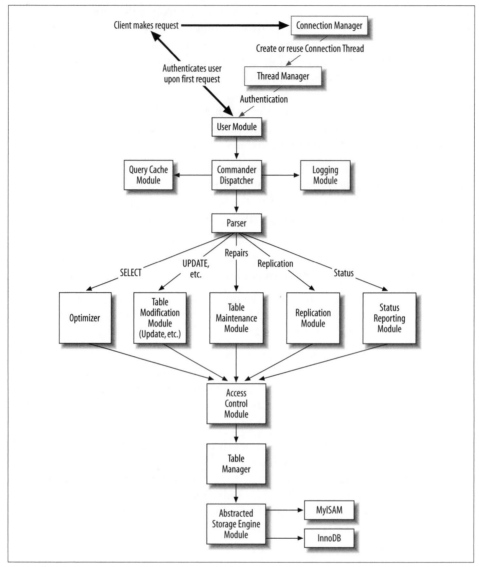

Figure 1-1. High-level view of MySQL modules

Detailed Look at the Core Modules

We will now take a closer look at each of the components. One purpose of the discussion is to connect the conceptual language used earlier with the actual source. In addition, we will cover the some of the history of each component and try to estimate its future development path.

Frequent references to the source will be made, and you may find it helpful to open the mentioned files in a text editor and locate the function references. This can also be done in a debugger, as shown in Chapter 3. That chapter will also tell you how to get the source code.

Server Initialization Module

The Server Initialization Module is responsible for the server initialization on startup. Most of the code is found in the file *sql/mysqld.cc*. The entry point is what a C/C++ programmer would expect: main( ). Some other functions of interest follow. If the file is not mentioned, the location is *sql/mysqld.cc*:

- init_common_variables( )
- init_thread_environment( )
- init_server_components( )
- grant_init( ) in *sql/sql_acl.cc*
- init_slave( ) in *sql/slave.cc*
- get_options( )

Although the code found in version 3.22 was never rewritten from scratch, it has been significantly refactored as new features were added to MySQL. One big chunk of initialization code that used to be under main( ) got reorganized gradually into a number of helper functions over the lifetime of the code. Additionally, the command line and configuration file option parsing got switched from the GNU getopt( ) to the MySQL Core API option parser once it became available in version 4.0.

In version 5.1, a significant portion was added to init_server_components( ) for plug-in initialization.

Overall, this area of the code is fairly stable. Based on the past history, we should anticipate possible incremental additions in the future as new features that require special initialization on startup are added. However, a rewrite of this code is unlikely.

Connection Manager

The Connection Manager listens for incoming connections from clients, and dispatches the requests to the Thread Manager. This module is really just one function in *sql/mysqld.cc*: handle_connections_sockets( ). However, it deserves to be classified as a separate module due to its critical role in the operation of the server. The abundance of #ifdef directives speaks to the challenge of porting networking code to a variety of operating systems.

Over time, the code evolved somewhat to accommodate quirks in the network system calls of different operating systems. Further changes might be necessary in the future as new ports are attempted, or as the different operating system vendors introduce new quirks into new versions of their products.

Thread Manager

The Thread Manager is responsible for keeping track of threads and for making sure a thread is allocated to handle the connection from a client. This is another very small module. Most of the code is found in *sql/mysqld.cc*. The entry point is create_new_thread( ). Another function of interest is start_cached_thread( ), defined in the same file.

One could perhaps consider the THD class defined in *sql/sql_class.h* and implemented in *sql/sql_class.cc* as a part of this module. Objects of the THD type are thread descriptors, and are critical in the operation of most of the server modules. Many functions take a THD pointer as their first argument.

The thread management code was significantly reworked in version 3.23 when the thread cache was added. Since then it has not been changed significantly. It is reasonable to expect that it will not receive any significant changes in the future.

However, if we, in our abstraction, consider the THD class itself as part of this module, we have a different story as far as changes are concerned. The addition of new features such as prepared statements, server-side cursors, and stored procedures led to a significant rework of THD in versions 4.1 and 5.0. It is now a super-class of the Query_arena, Statement, Security_context, and Open_tables_state classes, which are also defined in *sql/sql_class.h*.

Connection Thread

The Connection Thread is the heart of the work of processing client requests on an established connection. This module is also very small. It consists of just one function: handle_one_connection( ) in *sql/sql_parse.cc*. However, despite its size, it deserves to be classified as a module due to its role in the server.

The code evolved over time, gradually becoming more compact and readable as various initializations involving THD variables were moved under the THD class. It is reasonable to expect that the code will not change much in the future.

User Authentication Module

The User Authentication Module authenticates the connecting user and initializes the structures and variables containing the information on his level of privileges. The entry point for this module is check_connection( ) in *sql/sql_parse.cc*. However, the rest of the functionality is found in *sql/sql_acl.cc* and *sql/password.cc*. Some interesting functions to examine include:

- acl_check_host( ) in *sql/sql_acl.cc*
- create_random_string( ) in *sql/password.cc*
- check_user( ) in *sql/sql_parse.cc*
- acl_getroot( ) in *sql/sql_acl.cc*

The code has been significantly reworked only once, in version 4.1. Due to the possible impact of the changes, MySQL developers waited a while before they attempted the updates in the protocol needed to implement a more secure authentication.

Since then, there have not been many changes to this code. However, with the addition of plug-in capability in 5.1, MySQL developers are planning to add pluggable authentication and roles capabilities, which will require changes in this code.

Access Control Module

The Access Control Module verifies that the client user has sufficient privileges to perform the requested operation. Most of the code is in *sql/sql_acl.cc*. However, one of the most frequently used functions, check_access( ), is found in *sql/sql_parse.cc*. Some other functions of interest follow, all located in *sql/sql_acl.cc* unless otherwise indicated:

- check_grant( )
- check_table_access( ) in *sql/sql_parse.cc*
- check_grant_column( )
- acl_get( )

The code itself has not changed very much since version 3.22. However, new privilege types were added in version 4.0, which somewhat changed the way this module was used by the rest of the code. MySQL developers are planning to add support for roles, which will require significant changes to this module.

Parser

The Parser is responsible for parsing queries and generating a parse tree. The entry point is mysql_parse( ) in *sql/sql_parse.cc*, which performs some initializations and then invokes yyparse( ), a function in *sql/sql_yacc.cc* generated by GNU Bison from *sql/sql_yacc.yy*, which contains the definition of the SQL language subset understood by MySQL. Note that unlike many open source projects, MySQL has its own generated lexical scanner instead of using *lex*. The MySQL lexical scanner is discussed in detail in Chapter 9. Some files of interest, in addition to the ones just mentioned, include:

- *sql/gen_lex_hash.cc*
- *sql/lex.h*
- *sql/lex_symbol.h*
- *sql/lex_hash.h* (generated file)
- *sql/sql_lex.h*
- *sql/sql_lex.cc*
- The group of files under *sql/* with names starting in *item_* and extensions of *.h* or *.cc*

As the new SQL features are added, the parser keeps changing to accommodate them. However, the core structure of the parser is fairly stable, and so far has been able to accommodate the growth. It is reasonable to expect that while some elements will be added on, the core will not be changed very much for some time. MySQL developers have been, and sometimes still are, talking about a core rewrite of the parser and moving it away from *yacc*/Bison to make it faster. However, they have been talking about it for at least seven years already, and this has not yet become a priority.

Command Dispatcher

The Command Dispatcher is responsible for directing requests to the lower-level modules that will know how to resolve them. It consists of two functions in *sql/sql_parse.cc*: do_command( ) and dispatch_command( ).

The module kept growing over time as the set of supported commands increased. Small growth is expected in the future, but the core structure is unlikely to change.

Query Cache Module

The Query Cache Module caches query results, and tries to short-circuit the execution of queries by delivering the cached result whenever possible. It is implemented in *sql/sql_cache.cc*. Some methods of interest include:

- Query_cache::store_query( )
- Query_cache::send_result_to_client( )

The module was added in version 4.0. Few changes aside from bug fixes are expected in the future.

Optimizer

The Optimizer is responsible for creating the best strategy to answer the query, and executing it to deliver the result to the client. It is perhaps the most complex module in the MySQL code. The entry point is mysql_select( ) in *sql/sql_select.cc*. This module is discussed in detail in Chapter 9. Some other functions and methods of interest, all in *sql/sql_select.cc*, include:

- JOIN::prepare( )
- JOIN::optimize( )
- JOIN::exec( )
- make_join_statistics( )
- find_best_combination( )
- optimize_cond( )

As you descend into the depths of the optimizer, there is a cave worth visiting. It is the range optimizer, which was separate enough from the optimizer core and complex enough to be isolated into a separate file, *sql/opt_range.cc*. The range optimizer is responsible for optimizing queries that use a key with a given value range or set of ranges. The entry point for the range optimizer is SQL_SELECT::test_quick_select( ).

The optimizer has always been in a state of change. The addition of subqueries in 4.1 has added another layer of complexity. Version 5.0 added a greedy search for the optimal table join order, and the ability to use several keys per table (index merge). It is reasonable to expect that many more changes will be made in the future. One long-awaited change is improvements in the optimization of sub-queries.

Table Manager

The Table Manager is responsible for creating, reading, and modifying the table definition files (*.frm* extension), maintaining a cache of table descriptors called table cache, and managing table-level locks. Most of the code is found in *sql/sql_base.cc*, *sql/table.cc*, *sql/unireg.cc*, and *sql/lock.cc*. This module will be discussed in detail in Chapter 9. Some functions of interest include:

- openfrm( ) in *sql/table.cc*
- mysql_create_frm( ) in *sql/unireg.cc*
- open_table( ) in *sql/sql_base.cc*
- open_tables( ) in *sql/sql_base.cc*
- open_ltable( ) in *sql/sql_base.cc*
- mysql_lock_table( ) in *sql/lock.cc*

The code has not changed much since version 3.22 except for the new table definition file format in version 4.1. In the past, Monty has expressed some dissatisfaction with the inefficiencies in the table cache code, and wanted to rewrite it. For a while, this was not a top priority. However, some progress has finally been made in version 5.1.

Table Modification Modules

This collection of modules is responsible for operations such as creating, deleting, renaming, dropping, updating, or inserting into a table. This is actually a very significant chunk of code. Unfortunately, due to the space constraints, this book will not cover it in detail. However, once you become familiar with the rest of the code, you should be able to figure out the details by reading the source and using the debugger without too much trouble by starting from the following entry points:

- mysql_update( ) and mysql_multi_update( ) in *sql/sql_update.cc*
- mysql_insert( ) in *sql/sql_insert.cc*
- mysql_create_table( ) in *sql/sql_table.cc*

- `mysql_alter_table( )` in *sql/sql_table.cc*
- `mysql_rm_table( )` in *sql/sql_table.cc*
- `mysql_delete( )` in *sql/sql_delete.cc*

The Update and Delete modules have been changed significantly in version 4.0 with the addition of multi-table updates and deletes. Some reorganization also happened in Update, Insert, and Delete modules to support prepared statements in version 4.1 and triggers in 5.1. Otherwise, aside from fairly minor improvements from time to time, they have not changed much. It is reasonable to expect that for the large part the code will remain as it is in the future.

Table Maintenance Module

The Table Maintenance Module is responsible for table maintenance operations such as check, repair, back up, restore, optimize (defragment), and analyze (update key distribution statistics). The code is found in *sql/sql_table.cc*. The core function is `mysql_admin_table( )`, with the following convenience wrappers:

- `mysql_check_table( )`
- `mysql_repair_table( )`
- `mysql_backup_table( )`
- `mysql_restore_table( )`
- `mysql_optimize_table( )`
- `mysql_analyze_table( )`

`mysql_admin_table( )` will further dispatch the request to the appropriate storage engine method. The bulk of the work happens on the storage engine level.

The module was introduced in version 3.23 to provide an SQL interface for table maintenance. Prior to that table maintenance had to be performed offline. In version 4.1, significant changes were made to the Network Protocol Module to support prepared statements. This affected all the modules that talk back to the client, including the Table Maintenance Module. Otherwise, not much has changed since its introduction, and it is reasonable to expect that not much will in the future.

Status Reporting Module

The Status Reporting Module is responsible for answering queries about server configuration settings, performance tracking variables, table structure information, replication progress, condition of the table cache, and other things. It handles queries that begin with SHOW. Most of the code is found in *sql/sql_show.cc*. Some functions of interest, all in *sql/sql_show.cc* unless indicated otherwise, are:

- `mysqld_list_processes( )`
- `mysqld_show( )`

- `mysqld_show_create()`
- `mysqld_show_fields()`
- `mysqld_show_open_tables()`
- `mysqld_show_warnings()`
- `show_master_info()` in *sql/slave.cc*
- `show_binlog_info()` in *sql/sql_repl.cc*

The module has been constantly evolving. The addition of new functionality has created the need for additional status reporting. It is reasonable to expect that this pattern will continue in the future.

Abstracted Storage Engine Interface (Table Handler)

This module is actually an abstract class named `handler` and a structure called a *handlerton*. The handlerton structure was added in version 5.1 for plug-in integration. It provides a standardized interface to perform low-level storage and retrieval operations.

The table hander is defined in *sql/handler.h* and partially implemented in *sql/handler.cc*. The derived specific storage engine classes will have to implement all the pure virtual methods of this class. It will be discussed in greater detail in Chapter 9.

This module was introduced in version 3.23 to facilitate the integration of Berkeley DB tables. This move had far-reaching consequences: now a variety of low-level storage engines could be put underneath MySQL with a fair amount of ease. The code was further refined during the integration of InnoDB. The future of the module will largely depend on what new storage engines will be integrated into MySQL, and on the way the existing ones will change. For example, sometimes a new feature in some underlying storage engine may require an addition to the abstracted interface to make it available to the higher-level modules.

Storage Engine Implementations (MyISAM, InnoDB, MEMORY, Berkeley DB)

Each of the storage engines provides a standard interface for its operations by extending the `handler` class mentioned earlier. The methods of the derived class define the standard interface operations in terms of the low-level calls of the specific storage engine. This process and the individual storage engine will be discussed in detail in Chapter 10. Meanwhile, for a quick introduction, you may want to take a look at a few files and directories of interest:

- *sql/ha_myisam.h* and *sql/ha_myisam.cc*
- *sql/ha_innodb.h* and *sql/ha_innodb.cc*
- *sql/ha_heap.h* and *sql/ha_heap.cc*
- *sql/ha_ndbcluster.h* and *sql/ha_ndbcluster.cc*

- *myisam/*
- *innobase/*
- *heap/*
- *ndb/*

When the storage engine interface was first abstracted (version 3.23), there were only three fully functional storage engines: MyISAM, ISAM (older version of MyISAM), and MEMORY. (Note that the MEMORY storage engine used to be called HEAP, and some of the file and directory names in the source tree still reflect the earlier name.) However, the list grew rapidly with the addition of BerkeleyDB, MERGE, InnoDB, and more recently, NDB for the MySQL Cluster. Most storage engines are still in fairly active development, and we may see some new ones added in the future.

Logging Module

The Logging Module is responsible for maintaining higher-level (logical) logs. A storage engine may additionally maintain its own lower-level (physical or logical) logs for its own purposes, but the Logging Module would not be concerned with those; the storage engine itself takes charge. The logical logs at this point include the binary update log (used mostly for replication, otherwise), command log (used mostly for server monitoring and application debugging), and slow query log (used for tracking down poorly optimized queries).

Prior to version 5.1, the module was contained for the most part by the class MYSQL_LOG, defined in *sql/sql_class.h* and implemented in *sql/log.cc*. Version 5.1 brought a rewrite of this module. Now there exists a hierarchy of log management classes, and MYSQL_LOG is a super-class of TC_LOG, both of which are defined in *sql/log.h*.

However, most of the work in logging happens in the binary replication log. The classes for log event creation and reading for the binary replication log are defined in *sql/log_event.h* and implemented in *sql/log_event.cc*. Both the Replication Master and Replication Slave modules rely heavily on this functionality of the Logging Module.

Significant changes were made to this module with the introduction of replication. Version 5.0 brought on some changes required for XA transactions. Version 5.1 added the capability to search logs as if they were an SQL table, which required a significant refactoring of this code. The binary logging part required significant changes to accommodate row-based replication. At this point it is hard to anticipate where this code is going in the future.

Replication Master Module

The Replication Master Module is responsible for the replication functionality on the master. The most common operation for this module is to deliver a continuous feed of replication log events to the slave upon request. Most of the code is found in *sql/sql_repl.cc*. The core function is mysql_binlog_send( ).

The module was added in version 3.23, and it has not experienced any major changes other than a thorough cleanup to isolate chunks of code into functions. In the beginning, the code had very ambitions development plans for fail-safe replication. However, before those plans could be realized, MySQL acquired NDB Cluster code from Ericsson, and began pursuing another route to the eventual goal of automatic failover. In light of those developments, it is not clear at this point how the native MySQL replication will progress.

This module will be discussed in greater detail in Chapter 12.

Replication Slave Module

The Replication Slave Module is responsible for the replication functionality of the slave. The role of the slave is to retrieve updates from the master, and apply them on the slave. The slave starting in version 4.0 is two-threaded. The network I/O thread requests and receives a continuous feed of updates from the master, and logs them in a local relay log. The SQL thread applies them as it reads them from the relay logs. The code for this module is found in *sql/slave.cc*. The most important functions to study are handle_slave_io( ) and handle_slave_sql( ).

The module was added in 3.23 along with the Replication Master module. It went through a substantial change in version 4.0 when the monolithic slave thread was broken down into the SQL thread and the I/O thread.

This module will be discussed in greater detail in Chapter 12.

Client/Server Protocol API

The MySQL client/server communication protocol sits on top of the operating system protocol (TCP/IP or local socket) in the protocol stack. This module implements the API used across the server to create, read, interpret, and send the protocol packets. The code is found in *sql/protocol.cc*, *sql/protocol.h*, and *sql/net_serv.cc*.

The files *sql/protocol.h* and *sql/protocol.cc* define and implement a hierarchy of classes. Protocol is the base class, and Protocol_simple, Protocol_prep, and Protocol_cursor are derived from it. Some functions of interest in this module are:

- my_net_read( ) in *sql/net_serv.cc*
- my_net_write( ) in *sql/net_serv.cc*
- net_store_data( ) in *sql/protocol.cc*
- send_ok( ) in *sql/protocol.cc*
- send_error( ) in *sql/protocol.cc*

In version 4.0 the protocol was changed to support packets up to 4 GB in size. Prior to that, the limit was 24 MB. The Protocol class hierarchy was added in version 4.1 to deal with prepared statements. It appears that at this point most of the problematic areas in the protocol at this level have been addressed, and it is reasonable to expect that this code will not be changing much in the near future. However, MySQL developers are thinking about adding support for notifications.

This module will be discussed in greater detail in Chapter 5.

Low-Level Network I/O API

The Low-Level Network I/O API provides an abstraction for the low-level network I/O and SSL sessions. The code is found in the *vio/* directory. All functions in this module have names starting with vio_.

This module was introduced in 3.23, spurred by the need to support SSL connections. Abstracting the low-level network I/O also facilitated porting to new platforms and maintaining the old ports.

Core API

The Core API is the Swiss Army knife of MySQL. It provides functionality for portable file I/O, memory management, string manipulation, filesystem navigation, formatted printing, a rich collection of data structures and algorithms, and a number of other things. If a problem ever arises, there is usually a solution for it in the Core API Module. If there is not, it will be coded up. This module is to a great extent an expression of Monty's ability and determination to never solve just one problem. It is perhaps the core component of the Miracle of MySQL.

The code is found in the *mysys/* and *strings/* directories. Many of the core API functions have names starting with my_.

The module has always been in a state of growth and improvement. As the new functionality is added, great care is put into preserving its stability and high level of performance. It is reasonable to expect that this pattern will continue in the future.

This module will be discussed in greater detail in Chapter 3.

Nuts and Bolts of Working with the MySQL Source Code

Much can be learned about MySQL by studying its source. Monty Widenius, the creator of MySQL, once half-jokingly remarked that the source is the ultimate documentation. Indeed, assuming that the hardware and the compiler are functioning properly, the software will do exactly what the source tells it to. However, understanding the source of a complex program such as MySQL can be a challenge. The purpose of this chapter is to give you a head start in your study of the source.

Unix Shell

Although MySQL runs on a number of different platforms, you will find it easier to study the source if you get an account on some Unix-like system, such as Linux, FreeBSD, Mac OS X, or Solaris. If you do not have a preference to start with, I recommend Linux. It could be either a remote server, or running on your desktop. The examples in this chapter assume you are logged in to a Unix command shell, and that your shell is Bourne-compatible to some degree. One way to get such a shell is to execute:

```
/bin/sh
```

right after you log in.

BitKeeper

MySQL developers use BitKeeper (*http://www.bitmover.com*) for source revision control. A BitKeeper repository containing MySQL source code is publicly available with read-only access. Although MySQL source code can also be obtained by downloading a compressed archive, using BitKeeper offers a number of advantages:

- You get the most recent source version and can stay up to date with all the developments on a daily basis.
- BitKeeper tools allow you to easily keep track of changes.
- You can easily keep track of your own changes and submit patches to MySQL developers.

Unfortunately, there are also some disadvantages:

- The initial setup requires a download of over 30 MB of data if you are down-loading the revision history.
- Special tools such as *autoconf*, *automake*, and *bison* have to be installed in order to build MySQL.
- Since BitMover decided to discontinue the Open Logging License, it is not possi-ble to automatically integrate your changes, submit patches, and do other tasks without buying a commercial license.

If the disadvantages of using BitKeeper in your situation outweigh the advantages, please refer to the "Building from Source Distribution" section in this chapter. Other-wise, the first step is to make sure that BitKeeper is installed on your system.

Without a commercial license, the only advantage of using BitKeeper is being able to get the most recent development source. If you are not planning to use the commer-cial version of BitKeeper, follow these instructions to download the free BitKeeper client:

1. Download *http://www.bitmover.com/bk-client.shar*.
2. Unpack it by running */bin/sh bk-client.shar*.
3. Execute *cd bk_client-1.1; make* to build it.
4. Set *PATH=$PWD:$PATH* to get around some quirks in *sfioball*.

To get the MySQL source code, execute:

```
$ sfioball bk://mysql.bkbits.net/mysql-version some-directory
```

where *version* is the version number of MySQL of interest, such as 5.1, and *some-directory* is where you want to keep the source. For example, you might enter:

```
$ sfioball bk://mysql.bkbits.net/mysql-5.1 /home/devel/mysql-5.1
```

If you want the entire revision history, which will make the download take longer, enter:

```
$ sfioball -r+ bk://mysql.bkbits.net/mysql-5.1 /home/devel/mysql-5.1
```

To update your version (assuming you have 5.1), execute:

```
$ update bk://mysql.bkbits.net/mysql-5.1 /home/devel/mysql-5.1
```

You can also browse the change sets online at *http://mysql.bkbits.net* for different MySQL version trees.

If you are willing to invest in the commercial version of BitKeeper, visit *http://www.bitmover.com/cgi-bin/license.cgi* and follow the instructions, which call for you to fill out a form and get an email response with details about downloading.

Once you have BitKeeper installed, I would recommend running *bk helptool* to famil-iarize yourself with the following basic commands:

- *bk clone*
- *bk edit*
- *bk new*
- *bk rm*
- *bk citool*
- *bk commit*
- *bk pull*
- *bk push*
- *bk diffs*

Once you get comfortable with BitKeeper, the next step is to clone the repository of the MySQL version you would like to study. As of this writing, there are six version repositories available. They are summarized in Table 2-1.

Table 2-1. Versions of MySQL maintained through BitKeeper

MySQL version	Description	BitKeeper repository URL
3.23	Historically old unsupported version	*bk://mysql.bkbits.net/mysql-3.23*
4.0	Old unsupported version	*bk://mysql.bkbits.net/mysql-4.0*
4.1	Old supported version to be phased out soon	*bk://mysql.bkbits.net/mysql-4.1*
5.0	Current stable version	*bk://mysql.bkbits.net/mysql-5.0*
5.1	Current beta version	*bk://mysql.bkbits.net/mysql-5.1*
5.2	Current development version	*bk://mysql.bkbits.net/mysql-5.2*

The following directions and discussion apply mostly to the commercial version of BitKeeper.

To create a local copy of the repository, execute the *clone* command:

```
$ bk clone url
```

For example, if you want to get a copy of the 5.1 version repository, enter:

```
$ bk clone bk://mysql.bkbits.net/mysql-5.1
```

To clone the repository or access it via *sfioball*, your local instance of BitKeeper has to connect to port 7000 on *mysql.bkbits.net*. If you are behind a restrictive firewall, it might block an outgoing connection on that port. Fortunately, in the commercial version there's a workaround if you happen to have a local HTTP proxy (substitute the proper host name and port in the first command):

```
$ http_proxy="http://proxy_host_name:proxy_port/"
$ export http_proxy
```

If you do not have the commercial version, you may still be able to overcome the restriction with creative tunneling and port-forwarding.

The initial clone operation will transfer over 30 MB of data, so it could take a while depending on the speed of your connection and the overall network traffic congestion. When I did the previous clone around 11 P.M. EST on a 640 MBit/s DSL connection in Provo, Utah, the whole process completed in nine minutes.

Once the clone has been completed, you will see a subdirectory in your current directory corresponding to the name of the repository. For example, if you cloned version 5.1, the name of the directory will be *mysql-5.1*. If you prefer a different name, add an argument to the original command, for example:

```
$ bk clone bk://mysql.bkbits.net/mysql-5.1 src/mysql
```

Preparing the System to Build MySQL from BitKeeper Tree

Once you have cloned the BitKeeper repository, the following tools must be installed for the build scripts to work:

- *autoconf*
- *automake*
- *m4*
- *libtool*
- GNU *make*
- *bison*
- *gcc* or some other C++ compiler

The required version's utilities will be present on most Linux distributions that were put together in the second half of 2003 or later. If you have an older or a very customized Linux installation, or if you are using a different Unix variant, refer to Table 2-2 to verify that you have the required version of each tool.

Table 2-2. Versions of required build tools

Tool	Minimum required version	URL
autoconf	2.53	http://www.gnu.org/software/autoconf/
automake	1.8	http://www.gnu.org/software/automake/
m4	No version limit	http://www.gnu.org/software/m4/
libtool	1.5	http://www.gnu.org/software/libtool/
GNU make	3.79	http://www.gnu.org/software/make/
bison	1.75	http://www.gnu.org/software/bison/
gcc	2.95	http://www.gnu.org/software/gcc/

Note that the executable binary for each tool must be in your PATH. The following Bourne shell script will provide a helpful summary that you can use to evaluate whether your system is ready:

```
#! /bin/sh
for tool in autoconf automake m4 libtool make  bison gcc
do
    echo "Checking for $tool:"
    $tool -version
done
```

If the tools are installed and in your path, the script produces output similar to this:

```
Checking for autoconf:
autoconf (GNU Autoconf) 2.59
Written by David J. MacKenzie and Akim Demaille.

Copyright (C) 2003 Free Software Foundation, Inc.
This is free software; see the source for copying conditions.  There is NO
warranty; not even for MERCHANTABILITY or FITNESS FOR A PARTICULAR PURPOSE.
Checking for automake:
automake (GNU automake) 1.8.5
Written by Tom Tromey <tromey@redhat.com>.

Copyright 2004 Free Software Foundation, Inc.
This is free software; see the source for copying conditions.  There is NO
warranty; not even for MERCHANTABILITY or FITNESS FOR A PARTICULAR PURPOSE.
Checking for m4:
GNU m4 1.4o
Checking for libtool:
ltmain.sh (GNU libtool) 1.5.6 (1.1220.2.94 2004/04/10 16:27:27)

Copyright (C) 2003  Free Software Foundation, Inc.
This is free software; see the source for copying conditions.  There is NO
warranty; not even for MERCHANTABILITY or FITNESS FOR A PARTICULAR PURPOSE.
Checking for make:
GNU Make version 3.79.1, by Richard Stallman and Roland McGrath.
Built for i686-pc-linux-gnu
Copyright (C) 1988, 89, 90, 91, 92, 93, 94, 95, 96, 97, 98, 99, 2000
        Free Software Foundation, Inc.
This is free software; see the source for copying conditions.
There is NO warranty; not even for MERCHANTABILITY or FITNESS FOR A
PARTICULAR PURPOSE.

Report bugs to <bug-make@gnu.org>.

Checking for bison:
bison (GNU Bison) 1.875
Written by Robert Corbett and Richard Stallman.

Copyright (C) 2002 Free Software Foundation, Inc.
This is free software; see the source for copying conditions.  There is NO
warranty; not even for MERCHANTABILITY or FITNESS FOR A PARTICULAR PURPOSE.
Checking for gcc:
2.95.3
```

Determine the versions of each utility from the output of the script, and compare them against the table. If the numbers are less than the version numbers required, perform the necessary upgrades.

Building MySQL from BitKeeper Tree

MySQL developers have created a number of scripts to build different types of MySQL binaries on different platforms. They are found in the *BUILD* directory of the BitKeeper tree. Unfortunately, at the time of this writing, I could not find the one that would build a debugging-enabled binary on any architecture. To solve the problem, I will provide instructions on how to create one:

1. Copy *compile-pentium-debug* to *compile-generic-debug*.
2. Open *compile-generic-debug* in a text editor.
3. Change the line extra_flags="$pentium_cflags $debug_cflags" to extra_flags="-g $debug_cflags".
4. Remove all lines starting with: extra_configs= .
5. Add a line extra_configs="" before the line . "$path/FINISH.sh".
6. Save the edited file.

After the edit, *compile-generic-debug* will look like this:

```
#! /bin/sh

path='dirname $0'
. "$path/SETUP.sh" $@ --with-debug=full

extra_flags="-g $debug_cflags"
c_warnings="$c_warnings $debug_extra_warnings"
cxx_warnings="$cxx_warnings $debug_extra_warnings"
extra_configs=""


. "$path/FINISH.sh"
```

Now you are ready to use *compile-generic-debug* for the build. At the shell prompt from the root of the cloned repository, execute the following:

```
$ BUILD/compile-generic-debug
```

The script will generate the make files, create the necessary headers with definitions, and then compile the MySQL server, client, and miscellaneous utilities. This is a fairly long process. It took 12 minutes on my desktop (Athlon 2200+, 1.5 GB RAM, Linux).

During the build, you may see a number of warnings from different tools engaged in the process. Those are usually safe to ignore if the build does not abort. To verify that the build was successful, type at the shell prompt:

```
$ make test
```

Ideally, you will see all of the tests either pass or be skipped. Some tests, especially the ones that test replication, might fail on some systems due to the difficulties with server shutdown and restart. Since the BitKeeper repository may contain source in between releases, on occasion a developer may check in a test case for the bug that has not yet been fixed. So if a couple of the tests fail, this is not something to worry about for somebody studying how MySQL works. If the majority of the tests pass, consider the built binary fit for at least your educational use.

The tests take about 20 minutes to run. If you do not want to wait that long, you may simply check to see whether the *mysqld* binary was created:

```
$ ls -l sql/mysqld
```

If the build was successful, the command will produce output similar to:

```
-rwxr-xr-x   1 sasha    sasha    5001261 Jul 29 12:23 sql/mysqld
```

If the build process succeeds in creating a binary out of the unmodified clone of the public BitKeeper tree, the test suite also succeeds 95 percent of the time.

Building from Source Distribution

Although it is preferred that you use the BitKeeper repository, in some cases it might be desirable for you to use another method to build MySQL. You can use the source distribution in such cases. Although in most of the situations you will need only *gcc*, *gdb*, and GNU *make*, there are times when other tools mentioned in the section "Preparing the System to Build MySQL from BitKeeper Tree" are necessary. For example, you will need Bison to change the parser, and adding another file to the source will require the use of *autoconf*, *automake*, and *m4*. Therefore, it is still recommended that you follow the same procedures outlined in that section to prepare your system to the fullest extent possible.

Additionally, you will need the *tar* (*http://www.gnu.org/software/tar*) and *gzip* (*http://www.gnu.org/software/gzip*) utilities to unpack the archive. If you have a non-GNU *tar* already installed, it is recommended that you still install GNU *tar*. MySQL is archived using GNU *tar*, and some variants of *tar* are not compatible with it.

The following instructions explain how to download and compile MySQL using the source distribution:

1. Refer to the table listing MySQL versions in the "BitKeeper" section of this chapter, and decide which version of MySQL you would like to work with. Steps 2–5 assume you have chosen version 4.1. If you have chosen a different version, you will need to make the appropriate modifications to the following procedures, replacing *4.1* with the version you have chosen.

2. Visit *http://dev.mysql.com/downloads/mysql/4.1.html* (note the version number in the URL), scroll down to the bottom of the page where it says "Source downloads," and click on the link that says "Pick a mirror" on the "Tarball" line.

3. Optionally fill out the form at the top of the next page and submit it, or just scroll down to the bottom of the page, pick the mirror closest to you, click on the link, and proceed with the download. You will be downloading about 19 MB of data.

4. In the Unix shell, change to the directory where you plan to keep your MySQL sources, and execute the following commands:

```
$ gunzip -d downloaded-archive-name | tar xvf -
$ cd mysql-full-version-name
```

5. Follow the instructions in the section "Building MySQL from BitKeeper Tree." If you have not installed all of the required tools for a BitKeeper Tree build, additionally edit *BUILD/FINISH.sh* to comment out the following lines by adding # to the beginning:

```
aclocal    || (echo \"Can't execute aclocal\"     && exit 1)
autoheader || (echo \"Can't execute autoheader\"  && exit 1)
aclocal    || (echo \"Can't execute aclocal\"     && exit 1)
automake   || (echo \"Can't execute automake\"    && exit 1)
autoconf   || (echo \"Can't execute autoconf\"    && exit 1)
(cd bdb/dist && sh s_all)
(cd innobase && aclocal && autoheader && aclocal && automake && autoconf)
if [ -d gemini ]
then
    (cd gemini && aclocal && autoheader && aclocal && automake && autoconf)
fi"
```

Installing MySQL into a System Directory

If desired, you may install MySQL into a system directory by executing:

```
$ make install
```

as the *root* user. By default, the install prefix is */usr/local*. This can be changed by adding -prefix=*/path/to/other-prefix* to the extra_configs variable in the build script. If you do not have *root* privileges on the system, another build configuration option will be helpful: add --with-mysqld-user=*your_user_name* to extra_configs. A full listing of build configuration options can be obtained by executing:

```
# ./configure -help
```

in the root directory of the source tree.

If you do not plan to deploy the MySQL server binary you have built on this system, installing it into a system directory is not necessary. The *mysql-test-run* script permits you to start up the binary you have built and test it while it is located in the directory where it was created.

Source Code Directory Layout

Table 2-3 lists the top-level subdirectories in the MySQL source tree, with a brief explanation of each. Note that some reorganization is possible in the future versions, but most of the structure should be fairly stable.

Table 2-3. Top-level directories in MySQL source tree

Subdirectory	Description
BUILD	Developer build scripts.
Build-tools	Mostly scripts for building binary distributions.
Docs	Documentation.
NEW-RPMS	Used by the distribution build scripts to hold new RPMs.
SSL	Some configuration files from early SSL development.
VC++Files	Used for building MySQL binaries on Windows.
bdb	Berkeley DB storage engine code. Berkeley DB supports transactions and page locks. However, the interface between Berkeley DB and core MySQL is not very well developed, and InnoDB storage engine is a better choice when transactions are needed. Removed in version 5.1.
client	Command-line client utilities code.
cmd-line-utils	External libraries to enhance the command-line client (*libedit* and *recdline*).
dbug	Debugging library. I personally do not like using it because it alters execution and obscures the time-sensitive bugs, but some developers, including Monty, love it for its ability to print out the execution trace. To enable it, add *–with-debug* to `extra_configs` in your build script.
extra	Code for miscellaneous tools.
heap	Code for the in-memory tables. Moved to the *storage/* directory in 5.1.
isam	ISAM storage engine code (deprecated by MYISAM, removed in 5.0).
include	Include files.
innobase	Code for the InnoDB storage engine, which supports transactions and row-level locking. Moved to the *storage* directory in 5.1.
libmysql	Code for the client library for interfacing with the server.
libmysql_r	Thread-safe version of the client library.
libmysqld	Library for using MySQL server functionality in a standalone (embedded) mode without connecting to a server.
man	Unix manpages.
merge	Code to support ISAM-MERGE tables, which allow you to use several ISAM tables of identical structure as if they were one table. Removed in 5.1.
myisam	MyISAM storage engine code. MyISAM is the latest version of the original MySQL storage engine. It does not support transactions and requires table locks, but it uses less disk space and is faster on a number of queries than InnoDB, the transactional storage engine. Moved to the *storage* directory in 5.1.

Table 2-3. Top-level directories in MySQL source tree (continued)

Subdirectory	Description
myisammrg	Code to support MyISAM-MERGE tables, which allow you to use several MyISAM tables of identical structure as if they were one table. Moved to the *storage* directory in 5.1.
mysql-test	Regression test suite.
mysys	Core portability/helper API code.
ndb	MySQL Cluster code, utility scripts, and documentation. Moved to the *storage* directory in 5.1.
netware	Files used by the Netware port.
os2	Files used by the OS/2 port.
pstack	Code for the *pstack* library that allows the executable to unwind and resolve its own stack. Useful in a segmentation fault signal handler.
regex	Code for the *regex* library, which enables the programmer to manipulate regular expressions.
scripts	A collection of utility scripts used for a number of different purposes. When a developer writes a script and does not know where to put it, it ends up in this directory. Note, however, that this is the home of *mysqld_safe*, the king of all scripts. It is used to start the server from the command line.
sql	Catch-all directory for the core server code written in C++. This includes the parser and optimizer, the abstracted table handler (storage engine) interface, replication, query cache, table lock manager, the code to read and write table definitions, the logging code, and a number of other pieces. It does have a few stray C files that could not find a home in other directories. This is also the home of *mysqld.cc*, the file that defines `main( )`, where the execution starts when the server is launched.
sql-bench	Scripts for SQL benchmarks.
sql-common	Some of the files that are used in both the client and the server code.
strings	Custom string library to suit the needs of MySQL.
storage	Directory for storage engine code. Added in 5.1.
support-files	Miscellaneous example configuration files and utility scripts. Also contains configuration files for package builds, such as the RPM spec files.
tests	Specialized tests usually for difficult-to-duplicate bugs that do not fit into the format of the standard regression suite.
tools	In the pre-5.1 versions, this directory contained *mysqlmanager*, a utility used to perform controlled start and shutdown of the server, and to test the replication. Removed in 5.1.
unittest	Unit tests for the core API.
vio	Low-level portability network I/O code.
zlib	Code for ZLIB compression library.

Preparing the System to Run MySQL in a Debugger

To fully enjoy the study of MySQL internals, and to be able to execute the examples in the subsequent sections of this chapter, you must have *gdb* (*http://www.gnu.org/software/gdb/*) installed on your system, and be present in your PATH. You also need to have the X Window System, including a terminal program such as *xterm*. There are a number of X standard implementations, perhaps the most popular of them being X.org (*http://www.x.org*).

The tools just mentioned will be preinstalled by default on most Linux distributions. However, to confirm that you can debug threaded programs under *gdb*, it is important to make sure that */lib/libpthread.so* and */lib/libthread_db.so* are not stripped. The following example illustrates how to check this:

```
$ file -L /lib/libthread_db.so
/lib/libthread_db.so: ELF 32-bit LSB shared object, Intel 80386, version 1, not
stripped
$ file -L /lib/libpthread.so
/lib/libpthread.so: ELF 32-bit LSB shared object, Intel 80386, version 1, not
stripped
```

As you can see in the output, both libraries are not stripped. If you happen to have the misfortune of having them stripped by default, and you are not able to find a package with unstripped versions for your distribution, you can fix the problem by recompiling *glibc*.

Debugger-Guided Source Tour

Now with the tedious but necessary preparation behind your back, you can actually start exploring the source code. I find it particularly helpful, when faced with large quantities of unfamiliar code, to start by running a very simple test case in a debugger. MySQL, being a threaded server, presents a number of difficulties in this respect. Fortunately, MySQL developers have created a set of tools to facilitate the process for their own use, which they make available to the public. In this section, you will learn how to use them.

Instructions for running a simple query in a debugger:

1. Change to the *mysql-test* subdirectory in the source tree.
2. Create a new file named *t/example.test*. It is important that the file be under the *t* subdirectory, have the extension *.test*, and be different from the names of the already existing test files in the *t* subdirectory. Outside of those restrictions, the name of the file can be anything you want. If you choose a different name, however, you must also change references to it accordingly in the rest of this example.
3. Put the following line in the edited file:
   ```
   select 1;
   ```
4. Save the file.
5. Execute the following command to create the master result file:
   ```
   $ ./mysql-test-run --local --record example
   ```
6. Execute the following command to load MySQL server into *gdb* in a separate *xterm* window (if you're running it on another computer via SSH, be sure to have SSH X-forwarding enabled. If it's not possible—e.g., because you're using Windows—use *--manual-gdb* instead of *--gdb*):
   ```
   $ ./mysql-test-run --gdb example
   ```

7. An *xterm* window will open with a *gdb* prompt inside. The MySQL server will be started with a preset breakpoint in the `mysql_parse( )` function in the file *sql/sql_parse.cc*. The *mysql-test-run* script will spawn a client that will connect to the server being debugged, and start executing the queries listed in *example.test*, in our case, `select 1`. Refer to the sections "Basics of Working with gdb," and "Interesting Breakpoints and Variables," later in this chapter, to set breakpoints of interest, then enter *c* at the *gdb* prompt to continue execution.

8. When the execution of *example.test* terminates, *mysql-test-run* returns. However, the debugger window will remain open. You may connect using a MySQL command client to port 9306 and manually issue various queries, set breakpoints in the debugger, and examine their execution. A few examples follow.

   From the Unix shell, enter:

   ```
   $ ../client/mysql -uroot –host=127.0.0.1 –port=9306 test
   ```

   You will enter the MySQL command-line client shell, from which you continue with:

   ```
   $ create table t1(n int);
   ```

   When the debugger breaks in `mysql_parse( )`, type into the debugger window:

   ```
   disa 1
   b mysql_insert
   c
   ```

   At the MySQL command-line client prompt, type:

   ```
   insert into t1 values(345);
   ```

   The debugger will break in `mysql_insert( )`. In the debugger window, type:

   ```
   bt
   ```

   The debugger shows you the stack trace at the current breakpoint.

9. When finished with this debugger-guided source tour, press Ctrl-C if you do not have the *gdb* prompt, execute the *quit* command in the debugger, confirm that you want to stop the program being run when prompted, and return to the shell prompt from which you have executed *mysql-test-run*.

10. To speed up the execution of your next debugger-guided source tour, execute the following command at the shell prompt to clean up:

    ```
    $ rm -f var/run/*.pid
    ```

Basics of Working with gdb

gdb has a command-line interface similar to a Unix shell. You type a command and then press the Enter key to execute it. If you have never worked with *gdb* before, begin by executing the *help* command, which produces the following output:

```
List of classes of commands:

aliases -- Aliases of other commands
breakpoints -- Making program stop at certain points
```

```
data -- Examining data
files -- Specifying and examining files
internals -- Maintenance commands
obscure -- Obscure features
running -- Running the program
stack -- Examining the stack
status -- Status inquiries
support -- Support facilities
tracepoints -- Tracing of program execution without stopping the program
user-defined -- User-defined commands

Type "help" followed by a class name for a list of commands in that class.
Type "help" followed by command name for full documentation.
Command name abbreviations are allowed if unambiguous.
```

The instructions in the preceding output give you a starting point from which you can continue a more in-depth study of *gdb*. For example, if you want to learn about how to run a program being debugged, execute *help running*, which in turn gives you the following:

```
Running the program.

List of commands:

advance -- Continue the program up to the given location (same form as args for break
command)
attach -- Attach to a process or file outside of GDB
continue -- Continue program being debugged
detach -- Detach a process or file previously attached
disconnect -- Disconnect from a target
finish -- Execute until selected stack frame returns
handle -- Specify how to handle a signal
info handle -- What debugger does when program gets various signals
interrupt -- Interrupt the execution of the debugged program
jump -- Continue program being debugged at specified line or address
kill -- Kill execution of program being debugged
next -- Step program
nexti -- Step one instruction
run -- Start debugged program
set args -- Set argument list to give program being debugged when it is started
set environment -- Set environment variable value to give the program
set follow-fork-mode -- Set debugger response to a program call of fork or vfork
set scheduler-locking -- Set mode for locking scheduler during execution
set step-mode -- Set mode of the step operation
show args -- Show argument list to give program being debugged when it is started
show follow-fork-mode -- Show debugger response to a program call of fork or vfork
show scheduler-locking -- Show mode for locking scheduler during execution
show step-mode -- Show mode of the step operation
signal -- Continue program giving it signal specified by the argument
step -- Step program until it reaches a different source line
stepi -- Step one instruction exactly
target -- Connect to a target machine or process
thread -- Use this command to switch between threads
thread apply -- Apply a command to a list of threads
```

```
apply all -- Apply a command to all threads
tty -- Set terminal for future runs of program being debugged
unset environment -- Cancel environment variable VAR for the program
until -- Execute until the program reaches a source line greater than the current

Type "help" followed by command name for full documentation.
Command name abbreviations are allowed if unambiguous.
```

Now you have a list of commands, related to running a program, to learn. Suppose you want to learn about the *run* command. Execute *help run*. The following output is produced:

```
Start debugged program.  You may specify arguments to give it.
Args may include "*", or "[...]"; they are expanded using "sh".
Input and output redirection with ">", "<", or ">>" are also allowed.

With no arguments, uses arguments last specified (with "run" or "set args").
To cancel previous arguments and run with no arguments,
use "set args" without arguments.
```

Using the preceding method, you can get a full listing of *gdb* commands and learn about each one. If you prefer reading the manual, it is available at *http://www.gnu.org/software/gdb/documentation*.

Table 2-4 is a list of commands that you may find particularly useful when studying the MySQL source. Note the abbreviated version column. Using abbreviated versions significantly speeds up the tasks even if you are a fast typist.

Table 2-4. Common gdb commands

Command	Common abbreviation	Description	Examples
breakpoint	*b*	Sets a breakpoint.	*b mysql_select*
			b sql_parse.cc:245
continue	*c*	Continues execution to the next breakpoint, until the program terminates. If an argument *n* is given and the execution continues from a breakpoint, stop on that breakpoint only on the *n*th pass.	*c*
			c 10
next	*n*	Executes the next line without stepping into subroutine calls. If an argument *n* is given, do this *n* times or until the program stops for another reason.	*n*
			n 15
step	*s*	Executes the next line, stepping into subroutine calls. If an argument *n* is given, do this *n* times or until the program stops for another reason.	*s*
			s 20
finish	*fin*	Executes until the current subroutine returns.	*fin*
backtrace	*bt*	Prints the stack trace. With the full argument, also prints the values of local variables in each stack frame.	*bt*
			bt full
enable	*ena*	Enables a disabled breakpoint.	*ena 3*
disable	*disa*	Disables an enabled breakpoint.	*disa 3*

Table 2-4. *Common gdb commands (continued)*

Command	Common abbreviation	Description	Examples
info breakpoints	*i b*	Prints a list of breakpoints with detailed information about each.	*i b*
info line	*i li*	Prints information about the current line being debugged if the argument is omitted, otherwise prints information about the specified line.	*i li* *i li main* *i li mi_open.c:83*
print	*p*	Prints the value of the variable or expression specified as an argument.	*p thd* *p *thd* *p thd->query* *p length*
list	*l*	Prints the source code based on the value of the argument.	*l mysql_query* *l sql_parse.cc:245*
info local	*i lo*	Shows the values of local variables of the current frame.	*info local*
up	*up*	Selects and prints the local variables of the frame above the current one. The argument tells the number of frames to go up; the default is 1.	*up* *up 2*
down	*down*	Selects and prints the local variables of the frame below the current one. The argument tells how many frames to go down; the default is 1.	*down* *down 3*
info threads	*i th*	Lists all running threads with some information about each.	*i th*
thread	*thr*	Switches to the specified thread.	*thr 10*
info registers	*i r*	Prints the contents of the processor registers.	*i r*
disassemble	*disas*	Disassembles the specified section of code. If no argument is given, disassembles the executable code surrounding the *pc* register of the current stack frame.	*disas* *disas mysql_select*

Finding Things in the Source

A typical question programmers ask when working with a large unfamiliar code base is "Where in the world is the function get_and_lock_X( ) defined?" There are many techniques to find the answer, and many programmers have their own favorites. For those who do not, or who are having a hard time adapting them to the MySQL source, I will share mine.

Suppose you need to find the definition of mysql_lock_tables( ). Follow these steps:

1. Start an instance of MySQL server in a debugger as outlined in the section "Debugger-Guided Source Tour."

2. Once the debugger window opens, type in the debugger window:

   ```
   i li mysql_lock_tables
   ```

The debugger responds with:

```
Line 86 of "lock.cc"
starts at address 0x8125540 <mysql_lock_tables__FP3THDPP8st_tableUi>
    and ends at 0x812554f <mysql_lock_tables__FP3THDPP8st_tableUi+15>.
```

This tells you that `mysql_lock_tables()` is defined on line 86 of *lock.cc*. Unfortunately, it doesn't say which directory the file is in, so one more step is necessary.

3. Execute the following command from the root of the source tree:

```
$ find . -name lock.cc | xargs ls -l
```

This command returns two filenames in the output:

```
lrwxrwxrwx   1 sasha    sasha          16 Jul 29 15:08 ./libmysqld/lock.cc -> ./../
sql/lock.cc
-rw-rw-r--   1 sasha    sasha       20863 Jul 14 21:40 ./sql/lock.cc
```

From the output, you can see that *libmysqld/lock.cc* is a just a symbolic link, while the actual file is *sql/lock.cc*.

Sometimes things do not go as smoothly as in the previous example. What appears to be a function could in reality be a preprocessor macro. If that happens, the debugger will tell you it knows nothing about the symbol. Fortunately, *grep* comes to the rescue. Suppose you need to find the definition of `ha_commit()`, and the debugger has already told you that there is no such symbol. Execute the following command from the root of the source tree:

```
$ find . -name \*.h | xargs grep ha_commit
```

The following output is returned:

```
./sql/handler.h:513:#define ha_commit_stmt(thd)
(ha_commit_trans((thd), &((thd)->transaction.stmt)))
./sql/handler.h:515:#define ha_commit(thd) (ha_commit_trans((thd),
&((thd)->transaction.all)))
./sql/handler.h:543:int ha_commit_complete(THD *thd);
./sql/handler.h:545:int ha_commit_trans(THD *thd, THD_TRANS *trans);
./sql/mysql_priv.h:859:extern ulong ha_commit_count,
ha_rollback_count,table_cache_size;
```

You can see from the output that the macro `ha_commit()` is defined on line 515 of *sql/handler.h* and is aliased to `ha_commit_trans()` with an additional argument.

Interesting Breakpoints and Variables

If you have ever worked with an unfamiliar code base of significant size, you have most certainly been confronted with the challenge of mentally penetrating the execution flow. Yes, I understand this `init_X()` function, but where in the world does the meat really begin when I do operation Y?

Table 2-5, along with debugger-guided source tours inspired by its contents, will hopefully help you answer a number of such questions. It is based on the 4.1 source, but for the most part should be applicable to other versions. Although MySQL developers could possibly change the names of the functions and the code organization at any time in future versions, in practice 95 percent of the functions continue to carry their original name and role once that section of the code has stabilized. The asterisks in the final column do not indicate C++ pointers; they mean "all variables whose names match."

Table 2-5. Key functions and variables involved in common MySQL operations

Operation	Good place for an entry breakpoint	Interesting variables to examine

Select query	`mysql_select()`	`*thd`
		`thd->query`
		`*tables`
		`*join`

Insert query	`mysql_insert()`	`*thd`
		`thd->query`
		`*table`
		`fields`
		`values_list`

Update query	`mysql_update()`	`*thd`
		`thd->query`
		`*table_list`
		`fields`
		`values`
		`*conds`

Delete query	`mysql_delete()`	`*thd`
		`thd->query`
		`*table_list`
		`*conds`

Checking whether the query can be answered from a query cache	`Query_cache::send_result_to_client()`	`*this`
		`*thd`
		`sql`

Reading a communication packet from a client	`my_net_read()`	`*net`

Writing a communication packet to a client	`my_net_write()`	`*net`
		`packet`
		`len`

Authenticating a connection	`check_connection()`	`*thd` `thd->net`

Logging an update on a replication master	`MYSQL_LOG::write(Log_event *)`	`*event_info`
		`*event_info->thd`
		`event_info->thd->query`

Replication slave startup	`start_slave_threads()`	`*mi`
Execution of replication thread on the slave that handles network I/O	`handle_slave_io()`	`*mi`
Execution of replication thread on the slave that handles SQL commands	`handle_slave_sql()`	`*rli`

Table 2-5. Key functions and variables involved in common MySQL operations (continued)

Operation	Good place for an entry breakpoint	Interesting variables to examine
Opening a table	open_table( )	*thd thd->query db table_name alias
Reading the table definition file (.frm)	openfrm( )	name alias
Opening a MyISAM table	ha_myisam::open( )	*this name
Opening an InnoDB table	ha_innobase::open( )	*this name
Acquiring a table lock	mysql_lock_tables( )	*thd thd->query **tables
Committing a transaction	ha_commit_trans( )	*thd *trans

Making a Source Modification

If you have not added any extra files to the source, after making the change, simply execute:

```
$ make
```

from the root of the source tree, and wait for the recompilation and relinking to finish. If the only files you have changed are in the *sql* directory, it is sufficient to run *make* only in that directory, which will reduce the time of the process because *make* would doesn't check other directories to see whether anything needs to be done there.

If you have added new files, follow these steps:

1. For each directory where you added files, edit *Makefile.am* in that directory.

2. In each *Makefile.am*, find the appropriate variable that ends in SOURCES. For example, in the *sql* directory, the variable is called mysqld_SOURCES, and in the *myisam* directory, libmyisam_a_SOURCES.

3. Add the names of your C/C++ files that you have added to the SOURCES variable.

4. In each *Makefile.am* file, find the variables INCLUDES and noinst_HEADERS. Add the names of the new headers that you want to be installed by a *make install* command to INCLUDES, and the ones that do not need to be installed to *noinst_ HEADERS*.

5. Execute *BUILD/compile-generic-debug* (or its equivalent) as described in the section "Building MySQL from BitKeeper Tree."

Coding Guidelines

If you are making changes to MySQL, it is recommended that you follow the same coding guidelines as MySQL developers. This will make it easier for your code to work with what's already written, help you avoid bugs, and increase the chances of your patches being accepted by MySQL developers without serious modifications.

MySQL developers make their coding guidelines publicly available at *http://dev. mysql.com/doc/internals/en/index.html*.

In addition, I will provide a reorganized summary with some extra tips and comments from my own experience.

Stability

Here are some guidelines for preserving the code's stability while making changes:

- Always remember that, more often than not, you are in a thread and must follow the rules of thread-safe programming.

- Most global variables have an associated mutex that other threads will lock before accessing it. Make sure to learn which mutex is associated with each global variable, and lock it when accessing that variable.

- Be aware that you have very little stack space available. Chunks of memory larger than 100 bytes or so should be allocated with sql_alloc( ) or my_malloc( ).

- When possible, choose sql_alloc( ) over my_malloc( ) for small allocations. sql_alloc( ) allocates memory from a pre-allocated connection memory pool, while my_malloc( ) is just a wrapper around the regular malloc( ) call. sql_alloc( ) can be called anywhere in the stack of execution below do_command( ). To verify the stack position in question, set a breakpoint there in the debugger, and when it is reached, run the *bt* command. Note that the memory allocated with sql_alloc( ) lasts until the end of the query execution. If you want your allocation to persist past that, use my_malloc( ).

- Perform large allocations with my_malloc( ), and free the allocated blocks with my_free( ) as soon as possible.

- Do not free pointers allocated with sql_alloc( ). The memory pool will be freed at once with a call to free_root( ) at the end of the query.

- If a pointer was allocated with my_malloc( ), free it with my_free( ).

- Do not use exceptions. Whenever possible, the code is compiled with exceptions disabled.

- Do not use STL, *iostream*, or any other C++ extension that would require linking against *libstdc++*.

- Do not introduce dependencies on additional external libraries whenever possible.

- Try to reuse the existing MySQL code as much as possible.

Portability

Following these suggestions increases the likelihood that your code will work on systems other than the one you write and test on:

- Do not use direct *libc* calls. Instead, use the portability wrappers from *mysys* and *strings*. Usually a wrapper call from *mysys* will have the same name as the *libc* call prefixed with my_: for example, my_open( ), my_close( ), my_malloc( ), my_free( ).

- Be aware of differences in byte order across systems. Use macros such as int4store( ) and int4korr( ) if the data string created on one system could be transferred to another or shared among systems in any way.

- Be aware of alignment issues. Do not assign integer values to a pointer that could be unaligned. For example, instead of:

    ```
    *((char*)p+1) = n
    ```

    write:

    ```
    memcpy((char*)p+1,&n, 4)
    ```

    or for machine-independent byte-order:

    ```
    int4store((char*)p+1,n);
    ```

- When introducing a system or compiler-specific optimization that might not be supported on another system, make sure to enclose it in an #ifdef block, and provide an alternative if that optimization is not available.

- Do not put C++ style comments into C files, even though some C compilers support it.

- Use predefined types from *include/my_global.h* (e.g., uint8, uint32) if you need to control the byte size of the variable.

Performance

The following suggestions can help you maximize your code's memory and processor use:

- Develop a habit of thinking about performance naturally and coding that way. Learn the basics of how the CPU works and visualize what happens to it on the assembly level when your C/C++ code is executed.

- Reuse the existing MySQL code as much as possible.

- Be aware of what is going on inside the calls you are making.

- Avoid unnecessary system calls. Think of ways to combine several into one; for example, use IO_CACHE functions and macros instead of my_read( ) and my_write( ).

- Avoid unnecessary instantiation of objects.

- Do not declare large functions inline.

Style and Ease of Integration

Following are some conventions established by the MySQL developers for general consistency.

- Follow the indentation, variable naming, and commenting guidelines in *internals.html*.

- Do not reformat the code you did not write. Make sure your editor is not configured to do that automatically.

- In your functions, return 0 on success, and a non-zero value on failure.

- When possible, use the following syntax to call several functions short-circuiting out if one fails:

```
if (a() || b() || c())
    goto err;
```

- Use TRUE and FALSE instead of true and false.

- Use my_bool in C and bool in C++ source files.

- Pass by pointer instead of by reference in the C++ code.

- Write optimized code even in the sections where performance is not critical.

Keeping Your BitKeeper Repository Up to Date

MySQL source keeps changing with time—a lot during the alpha stage, less during beta, and only very little once it reaches the stable status. It is recommended that you stay current with the recent developments whether you are just studying or are making modifications to the MySQL source.

Instructions follow on how to update your local BitKeeper repository. This section applies to the commercial version of BitKeeper.

1. If you have not previously committed a change, edit *BitKeeper/triggers/post-commit* and replace its contents with the following:

```
#! /bin/sh
exit 0
```

This script executes every time you commit a change, and in its original version it will notify MySQL developers and the public about the details of your change. This notification is desirable when a MySQL developer makes a commit, but may not be so desirable for you. If you do want the world to be notified every time you commit, you may keep this script the way it is.

2. At the Unix shell prompt, from anywhere inside the repository tree, execute:

```
$ bk citool &
```

BitKeeper will take a couple of minutes to examine the changed files, and then it will present a GUI dialog asking you to comment on each change you have made.

3. After you have commented your changes to each individual file, as well as to the entire change set, press the Commit button twice and wait for the BitKeeper window to disappear.

4. Execute the following command at the Unix shell prompt from anywhere inside the repository tree:

    ```
    $ bk pull
    ```

5. In some rather rare cases, the pull may result in conflicts. This usually happens when you change the same lines at the same time that some MySQL developer does. In this event, BitKeeper will print a message on the standard output about failed conflicts and instruct you to run *bk resolve*. Do so, and follow the prompts that BitKeeper gives you. If needed, refer to the BitKeeper documentation by running *bk helptool*.

Submitting a Patch

If you have added a feature or fixed a bug, and would like MySQL developers to consider it for submission, follow the steps in this section. The instructions assume you have used the commercial version of BitKeeper. If you have not, you will have to *diff* your source against an unmodified copy in step 1.

1. Execute the following command from the directory inside the source tree:

    ```
    $ bk -r diffs -c > /tmp/mysql-patch.diff
    ```

2. Examine the contents of */tmp/mysql-patch.diff* to make sure the patch makes sense to you.

3. Send a message to *internals@lists.mysql.com*. If the patch is reasonably small (under a few kilobytes), include it in the body of the message. Otherwise, post it at a URL and include the URL in the body of the message. Make sure to include a brief description of the patch.

## CHAPTER 3

Core Classes, Structures, Variables, and APIs

The MySQL source code contains several hundred thousand lines and continues to grow. Finding your way in it is quite a challenge. However, the task is not as difficult and daunting as it appears initially, if you are familiar with the core elements of the code and their respective roles. The purpose of this chapter is to give you a foundation that will enable you to read most sections of the code with some degree of ease.

This chapter is meant to be a literacy crash course. We will focus on the core elements of the code that are critical to understanding what is generally going on. The more specific details of various modules will be discussed in later chapters dedicated to them.

In the discussion of the various code elements, I will inevitably have to leave out a number of less significant class members, API calls, and global variables due to space constraints. Additionally, by the time this book is printed, a number of new code elements might appear, and a few might change names or functions to some extent. However, it is reasonable to expect that such cases will be minimal. The major part of the code we will discuss in this chapter has already stabilized and will not change significantly.

I must also note that again for reasons of space constraints we will have to leave out a large number of vital classes, structures, and macros. However, I hope that once you become familiar with what we have covered, you will have sufficient background to elicit the additional information through your own study of the code.

THD

The THD class defines a thread descriptor. It contains the information pertinent to the thread that is handling the given request. Each client connection is handled by a thread. Each thread has a descriptor object. Handling client requests is not the only time a thread is created. MySQL has a number of system threads, such as the replication slave threads and delayed insert threads. Additionally, there exists a special case when a thread descriptor object is created without a thread—the server running in bootstrap mode to create the necessary system tables during installation.

Due to the close relationship between client connections and threads, the terms *thread* and *connection* are often used synonymously by MySQL developers. I will do so in the discussion of this class.

THD is perhaps the most frequently referenced type in the server code. It is passed as the first argument in most of the higher-level calls. With the exception of low-level storage and retrieval operations, few things of significance happen inside the server without some involvement of this class. Familiarity with its members will give you a good idea of the overall architecture and capabilities of the server.

THD is defined in *sql/sql_class.h* and implemented in *sql/sql_class.cc*.

Most commonly, an instance of THD is pointed to by a variable thd of type THD*. Therefore, if you are trying to find places in the code where a particular member of this class is used, the following command will work almost without fail:

```
grep "thd->var_name" sql/*.cc
```

The class consists mostly of data members, which will be the primary focus of this discussion. There are a few fairly simple and infrequently used methods, which we will not discuss due to the space constraints. However, once you understand the role of the data members we will discuss, the function of the methods will become apparent to you from their source.

Table 3-1 lists the most prominent members of the THD class. Note that in version 4.1, part of THD was moved into the newly created class Statement, and THD was made a subclass of Statement. The table also lists the public members of Statement that were in THD and are still frequently referenced as members of THD.

Table 3-1. Members of the THD class

Member definition	Description
LEX* lex	Parse tree descriptor for the current query. It is a member of Statement in version 4.1 and later.
char* query	Current query in plain text. In version 4.1 and later, a member of Statement.
uint32 query_length	Length (in bytes) of the current query. In version 4.1 and later, a member of Statement.
Item* free_list	A linked list of all parse tree nodes of the current query. Used during post-execution cleanup (free_items( ) in *sql/sql_parse.cc*). In version 4.1 and later, a member of Statement.
MEM_ROOT mem_root	Thread memory pool. Used by alloc_root( ) and free_root( ). In version 4.1 and later, a member of Statement.
NET net	Client connection descriptor.
MEM_ROOT warn_root	Memory pool used for issuing warnings and errors. New in version 4.1.
Protocol* protocol	Client/server communication protocol descriptor. Will point to a different object type based on whether the current query is a prepared statement or not. New in version 4.1.
HASH user_vars	Hash to store user variables used in queries like this: SET @a:=31; SELECT col1 FROM t1 WHERE col2=@a;

Table 3-1. Members of the THD class (continued)

Member definition	Description
`String packet`	Dynamic buffer used for network I/O.
`struct system_ variables variables`	System variables local to this connection that can be changed by the client. For example, `SET LOCAL sort_buffer_size=256000` will set the value of `variables.sortbuff_size` to 256,000 and affect the processing of the ORDER BY and GROUP BY queries that require sorting. New in version 4.0.
`Statement_map stmt_map`	A hash of all the prepared statements and cursors on this connection. New in version 4.1.
`char* host`	The host the client is connecting from.
`char* priv_host`	The client host value, which is obtained by matching the host identification from the connection socket parameters against the contents of *mysql.user* table. In other words, the first matching host column value from the *mysql.user* table. Usually the same as `host`. Note that in MySQL, a user entity consists of two parts: a username and a host name. So for example, *john@localhost* is separate from *john@www*.
`char* user`	The user the client has passed to the access control system.
`char* priv_user`	The user value match in the *mysql.user* table for the user value passed to the access control system. Usually the same as `user`.
`char* db`	Currently selected database.
`uint32 db_length`	Length of the string pointed to by `db`.
`char* ip`	The IP address the client has connected from in alphanumeric form.
`char* host_or_ip`	Points to the host the client has connected from if available, otherwise (for example, if the reverse DNS lookup failed) points to an alphanumeric string containing the client's IP address.
`const char* proc_info`	Points to the value of the `Info` column in the output of SHOW PROCESSLIST. Will usually be set before an operation that could take a long time. Very useful for troubleshooting performance problems.
`ulong client_ capabilities`	A bit mask of client capabilities. As far as the client-server protocol is concerned, aside from some minor limitations, all MySQL versions are forward and backward compatible. Any client can talk to any server, regardless of the version. This variable helps the server know how to not confuse clients of older versions. It also keeps track of whether the client is prepared to use SSL or compression.
`ulong master_access`	In the MySQL access control system, privileges can be granted to a user either on the global level, or on the database, table, or column level. This variable is a bit mask of the global privileges for the current connection.
`ulong db_access`	Client privilege bit mask for the currently selected database on the current connection.
`ulong col_access`	The name of the variable is somewhat misleading. One would think that just like the other two, it would be a bit mask for some kind of column access. However, this happens to be just a temporary variable used to determine whether the user has some privilege on a table when processing SHOW TABLES. If she does not have any, the table will be excluded from the output.
`TABLE* open_tables`	Linked list of regular tables in use by this thread. A regular table is a non-temporary table that was referenced with a higher-level query such as SELECT, UPDATE, DELETE, INSERT, REPLACE, or ALTER. Tables used in HANDLER queries, and derived tables in subqueries, do not fit into this category (see `handler_tables` and `derived_ tables`). Tables listed here are automatically closed at the end of the query.

Table 3-1. Members of the THD class (continued)

Member definition	Description
`TABLE* handler_tables`	Linked list of tables opened with HANDLER OPEN by this thread. HANDLER commands provide a direct interface to the low-level storage engine bypassing the optimizer. New in version 4.0.
`TABLE* temporary_tables`	Linked list of temporary tables created by this thread. A temporary table exists in the scope of the given connection, and can be created either manually with CREATE TEMPORARY TABLE, or inside the optimizer when it is unable to retrieve the results of a SELECT by merely examining the query tables.

`TABLE* derived_tables`	Linked list of derived tables created in this query. A *derived table* is a table resulting from a sub-query in the FROM clause of a SELECT statement. For example, in
	
	`SELECT  AVG(a) FROM (SELECT COUNT(*) AS a, b`
	`FROM t1 GROUP BY b) AS t_derived WHERE n > 100`
	
	t_derived is a derived table. Note that the term *derived table* is not precisely defined in the SQL standard, and therefore MySQL documentation refers more precisely to a "sub-query in the FROM clause." However, for historical reasons, "derived" is being used throughout the code. New in version 4.1.

`MYSQL_LOCK* lock`	A descriptor structure containing the list of all the tables automatically locked by this thread without the use of the LOCK TABLES command. This type of locking occurs when the server processes regular queries such as SELECT, INSERT, or UPDATE and the need for a lock is discovered. Only one group of tables may be locked at any given time. The lock must be acquired and released for the entire group at once. If set to a nonzero value, locked_tables (see later) must be set to 0.
`MYSQL_LOCK* locked_tables`	A descriptor structure containing a list of all the tables locked with LOCK TABLES. If set to a nonzero value, lock must be set to 0.
`struct st_my_thread_var *mysys_var`	A structure used to store the information about the current POSIX Threads condition that this thread might be waiting for. Used to wake sleeping threads during shutdown or when they are being killed with the KILL command. The condition gets artificially broadcast, and the threads awaken, check their killed flag, and realize that they are supposed to exit. For details, see THD::enter_cond( ) and THD::exit_cond( ) in *sql/sql_class.h*, as well as THD::awake( ) in *sql/sql_class.cc*. If a thread is not waiting for anything, mysys_var is set to 0. Any time you plan to wait using a call to pthread_cond_wait( ), call THD::enter_cond( ) first, and once you are done waiting, THD::exit_cond( ).
`enum enum_server_command command`	Type of the current server command. The most common one is COM_QUERY. All possible types are listed in *include/mysql_com.h* under the definition of the enum_server_command type.
`uint32 server_id`	This variable is used in the slave SQL thread during replication. Each server participating in replication must be assigned a unique ID in its configuration file. When a master performs an update, it logs the originating server ID to the binary update log. When updates are performed by a regular client, the originating ID is the same as the server ID. However, the slave thread must preserve the originating ID of the master to avoid infinite update loops. If this is done, the slave can break the potentially infinite replication loop by skipping update events that have the same ID as the server ID. By setting the value of this variable during query initialization, the caller is able to control which server ID gets logged with the update.

Table 3-1. Members of the THD class (continued)

Member definition	Description
delayed_insert *di	Current delayed insert descriptor. Used for processing INSERT DELAYED queries, which permit the client to request that the rows be inserted some time in the future when the table becomes available.
struct st_transactions transaction	Transaction descriptor. Used to manage logical update logging, keeping track of changed tables (for the query cache).
Statement *current_ statement	Current prepared statement descriptor. Set to 0 if there is no prepared statement. New in version 4.1.
uint server_status	A bit mask used to report status messages to the client. Examples of when status messages might occur: if the server is in the middle of a transaction, if there exists some additional query result data to retrieve, or if the query did not use a key efficiently.
ulonglong next_ insert_id	MySQL supports the generation of automatically incrementing unique keys. Only one such key is allowed per table. The client, however, is allowed to set the value of the next generated key by executing SET INSERT_ID=*value*. When this command is executed, next_insert_id is set to the specified value.
ulonglong last_insert_ id	Set to the value of the last generated automatically incrementing unique key. Available to the client through the SQL function LAST_INSERT_ID( ). Can also be set manually by the client by executing SET LAST_INSERT_ID=*value*.
table_map used_tables	A bit mask to keep track of which tables actually need to be examined in order to answer the query. Heavily used by the optimizer.
USER_CONN *user_connect	Descriptor of user resource limits. MySQL has the capability to restrict the number of connections and queries per hour that a particular user is allowed to perform. New in version 4.0.
CHARSET_INFO *db_ charset	Character set descriptor for the current database. New in version 4.1.
List <MYSQL_ERROR> warn_list	Some queries may produce warnings. They will be stored in this variable and can be viewed later with SHOW WARNINGS. New in version 4.1.
ulong query_id	Internal ID of the currently executed query. Every new query will have a value one higher than the previous query.
ulong thread_id	A server-assigned numeric ID for this thread. This value shows up in the Id column of SHOW PROCESSLIST output and is used as an argument to the KILL command.
pthread_t real_id	POSIX Threads ID for this thread.
uint system_thread	Set to a nonzero value indicating thread type for nonclient threads. Examples of such threads include delayed insert threads, replication slave threads, event scheduler and worker threads, and the NDB cluster binlog thread. Set to 0 for client threads.
bool slave_thread	Set to 1 (true) for slave threads.
bool bootstrap	Set to 1 (true) for the bootstrap thread. The bootstrap thread is not really a thread. When mysqld is started with the –bootstrap option, it merely executes queries read from the standard input, and exits once the standard input is closed. However, an instance of THD is created and marked as a special case by setting this variable. The bootstrap execution mode is used during installation to create the system tables necessary for server operation.
bool volatile killed	Set to 1 (true) when a thread is asked to terminate. Each thread is responsible for checking this variable frequently during time-consuming operations. If set, the thread must perform the cleanup as quickly as possible and exit.

NET

The NET structure defines a network connection descriptor. MySQL uses a fairly complex protocol on top of the one already provided by the operating system for client/server communication. This structure lies at the core of the protocol's implementation.

The protocol defines its own packet format. A packet can send a command, a message, or a block of data. Packets can be compressed, or transmitted over the SSL layer.

All network communication functions use NET one way or the other, usually by accepting it as an argument. Becoming familiar with the members of NET is a major step toward understanding the client/server communication protocol.

NET is a rather small structure, which permits us to cover it in its entirety. It is defined in *include/mysql_com.h*. The same definition is also used by the client library, which is written in C. This would exclude any possibility for NET to have any methods. However, there are a number of functions that accept NET* as an argument, which will be covered in Chapter 5.

Table 3-2 lists the NET members.

Table 3-2. Members of the NET class

Member definition	Description
Vio* vio	Low-level network I/O socket descriptor. V stands for virtual. The VIO abstraction was originally created to support SSL. Now it is also used to support Windows shared memory and named pipe connections. It also facilitates cross-platform porting in many other ways.
unsigned char *buff	Start of the data buffer.
unsigned char *buff_end	End of the data buffer.
unsigned char* write_pos	Points to the position in the data buffer from which the next write will take the data.
unsigned char* read_pos	Points to the position in the data buffer to which the next read will put the data.
my_socket fd	A variable needed to support Perl DBI/DBD client interface. Contains the number of the operating system socket descriptor.
unsigned long max_packet	Current size of the network packet buffer. Initially set to the value of net-buffer-length configuration variable, but may be increased to accommodate a larger packet up to the value of max-allowed-packet configuration variable.
unsigned long max_packet_size	Maximum allowed packet size on this connection. Set to the value of max-allowed-packet configuration variable.
unsigned int pkt_nr	Current packet sequence number for the uncompressed protocol. Packet sequence numbers are mainly used for sanity checks in the protocol. An out-of-order packet sequence number can be caused only by a bug, barring hardware and operating system problems.

Table 3-2. Members of the NET class (continued)

Member definition	Description
`unsigned int compress_pkt_nr`	Current packet sequence number for the compressed protocol.
`unsigned int write_timeout`	Maximum amount of time one network write operation is allowed to take before it times out with an error. Set to the value of `net-write-timeout` configuration variable.
`unsigned int read_timeout`	Maximum amount of time one network read operation is allowed to take before it times out with an error. Set to the value of `net-read-timeout` configuration variable.
`unsigned int retry_count`	How many times a failed network I/O operation should be retried before considering that it has failed. Many platforms interrupt potentially successful network I/O with an error for a number of peculiar reasons. Failing once, therefore, is not a good reason to give up. Set to the value of `net-retry-count` configuration variable.
`int fcntl`	Currently not used. Might be removed in future versions.
`my_bool compress`	Set to 1 when data compression is used.
`unsigned long remain_in_buf`	In the compressed protocol, the reading peer will attempt a read from the socket that may exceed the compressed length of the packet. Thus, it will read a portion of the next packet. This variable keeps track of how many extra bytes were read. When compression is not enabled, the reading peer will try only the exact length of the packet after reading the header first. No extra bytes will be read, so this variable is not used if there is no compression. However, this algorithm is not very efficient for small packets. It is reasonable to suppose that it will be optimized in the future to attempt a larger read from the start. If this happens, it is very likely that this variable will be used to keep track of how many bytes past the first packet boundary have been read.
`unsigned long length`	Contains the length of the current packet in bytes. Does not include the header.
`unsigned long buf_length`	Contains the length of the packet buffer. Not to be confused with the length of the packet itself, which for instance does not include the header. Additionally, the buffer may contain a carryover from the next packet if compression is used.
`unsigned long where_b`	The value of `read_pos - buff`, or in other words, the offset of the current reading position in the buffer.
`unsigned int *return_status`	Points to the `server_status` variable in the THD thread descriptor associated with the connection.
`unsigned char reading_or_writing`	Set to 0 when there is no ongoing I/O operation, to 1 when a read is in progress, and 2 when a write is in progress. Used in the handling of SHOW PROCESSLIST query.
`char save_char`	Some client routines can achieve better performance if they can assume a zero byte immediately after the end of the packet data in the buffer. When compression is used, that byte is not safe to overwrite with a zero without saving it first. This variable is used to save that byte and restore it later.
`my_bool no_send_ok`	Most of the time, a successful operation on the server is reported with the OK packet to the client. However, sometimes this is not desirable. If this variable is set to 1, no OK packet will be sent.

Table 3-2. Members of the NET class (continued)

Member definition	Description
char last_error[MYSQL_ERRMSG_SIZE]	A buffer containing the text of the last error message sent to the client. If there was none, the first byte will be set to 0.
char sqlstate[SQLSTATE_LENGTH+1]	Buffer containing the value of SQL state used by ODBC and JDBC drivers. New in version 4.1. In earlier versions, the drivers had to figure out the state themselves from the value of the error code. Since 4.1, the server does it for them.
unsigned int last_errno	The value of MySQL error code from the last error message sent to the client. Set to 0 if there was no error.
unsigned char error	Set to 0 if the I/O operation happened successfully, to 1 if there was some logical error on the protocol level, to 2 if there was a system call or standard library failure, and to 3 in a special case when a large packet is successfully skipped after a failed attempt to expand the buffer to accommodate it.
gptr query_cache_query	Used for proper synchronization between the network I/O code and the query cache. New in version 4.0.
my_bool report_error	Set to 1 if the error should be reported to the client.
my_bool return_errno	Set to 1 if the MySQL error code value should be reported to the client. In version 4.1, this would also include the reporting of SQL state.

TABLE

The TABLE structure defines a database table descriptor. A table can exist in an open or closed state. In order to be used in the server, it has to be opened. Whenever this happens, a table descriptor is created, and placed in the table cache to be reused later when another request is made that references the same table.

Instances of TABLE are frequently referenced in the parser, optimizer, access control, and query cache code. It glues things together in a number of ways. Studying its members is a good way to become acquainted to a degree with the low-level details of the server implementation.

This structure is defined in *sql/table.h* as struct st_table, but then is aliased to TABLE with a typedef in *sql/handler.h*.

Note that in version 5.1 TABLE was refactored, and portions of it were moved to TABLE_SHARE class, which is shared between the instances of the same physical table. TABLE_SHAREs are cached in the table definition cache.

TABLE is a large structure. We will cover only the most essential parts. Table 3-3 lists some of its members.

Table 3-3. Members of the TABLE class

Member definition	Description
`handler *file`	Pointer to the storage engine (handler) object for this table. The object is used for all low-level data storage and retrieval operations.
`Field **field`	Array of field descriptors for each field in this table. The number of fields in the `fields` variable.
`HASH  name_hash`	A hash for locating fields by name. Will be used if the number of fields is at least `MAX_FIELDS_BEFORE_HASH`, which is currently defined in *sql/mysql_priv.h* and set to 32.
`byte *record[2]`	A pair of temporary buffers used for record operations by the optimizer.
`uint fields`	Number of fields in the table.
`uint reclength`	Length of the record in bytes. Note that this refers to the length of the record when it is processed in memory on the optimizer level, not when it is stored by the storage engine.
`uint rec_buff_length`	Length of the temporary buffer allocated for manipulating one record.
`uint keys`	Number of keys in the table.
`uint key_parts`	A column that is a part of a key is called *key part* in MySQL terminology. This variable stores the number of key parts. A column is counted once for each key it is a part of.
`uint primary_key`	Array index of the primary key in the key array. 0 if the primary key exists, and `MAX_KEY` otherwise, which is defined to be 64 in versions 4.1 and later, and 32 in 4.0 and earlier. The location of the definition is *sql/unireg.h*.
`uint null_fields`	Number of fields in the table that can contain `NULL` values.
`uint blob_fields`	Number of fields of type `BLOB` or `TEXT` in the table.
`key_map keys_in_use`	A map showing which keys are available for use in queries. This would include all the keys present in the table that have not been taken offline with `ALTER TABLE...DISABLE KEYS` or some other way. Note that in 4.0 and earlier, the map is implemented through a simple bit mask. Starting in 4.1, `key_map` became an object to meet the need to support a large number of keys.
`key_map quick_keys`	A map of keys that can be used for range optimizations for the current query. If we have a key on `last_name`, for example, then `SELECT * FROM` phonebook `WHERE last_name > 'A' AND last_name < 'B'` permits a range optimization if the storage engine supports reading keys based on a range.
`key_map used_keys`	A map of keys that can be used in the current query. This is basically the value of `keys_in_use` after some filtering that comes from taking into account the `FORCE KEY` and `IGNORE KEY` directives in the query.
`key_map keys_in_use_for_query`	A map of keys that can be used for the query according to the `FORCE KEY` and `IGNORE KEY` directives.
`KEY  *key_info`	Array of key descriptors for the table. The length of the array is stored in the variable `keys`.

TABLE | 49

Table 3-3. Members of the TABLE class (continued)

Member definition	Description
`TYPELIB keynames`	A lookup table to find the key number by its name.
`ha_rows max_rows`	The value of `MAX_ROWS` that the table was created with. This is not necessarily a hard limit on how many rows the table can have, but more of a hint to help the storage engine figure out the best record storage format.
`ha_rows min_rows`	The value of `MIN_ROWS` that the table is created with. Currently stored in the table definition file (*.frm*), but otherwise not used.
`ulong    avg_row_length`	The value of `AVG_ROW_LENGTH` that the table is created with. This is a hint to the storage engine as to what the average length of a record in a variable length record table is expected to be.
`TYPELIB fieldnames`	A lookup table to find the field number by its name.
`enum db_type db_type`	Storage engine type for this table.
`enum row_type row_type`	Indicates whether the record is fixed length or dynamic length.
`uint db_create_options`	A bit mask of options the table was created with.
`uint db_stat`	A bit mask of various capabilities and operations for this table.
`uint status`	A bit mask showing the status of the last record operation. Provides an idea of what is found in the `record` variable.
`enum tmp_table_type tmp_table`	Set to `NO_TMP_TABLE` for non-temporary tables, `TMP_TABLE` for non-transactional temporary tables, and `TRANSACTIONAL_TMP_TABLE` for transactional temporary tables.
`my_bool force_index`	Set to 1 if this table has an index that was referenced with a `FORCE INDEX` directive in the current query.
`my_bool key_read`	A flag used by the optimizer to mark that a key will be used to retrieve the data from this table in the current query.
`my_bool db_low_byte_first`	Indicates the byte order of integer fields for the storage engine of this table. Set to 1 if the low byte goes first.
`my_bool fulltext_searched`	A flag used by the optimizer to mark that the table will be searched with a full-text key lookup.
`my_bool crashed`	This flag is set to 1 if at any point the storage engine reports that the internal structure of the table is corrupt.
`my_bool no_keyread`	A flag to communicate to the optimizer that keys should not be used to read from this table because of some special case situation.
`Field *next_number_field`	If the field has an auto-increment field (there can be only one), points to its descriptor. Otherwise, it is set to 0.
`Field_timestamp *timestamp_field`	If the field has a timestamp field (there can be only one), this points to its descriptor. Otherwise, it is set to 0.
`CHARSET_INFO *table_charset`	The descriptor of the character set of this table.
`MEM_ROOT mem_root`	Memory pool used for various members of the table descriptor.
`GRANT_INFO grant`	Access control information descriptor for this table.
`char *table_cache_key`	Hash key value used for locating this table descriptor in the table cache. It is formed by concatenating database name, `'\0'`, table name, `'\0'`, and an optional string for temporary tables. So `table_cache_key` is often used in the code to reference the name of the database.

Table 3-3. Members of the TABLE class (continued)

Member definition	Description
char *table_name	If the table is not aliased, same as `real_name`. Otherwise, the name of the alias. For example, in `SELECT t1.* FROM names AS t1`, this variable is set to `t1`.
char *real_name	The name of the table. If aliased, the nonaliased name. See example under `table_name`.
char *path	The full path to the table's *.frm* file on the filesystem without the *.frm* extension relative to `datadir`. For example, if the table is in the database `db1`, and the name of the table is *t1*, this variable is set to `./db1/t1`.
uint key_length	The length of `table_cache_key` in bytes.
table_map map	During a join, each table instance is assigned a number. This variable is a bit mask with the one bit corresponding to the table number set, and all others cleared.
ulong version	Used to check if the table cached in memory is up to date. If another thread performs `FLUSH TABLES`, the table descriptor is no longer valid. This is detected by comparing the value of this variable against the global `refresh_version`.
FILESORT_INFO sort	Descriptor structure used for record pointer sorting. Utilized in solving `GROUP BY` and `ORDER BY` queries.
ORDER *group	Used by the optimizer for solving `GROUP BY` queries through a temporary table. If this technique is used, the appropriate key is created in the temporary table. In that case this field is set to the descriptor of the `GROUP BY` expression.
ha_rows quick_rows[MAX_KEY]	Used by the range optimizer to store the estimate of how many records the key range will match for each key in the table.
ulong query_id	The ID of the query that is currently using this table descriptor.
uchar frm_version	Version of the table definition file (*.frm*) format.
THD *in_use	Points to the descriptor of the thread that is currently using this table.
struct st_table *next	Points to the next table in the linked list of tables.
struct st_table *prev	Points to the previous table in the linked list of tables.

Field

The `Field` class defines a field descriptor. It is actually a base abstract class for a number of subclasses defined for each specific field type, such as integer, string, or timestamp.

This class naturally plays a critical role in the parser and optimizer, because most of the operations in processing a query involve table fields.

`Field` is defined in *sql/field.h*, and partially implemented in *sql/field.cc*. The implementation is partial because it is an abstract class. Its subclasses, which all have names beginning with `Field_`, complete the implementation.

This class has only a few data members, but on the other hand does contain many methods. We will, therefore, cover all of the data members, and only the most important methods. Table 3-4 lists the members of `Field`.

Table 3-4. Members of the Field class

Member definition	Member description
`char *ptr`	Points to the field data in the in-memory copy of the record.
`uchar *null_ptr`	Points to the byte in the in-memory copy of the record that contains the bit indicating whether the value of this field is NULL.
`const char *table_name`	The name of the table containing this field.
`const char *field_name`	The name of this field.
`LEX_STRING comment`	The contents of the comment on this field. The comment can be entered in the CREATE TABLE statement when the field is defined; for example, CREATE TABLE t1 (n INT COMMENT 'some integer value').
`ulong query_id`	The ID of the query currently using this field descriptor.
`key_map key_start`	If the *n*th bit of this bit mask is set, this field is the first part of the *n*th key in the table.
`key_map part_of_key`	If the *n*th bit of this bit mask is set, this field is a part of the *n*th key in the table.
`key_map part_of_sortkey`	If the *n*th bit of this bit mask is set, this field is a part of the *n*th key in the table, and the key is capable of being traversed in the ascending or descending order of its values. This would be the case for a B-tree key, but not for a hash or full-text key, for example.
`utype unireg_check`	Field type code stored in the table definition file (.frm).
`uint32 field_length`	Maximum length in bytes of the data that can be stored in this field.
`uint16 flags`	A bit mask of the special attributes of the field set in the field definition in CREATE TABLE, for example NOT NULL, AUTO INCREMENT, or ZEROFILL.
`uchar null_bit`	A bit mask with just one bit set, corresponding to the bit in the record prefix that indicates that the value of this field is NULL. See also null_ptr.
`int store(const char *from, uint length, CHARSET_INFO *cs)`	Stores the string pointed to by from in the in-memory copy of the record associated with this field descriptor.
`int store(double nr)`	Stores the value of the double precision floating-point number nr in the in-memory copy of the record associated with this field descriptor.
`int store(longlong nr)`	Stores the value of the 64-bit integer number nr in the in-memory copy of the record associated with this field descriptor.
`void store_time(TIME *ltime,timestamp_type t_type)`	Stores the time value specified by ltime in the in-memory copy of the record associated with this field descriptor.
`double val_real(void)`	Returns the value stored in the in-memory copy of the record associated with this field descriptor, converting it to a double-precision floating-point number.

Table 3-4. Members of the Field class (continued)

Member definition	Member description
`String *val_str(String *str)`	Returns the value stored in the in-memory copy of the record associated with this field descriptor, converting it to a string. The value is stored in the argument-supplied buffer. Note that the caller must pass a pointer to a preallocated String object. Calling `val_str( )` with `str` set to 0 will result in a crash.
`Item_result result_type ( )`	Returns the data type stored in the field. Currently used by the range optimizer to decide whether the range optimization would be appropriate. For example, if a is a string, we have a key on a, and the query is `SELECT * FROM t1 WHERE a > 1 AND a < 5`, then reading the keys in the (`'1'`,`'5'`) range would give incorrect results if we have a record with a equal to `'10'`. Because a is stored as a string, the key order will be lexicographic, and `'10'` would make it into the range. However, the syntax of the query asks for a numeric comparison. So the record with a equal to `'10'` should be excluded.
`Item_result cmp_type ( )`	Returns the data type stored in the field that should be examined to decide how comparisons with other values should be made. Usually the same as `result_type( )`. One exception is timestamps. Their `result_type( )` is `STRING_RESULT`, while their `cmp_type( )` is `INT_RESULT`. This is so that they could be compared with integers as integers rather than converting the integer to a string and performing string comparisons.
`void reset(void)`	Clears the value set in the in-memory copy of the record associated with this field descriptor.
`bool binary( )`	Reports whether the comparisons of field values are performed in a binary or the byte-for-byte manner. A `char(N)` field with default attributes, for example, would not be such a field: the comparison is case-insensitive, and the trailing spaces are ignored.
`uint32 key_length( )`	Returns the length of the field for the purpose of in-memory operations on keys.
`enum_field_types type( )`	Returns the field type in the table definition context.
`int cmp(const char *str)`	Returns the result of comparison of `str` against the value in the in-memory copy of the record associated with this field descriptor. Returns −1 if the field value is less than `str`, 0 if they are equal, and 1 if the field value is greater than `str`. `str` is assumed to be `field_length` bytes long.
`int key_cmp (const byte *str, uint length)`	Returns the result of comparison of `str` against the value in the in-memory copy of the record associated with this field descriptor in the context of keys. Returns −1 if the field value is less than `str`, 0 if they are equal, and 1 if the field value is greater than `str`.
`bool is_null(uint row_offset=0)`	Returns true if the value of the field in the in-memory copy of the record associated with this field descriptor is NULL in the SQL sense.
`void set_null(int row_offset=0)`	Marks the field value in the in-memory copy of the record associated with this field descriptor as NULL in the SQL sense.
`bool maybe_null(void)`	Returns true if the field could contain NULL values in the SQL sense.
`void move_field(char *ptr_arg)`	Redirects the internal field data pointer to a different location.

Utility API Calls

A number of core jobs, such as memory allocation, string operations, or file management, are performed by a group of internal API calls. Due to portability requirements, the standard C library is used very sparingly, and the C++ libraries are not used at all.

There are a large number of utility functions. I cannot cover them all in this book, but I provide a representative sample in Table 3-5.

Table 3-5. Common utility functions

Prototype	Defined in	Description
gptr my_malloc (uint Size, myf MyFlags)	*mysys/my_malloc.c*	Portability wrapper around malloc( ). Used for allocating memory blocks for global buffers and other objects that have a lifetime of more than one query, as well as large memory blocks.
void my_free (gptr ptr, myf MyFlags)	*mysys/my_malloc.c*	Frees the blocks allocated with my_malloc( ). Note that my_free( ) has evolved into a macro alias for my_no_flags_free( ), so you should look for the definition of my_no_flags_free( ) rather than my_free( ) in *mysys/my_malloc.c*. Nevertheless, my_free( ) is still what is used throughout the code to free memory blocks.
gptr my_multi_malloc (myf myFlags, ...)	*mysys/mulalloc.c*	Allocates memory for a set of pointers, and points each to its respective part of one big block. Consider the example: ```char *p1,*p2,*block;\nif (!(block = my_multi_malloc\n(MYF (MY_WME),\n&p1,10,&p2,20,NULL))\n goto err;``` block points to the start of the allocated block, p1 points to a part of it with 10 bytes reserved, and p2 points to another part with 20 bytes reserved. When the work is done, block should be freed using my_free( ).
void init_alloc_root (MEM_ROOT *mem_root, uint block_size, uint pre_alloc_size)	*mysys/my_alloc.c*	Initializes the memory pool with the descriptor pointed to by mem_root.
gptr alloc_root (MEM_ROOT *mem_root, unsigned int Size)	*mysys/my_alloc.c*	Allocates memory from the pool specified by mem_root. Returns a pointer to the allocated block, or 0 on failure.
void free_root (MEM_ROOT *mem_root, myf MyFlags)	*mysys/my_alloc.c*	Frees the memory pool associated with mem_root.
File my_open (const char *FileName, int Flags, myf MyFlags)	*mysys/my_open.c*	A wrapper around open( ). The last argument contains MySQL API-specific flags. The File type is an alias for int.

Table 3-5. Common utility functions (continued)

Prototype	Defined in	Description
`int my_close` `(File fd, myf MyFlags)`	*mysys/my_open.c*	A wrapper around `close( )`. The last argument contains MySQL API-specific flags.
`uint my_read` `(File Filedes, byte` `*Buffer, uint Count,` `myf MyFlags)`	*mysys/my_read.c*	A fairly extensive wrapper around `read( )`. Among other capabilities, this will keep reading until all of the `Count` bytes have been successfully if `MY_FULL_IO` is set in `MyFlags`.
`uint my_write` `(int Filedes, const byte` `*Buffer, uint Count, myf` `MyFlags)`	*mysys/my_write.c*	A fairly extensive wrapper around `write( )`. Will keep writing until all the `Count` bytes have been written. If `MY_WAIT_IF_FULL` is present in `MyFlags`, will wait for the disk space to become available instead of just failing when the disk is full.
`int init_io_cache` `(IO_CACHE *info, File file,` `uint cachesize,` `enum cache_type type,` `my_off_t seek_offset,` `pbool use_async_io,` `myf cache_myflags)`	*mysys/mf_iocache.c*	Initializes the descriptor for an I/O cache. An I/O cache is somewhat similar to the standard C library structure `FILE`. Returns 0 on success, and a nonzero value of failure.
`int my_b_read` `(register IO_CACHE *info,` `byte *Buffer,` `uint Count)`	*mysys/mf_iocache.c*	Reads from the I/O cache associated with info. Technically speaking, this is actually a preprocessor macro that is aliased to the `_my_b_read( )` function when there is not enough data in the cache buffer to satisfy the request. Returns 0 on success, and a nonzero value of failure.
`int my_b_write` `(register IO_CACHE *info,` `const byte *Buffer, uint` `Count)`	*mysys/mf_iocache.c*	Writes to the I/O cache associated with info. Technically speaking, this is actually a preprocessor macro which is aliased to the `_my_b_write( )` function when there is not enough space in the buffer, and a physical write is required to satisfy the request. Returns 0 on success, and a nonzero value of failure.
`int flush_io_cache` `(IO_CACHE *info)`	*mysys/mf_iocache.c*	Writes out the data from the memory buffer to the file descriptor. Note that `flush_io_cache( )` is actually a macro alias for `my_b_flush_io_ cache( )`. Returns 0 on success, and a nonzero value of failure.
`int end_io_cache` `(IO_CACHE *info)`	*mysys/mf_iocache.c*	Closes the cache associated with the descriptor, performing all necessary cleanup.
`my_string fn_format` `(my_string to, const char` `*name, const char *dir,` `const char *extension, uint` `flag)`	*mysys/mf_format.c*	Constructs a path to the file, possibly adjusting the extension. The arguments should be formatted in the Unix style with forward slashes. On Windows, the slashes will be reversed in the result. The flags in the last argument allow a number of file path operations. For example, if `MY_RESOLVE_ SYMLINKS` is set, the resulting path written to the `to` argument will have the symbolic links followed and resolved.

Table 3-5. Common utility functions (continued)

Prototype	Defined in	Description
my_bool hash_init (HASH *hash,CHARSET_INFO *charset, uint size, uint key_offset, uint key_length, hash_get_key get_key, void (*free_element)(void*))	*mysys/hash.c*	Initializes a hash descriptor. Returns 0 on success, and a nonzero value on failure. Note that hash_init( ) is actually a macro alias for _hash_init( ). The method of obtaining the hash key for the given record may be specified with the key_offset and key_length arguments, or by the function pointer get_key.
gptr hash_search (HASH *hash,const byte *key, uint length)	*mysys/hash.c*	Finds the first record in the hash that is associated with the specified key value. Returns a pointer to the record on success, and 0 on failure.
gptr hash_next (HASH *hash, const byte *key, uint length)	*mysys/hash.c*	Finds the next record in the hash that is associated with the specified key value. Should be called repeatedly after the initial call to hash_search( ) for the retrieval of subsequent records associated with the key. Returns a pointer to the record on success. On failure (no more records), returns 0.
my_bool my_hash_insert (HASH *info,const byte *record)	*mysys/hash.c*	Inserts the record pointer into the hash. Returns 0 on success, and a nonzero value of failure. In the past, the function was called hash_insert( ). However, it was renamed due to a namespace conflict.
my_bool hash_delete (HASH *hash,byte *record)	*mysys/hash.c*	Deletes the record pointer from the hash. Note that the actual pointer value—not the key— is compared, and only one record is deleted.
void hash_free (HASH *hash)	*mysys/hash.c*	Frees the hash associated with the descriptor performing all necessary cleanup.
my_bool init_dynamic_array(DYNAMIC_ARRAY *array, uint element_size, uint init_alloc, uint alloc_increment)	*mysys/array.c*	Initializes a dynamic array descriptor. Note that unlike in the hash, the operations are conducted on the element data, as opposed to pointer references. So, it becomes necessary to know the size of the element.
my_bool insert_dynamic(DYNAMIC_ARRAY *array, gptr element)	*mysys/array.c*	Inserts an element into the dynamic array. Note that the second argument is a pointer from which the data will be copied into the array upon insertion.
void get_dynamic(DYNAMIC_ARRAY *array, gptr element, uint idx)	*mysys/array.c*	Copies the element data at index idx to the address pointed to by element. Note that element must point to a location with sufficient memory to cover the size of array element.
void delete_dynamic (DYNAMIC_ARRAY *array)	*mysys/array.c*	Frees the dynamic array resources and invalidates the descriptor. Used for cleanup after the caller is done using the array.
char *strmov (char *dst, const char *src)	*strings/strmov.c*	Like strcpy( ), except the return value points to the new terminating null character of dst.

Table 3-5. Common utility functions (continued)

Prototype	Defined in	Description
char* strxmov (char *dst, char* src1, ...)	*strings/strxmov.c*	Concatenates all of the arguments from the second to the next to last into dst, terminating it with a null character. The last argument must be NullS. Returns a pointer to the terminating null character of the result.
int my_snprintf (char* to, size_t n, const char* fmt, ...)	*strings/my_vsnprintf.c*	A stripped-down implementation of snprintf( ). snprintf( ) is a very nice function for securely copying formatted strings into buffers of restricted length. However, it is not available on all platforms. my_snprintf( ) also contains additional features not available in the standard implementation of snprintf( ).
gptr sql_alloc(uint Size)	*sql/thr_malloc.cc*	Allocates memory from the pool of the current thread descriptor. Should be used for all small memory allocations while processing a query. Note that all blocks allocated with sql_alloc( ) are freed when the query is finished. It is neither necessary nor possible to free individual blocks allocated with sql_alloc( ). If a block is used for a longer duration, or if it is large, it should be allocated with my_malloc( ) and freed with my_free( ).
my_string ip_to_hostname (struct in_addr *in, uint *errors)	*sql/hostaname.cc*	Converts the address structure into a string representation of the host, resolving it if possible. Unresolved IP addresses are converted into a string representation.

Preprocessor Macros

MySQL makes heavy use of the C preprocessor. A number of tasks are complex enough to justify some form of an alias rather than being spelled out in the code, but are still too simple to justify a function. Other tasks are performed differently—or in some cases, not at all—depending on the compilation options. Such tasks are performed with a preprocessor macro. Table 3-6 lists the most frequently used.

Table 3-6. Common preprocessor macros

Macro	Defined in	Description
sint2korr(A)	*include/my_global.h*	Returns a signed 2-byte integer stored at the location A with the low byte first. On a little-endian architecture, the macro is a mere pointer dereference. However, on a big-endian system it has to perform a computation to return the correct value.
sint3korr(A)	*include/my_global.h*	Returns a signed 3-byte integer stored at the location A with the low byte first.
sint4korr(A)	*include/my_global.h*	Returns a signed 4-byte integer stored at the location A with the low byte first.

Table 3-6. Common preprocessor macros (continued)

Macro	Defined in	Description
sint5korr(A)	*include/my_global.h*	Returns a signed 5-byte integer stored at the location A with the low byte first.
sint8korr(A)	*include/my_global.h*	Returns a signed 8-byte integer stored at the location A with the low byte first.
uint2korr(A)	*include/my_global.h*	Returns an unsigned 2-byte integer stored at the location A with the low byte first.
uint3korr(A)	*include/my_global.h*	Returns an unsigned 3-byte integer stored at the location A with the low byte first.
uint4korr(A)	*include/my_global.h*	Returns an unsigned 4-byte integer stored at the location A with the low byte first.
uint5korr(A)	*include/my_global.h*	Returns an unsigned 5-byte integer stored at the location A with the low byte first.
uint8korr(A)	*include/my_global.h*	Returns an unsigned 8-byte integer stored at the location A with the low byte first.
int2store(T, A)	*include/my_global.h*	Stores the value of A in 2 bytes starting at the location T with the low byte first regardless of the machine byte order.
int3store(T, A)	*include/my_global.h*	Stores the value of A in 3 bytes starting at the location T with the low byte first regardless of the machine byte order.
int4store(T, A)	*include/my_global.h*	Stores the value of A in 4 bytes starting at the location T with the low byte first regardless of the machine byte order.
int5store(T, A)	*include/my_global.h*	Stores the value of A in 5 bytes starting at the location T with the low byte first regardless of the machine byte order.
int8store(T, A)	*include/my_global.h*	Stores the value of A in 8 bytes starting at the location T with the low byte first regardless of the machine byte order.
LINT_INIT(var)	*include/my_global.h*	Some variables in the code are normally not initialized, while some programming error detection tools think they should be. Rather than waste the CPU by initializing them all the time, this macro exists to initialize them when the use of one of those tools is detected, or when FORCE_INIT_OF_VARS is defined.
swap_variables (t, a, b)	*include/my_global.h*	Swaps the contents of the variables a and b of type t.
set_if_ bigger(a, b)	*include/my_global.h*	Sets the value of a to b if b is greater than a.
set_if_ smaller(a, b)	*include/my_global.h*	Sets the value of a to b if b is less than a.
test_all_ bits(a, b)	*include/my_global.h*	Returns a nonzero value if all the bits set in a are also set in b.
array_ elements(A)	*include/my_global.h*	Returns the number of elements in the array A.
current_thd	*sql/mysql_priv.h*	Returns a pointer to the THD object associated with the current thread.
IF_WIN(A, B)	*sql/mysql_priv.h*	Expands into A on Windows and OS/2, and into B on all other systems.
PREV_BITS (type, A)	*sql/mysql_priv.h*	Returns a bit mask of type type with the lowest A bits set and others cleared.

Global Variables

MySQL code uses a large number of global variables for various purposes: configuration settings, server status information, various data structures shared among threads, and other things. Studying the global variables provides numerous insights on the server architecture. Often the very existence of the variable concisely tells a story about how and why different components work together.

Table 3-7 summarizes the most commonly used global variables. Many of those were moved under the system_status_var structure in version 5.0.

Table 3-7. Commonly used global variables

Variable definition	Defined in	Description
char *mysql_data_home	*sql/mysqld.cc*	Points to the path of the data directory, which is set by the datadir configuration parameter.
char server_version [SERVER_VERSION_LENGTH]	*sql/mysqld.cc*	Contains the server version string displayed in the connection greeting and in the log; for example, *mysql-4.1.5-log*.
char mysql_charsets_dir [FN_REFLEN]	*sql/mysqld.cc*	Contains the path to the configuration directory holding the character set definition files. The value is set by the character-sets-dir configuration parameter.
ulong refresh_version	*sql/mysqld.cc*	The value gets incremented every time the database administrator issues the FLUSH TABLES command. When a request is made to use an already open table, the value of table->refresh_version is checked against the global refresh_version to determine whether the table needs to be reloaded.
ulong thread_id	*sql/mysqld.cc*	A counter used for assigning unique ID values to the newly created threads. Each time a new thread is created, the current value of thread_id is assigned, and then the value is incremented by 1.
ulong query_id	*sql/mysqld.cc*	A counter used for assigning unique ID values to the new requests. Each time a new request is processed, the current value of query_id is assigned, and then the value is incremented by 1.
ulong opened_tables	*sql/mysqld.cc*	A counter that keeps track of how many table-opening operations were performed since the start of the server. The value is displayed in the output of SHOW STATUS under Opened_tables. Not to be confused with the value of Open_tables, which is the number of tables currently in the table cache.
ulong created_tmp_tables	*sql/mysqld.cc*	A counter that keeps track of how many temporary tables were created since the start of the server. The value is displayed in the output of SHOW STATUS under Created_tmp_tables.

Table 3-7. Commonly used global variables (continued)

Variable definition	Defined in	Description
`ulong created_tmp_disk_ tables`	*sql/mysqld.cc*	When possible, MySQL will try to keep the temporary table it creates in memory. However, it is not possible in some situations due either to the table size or the limitations of the in-memory storage engine. Then the table is created on disk, and this counter is incremented. The value of this counter is displayed in the output of SHOW STATUS under `Created_tmp_disk_tables`.
`ulong aborted_threads`	*sql/mysqld.cc*	Keeps track of the number of connections that were terminated abnormally after they have been successfully established. The value is displayed in the output of SHOW STATUS under `Aborted_clients`.
`ulong aborted_connects`	*sql/mysqld.cc*	Keeps track of the number of attempted connections that failed to progress past the authentication stage and reach the status of being able to issue requests. The value is displayed in the output of SHOW STATUS under `Aborted_connects`.
`ulong query_cache_size`	*sql/mysqld.cc*	New in version 4.0. Size of the query cache. Set by the `query-cache-size` configuration variable.
`ulong server_id`	*sql/mysqld.cc*	Each server participating in replication must have a unique ID among its replication peers. This variable contains the ID value for this server. Set by the `server-id` configuration parameter.
`ulong max_connections`	*sql/mysqld.cc*	Contains the limit on the maximum number of simultaneous connections the server will accept. Set by the `max-connections` configuration variable.
`ulong long_query_count`	*sql/mysqld.cc*	Counts the queries that were deemed slow by the optimizer. Displayed in the output of SHOW STATUS under `Slow_queries`.
`ulong what_to_log`	*sql/mysqld.cc*	Contains a bit mask of SQL commands that ought to be logged to the server activity log. This is currently an internal variable that cannot be set by the user.
`ulong com_stat [(uint) SQLCOM_END]`	*sql/mysqld.cc*	An array of counters for the different types of SQL commands. Can be viewed by the user with SHOW STATUS LIKE 'Com_%'.
`bool abort_loop`	*sql/mysqld.cc*	A flag set during shutdown to signal to all looping areas of code that it is time to exit the loop.
`bool shutdown_in_progress`	*sql/mysqld.cc*	A flag set during server shutdown. Primarily used to avoid initiating the shutdown process more than once.
`uint thread_count`	*sql/mysqld.cc*	Total number of threads currently existing in the server. Displayed in the output of SHOW STATUS under `Threads_connected`.
`uint thread_running`	*sql/mysqld.cc*	Total number of threads currently serving a request. Note that some of the existing threads might be just waiting for a request instead of processing one. Displayed in the output of SHOW STATUS under `Threads_running`.

Table 3-7. Commonly used global variables (continued)

Variable definition	Defined in	Description
`MYSQL_LOG mysql_log`	*sql/log.cc*	The log object associated with the plain text activity log.
`MYSQL_LOG mysql_bin_log`	*sql/log.cc*	The log object associated with the binary update log.
`MYSQL_LOG mysql_slow_log`	*sql/log.cc*	The log object associated with the slow query log.
`pthread_mutex_t LOCK_open`	*sql/mysqld.cc*	The lock variable for protecting critical regions that operate on the table cache and perform other operations related to opening a table that require mutual exclusion.
`pthread_mutex_t LOCK_thread_count`	*sql/mysqld.cc*	The lock variable for protecting critical regions that create or remove threads.
`pthread_mutex_t LOCK_status`	*sql/mysqld.cc*	The lock variable for protecting critical regions that read or modify the status variables visible via SHOW STATUS.
`pthread_cond_t COND_refresh`	*sql/mysqld.cc*	The POSIX Threads broadcast condition used for signaling to the waiting threads that the state of a table was changed in some way.
`pthread_cond_t COND_thread_count`	*sql/mysqld.cc*	The POSIX Threads broadcast condition used for signaling to the waiting threads that a new thread was created, or an old one was destroyed.
`I_List<THD> threads`	*sql/mysqld.cc*	A list of all threads that currently exist in the server. Can be viewed by the user with SHOW PROCESSLIST or SHOW FULL PROCESSLIST for more detail.
`I_List<NAMED_LIST> key_caches`	*sql/mysqld.cc*	New in version 4.1, which supports multiple key caches for MyISAM tables. A list of MyISAM key caches that exist in the server.
`struct system_variables global_system_variables`	*sql/mysqld.cc*	New in version 4.0. A descriptor of the collection of server configuration variables that can be modified by a client.
`struct system_variables max_system_variables`	*sql/mysqld.cc*	New in version 4.0. Contains the limits on the values of the server configuration variables that can be modified by a client.
`HASH open_cache`	*sql/sql_base.cc*	The table cache. When a table is opened, the descriptor is placed into the table cache. Subsequent requests to open the same table will be satisfied from the cache. The contents of the cache can be viewed with SHOW OPEN TABLES.
`uint protocol_version`	*sql/mysqld.cc*	Stores the version of the network communication protocol.
`uint mysqld_port`	*sql/mysqld.cc*	The TCP/IP port number that the server listens on for requests.
`struct my_option my_long_options[]`	*sql/mysqld.cc*	The descriptor of all the configuration options understood by the server.

## CHAPTER 4

Client/Server Communication

In this chapter we will discuss the details of the client/server communication in MySQL. The goal is to give you the ability to look at a binary dump of the client/server communication and be able to understand what happened. This chapter can also be helpful if you are trying to write a MySQL proxy server, a security application to audit MySQL traffic on your network, or some other program that for some reason needs to understand the low-level details of the MySQL client/server protocol.

Protocol Overview

The server listens for connections on a TCP/IP port or a local socket. When a client connects, a handshake and authentication are performed. If successful, the session begins. The client sends a command, and the server responds with a data set or a message appropriate for the type of command that was sent. When the client is finished, it sends a special command telling the server it is done, and the session is terminated.

The basic unit of communication is the application-layer packet. Commands consist of one packet. Responses may include several.

Packet Format

There are two types of packets: compressed and noncompressed. The decision on which one will be used for the session is made during the handshake stage, and depends on the capabilities and settings of both the client and the server.

Additionally, regardless of the compression option, the packets are divided into two categories: commands sent by the client, and responses returned by the server.

Server response packets are divided into four categories: data packets, end-of-data-stream packets, success report (OK) packets, and error message packets.

All packets share the common 4-byte header, documented in Table 4-1.

Table 4-1. Common 4-byte header for uncompressed packets

Offset	Length	Description
0	3	Packet body length stored with the low byte first.
3	1	Packet sequence number. The sequence numbers are reset with each new command. While the correct packet sequencing is ensured by the underlying transmission protocol, this field is used for the sanity checks of the application logic.

A compressed packet will have an additional 3-byte field, low byte first, containing the length of the compressed packet body part that follows. An uncompressed packet will have the body immediately after the header.

The compression is done with the use of ZLIB (see *http://www.zlib.net*). The body of the compressed packet is exactly what a call to compress( ) with the uncompressed body as argument would return. It is, however, possible for the body to be stored without compression when the compressed body would turn out no smaller than the uncompressed one, or when compress( ) fails for some reason—e.g., due to the lack of available memory. If this happens, the uncompressed length field will contain 0.

It is important to remember, though, that even in that case, the compressed format is still used, which unfortunately results in the waste of 3 bytes per packet. Therefore, a session that predominately uses small or poorly compressible packets goes faster if the compression is turned off.

As you may have noticed, the 3-byte field would limit the body length to 16 MB. What if you need to send a bigger packet? In version 3.23 and earlier, it is not possible. Version 4.0 added a compatible improvement to the protocol that overcame this limitation. If the length of the packet is greater than the value of MAX_PACKET_LENGTH, which is defined to be $2^{24}-1$ in *sql/net_serv.cc*, the packet gets split into smaller packets with bodies of MAX_PACKET_LENGTH plus the last packet with a body that is shorter than MAX_PACKET_LENGTH. The last short packet will always be present even if it must have a zero-length body. It serves as an indicator that there are no more packet parts left in the stream for this large packet.

Relationship Between MySQL Protocol and OS Layer

If you try to run a network sniffer on the MySQL port, you will notice that sometimes several MySQL protocol packets are contained in one TCP/IP packet, and sometimes a MySQL packet spans several TCP/IP layer packets, while some fit into exactly one TCP/IP packet. If you somehow manage to intercept the local socket traffic, you will observe a similar effect. Some buffer writes will have exactly one packet, while others may contain several. If the lower-level socket-buffer write operation has a limit on the maximum number of bytes it can handle in one chunk, you may also see one MySQL packet being transferred in several buffer writes.

To understand the mechanics of this phenomenon, let's examine the API the server or the client uses to send packets. Packets are put in the network buffer with a call to my_net_write( ), defined in *sql/net_serv.cc*. When the buffer has reached capacity, its contents will be flushed, which results in an operating system write( ) call on the socket—or possibly a sequence of them if the contents of the buffer cannot be written into the socket in one operation. On the operating system level this may result in sending one or more packets, depending on how much it takes to accommodate the data volume under the operating system protocol constraints.

In some cases, the data in the network buffer needs to be sent to the client immediately. In that case, net_flush( ), defined in *sql/net_serv.cc*, is called.

Authenticating Handshake

The session between a client and a server begins with an authenticating handshake. Before it can begin, the server checks whether the host that the client is connecting from is even allowed to connect to this server. If it is not, an error message packet is sent to the client notifying it that the host is not allowed to connect.

In the case of successful host verification, the server sends a greeting packet with the standard 4-byte header, the packet sequence number set to 0, and the body in the format shown in Table 4-2.

Table 4-2. Fields of the server's greeting packet

Offset in the body	Length	Description
0	1	Protocol version number. Decimal 10 (0x0A) in recent versions. Although some changes were made in the protocol in versions 4.0 and 4.1, the protocol version number remained the same because the changes were fully backward-compatible.
1	ver_len = strlen (server_version) + 1	Zero-terminated server version string. The length is variable, and is calculated according to the formula in the Length column. The subsequent offsets are a function of the length of this field.
ver_len + 1	4	Internal MySQL ID of the thread that is handling this connection. Low byte first.
ver_len + 5	9	In version 4.0 and earlier, the random seed string in its entirety. In 4.1 and later, the first 8 bytes of the 20-byte random seed string. At the end is a terminating zero. Starting in version 4.1, the length of this field is controlled by the value of SCRAMBLE_LENGTH_323, defined in *include/mysql_com.h*. In the earlier versions, the macro is SCRAMBLE_LENGTH, defined in *sql/sql_parse.cc*. With the terminating zero byte, the length of the string is one greater than the value of the macro.
ver_len + 14	2	Server capabilities bit mask with the low byte first. See Table 4-5 later for the meaning of different bits.

Table 4-2. Fields of the server's greeting packet (continued)

Offset in the body	Length	Description
ver_len + 16	1	Default character set code, or more precisely, the code of the default collation. A *character set collation* is a set of rules that defines a sequential order among characters. A list of available collations and their codes can be obtained by executing SHOW COLLATION LIKE '%' in version 4.1.
ver_len + 17	2	The server status bit mask with the low byte first. Reports whether the server is in transaction or autocommit mode, if there are additional results from a multistatement query, or if a good index (or some index) was used for query optimization. For details, see the SERVER_* values in *include/mysql_com.h*.
ver_len + 19	13	Reserved for future use. Currently zeroed out.
ver_len + 32	13	Present only in version 4.1 and later. The rest of the random seed string terminated with a zero byte. The length is equal to the value of SCRAMBLE_LENGTH - SCRAMBLE_LENGTH_323 + 1.

The client responds with a credentials packet. The format differs between versions up to and including 4.0, and versions 4.1 and later. Table 4-3 shows the format for the pre-4.1 era. Table 4-4 shows the format for versions 4.1 and later, if the client understands and is willing to use the 4.1 protocol.

Table 4-3. Fields of the client's credentials packet, up to MySQL version 4.0

Offset in the body	Length	Description
0	2	Protocol capabilities bit mask of the client, low byte first.
2	3	Maximum packet length that the client is willing to send or receive. Zero values means the client imposes no restrictions of its own in addition to what is already there in the protocol.
5	Varies; see description	Credentials string in following format: zero-terminated MySQL username, then if the password is not empty, scrambled password (8 bytes). This can be optionally followed by the initial database name, in which case a zero byte terminator is added immediately after the XOR encrypted password, followed by the database name string without a terminating zero byte.

Table 4-4. Fields of the client's credentials packet, MySQL version 4.1 and later

Offset in the body	Length	Description
0	4	Protocol capabilities bit mask of the client, low-byte first.
4	4	Maximum packet length that the client is willing to send or receive. Zero values means the client imposes no restrictions of its own in addition to what is already there in the protocol.
8	1	Default character set (or more precisely, collation) code of the client.
9	23	Reserved space; currently zeroed out.
32	Varies; see description	Credentials string in the following format: zero-terminated username, then the length of the SHA1 encrypted password (decimal 20), followed by its value (20 bytes), which is optionally followed by the zero-terminated initial database name.

If the SSL capability option is enabled both on the client and on the server, the client will first send the initial part of the response packet without the credentials string. When the server receives it, it will see the SSL capability bit enabled in the capabilities mask, and know that it should expect the rest of the communication in SSL. The client switches to the SSL layer, and resends the entire response packet securely this time. It would be more efficient, of course, to not resend the initial part of the response, but, for historical reasons, this small overhead allowed the code on the server to stay fairly clean without thorough rework.

Once the server receives the credentials packet, it verifies the information. From this point, it can respond in three different ways:

- If the check succeeds, the standard OK response packet is sent (for details, see the "Server Responses" section, later in the chapter).

- If the credentials did not meet the expectations of the server, the standard error message response is sent.

- The third possibility comes from the need to support the transition from 4.0 to 4.1. In some cases, the DBA may have upgraded both the client and the server to 4.1, but forgot or chose not to upgrade the user table in the mysql database, which contains user names and their respective password hashes. If the entry for that user has the old-style password hash, it is impossible to authenticate with the new authentication protocol.

    In that event, the server sends a special packet with the 1-byte-long body containing decimal 254, which means: "please send the authentication credentials in the old format." The client responds with a packet whose body contains a zero-terminated encrypted password string. The server responds with either OK or a standard error message.

At this point the handshake is complete, and the client begins to issue commands.

Authentication Protocol Security

Neither the old nor the new protocol ever sends the user password across the connection in plain text. However, there are a number of weaknesses in the old protocol. First, knowing the value of the password hash allows the attacker to perform authentication without actually knowing the password. This is possible due to a flaw in the way the expected response to the challenge is computed—it is uniquely determined by the value of the password hash and the value of the challenge (for details, see scramble_323( ) and check_scramble_323( ) in *sql/password.c*). Therefore, if the attacker can get read access to the user table in the mysql database, or obtain the value of the stored password hash some other way, she will be able to authenticate with a specially modified version of the MySQL client library.

Second, even without having access to the hash, the correct password can be guessed in a small number of attempts if the attacker can intercept the authentication traffic between the client and the server on a few occasions. This is possible due to the weakness in the encryption method of the old protocol. The encryption is done using a home-cooked XOR procedure (see the `scramble_323( )` function mentioned earlier), which lacks true cryptographic strength.

These weaknesses have been addressed in version 4.1. The authentication method now uses SHA1 hashes for encryption, which are much more resistant to cracking. Also, the changed challenge-verification algorithm removed the ability to authenticate by knowing just the value of the password hash rather than the actual password.

Despite the added improvements, do not feel complacent about the security of the new protocol. It is still recommended to block access to the MySQL port on the firewall, and if this is not possible, require the clients to use SSL.

Protocol Capabilities Bit Mask

During the authentication handshake, the client and the server exchange information on what the other is able or willing to do. This enables them to adjust their expectations of their peer and not send the data in some unsupported format. The exchange of information is accomplished through fields containing the bit mask of protocol capabilities.

The bit mask can be either 4 or 2 bytes long, depending on the context. The newer (4.1 and later) clients and servers understand 4-byte masks as well as 2-byte ones. The older (4.0 and earlier) ones can handle only 2-byte masks.

The server, regardless of the version, always announces its capabilities with a 2-byte bit mask. Although both newer clients and servers understand the 4-byte mask, the first packet in the dialog must be understood by any client regardless of the version. For this reason, even the newer clients expect the greeting packet to contain a 2-byte mask.

Once the client knows that it is talking to a newer server, it can announce its capabilities with a 4-byte mask. However, if the newer client detects that it is talking to an older server, it will announce the capabilities with only a 2-byte mask. Naturally, the older clients can only send a 2-byte mask; they are not aware of 4-byte ones.

Table 4-5 explains the meaning of the bits used in the capabilities' bit mask. The values are defined in *include/mysql_com.h*.

Table 4-5. Protocol capability bits

Bit macro symbol	Hex value	Description
CLIENT_LONG_PASSWORD	0x0001	Apparently was used in the early development of 4.1 to indicate that the server is able to use the new password format.
CLIENT_FOUND_ROWS	0x0002	Normally, in reporting the results of an UPDATE query, the server returns the number of records that were actually modified. If this flag is set, the server is being asked to report the number of records that were matched by the WHERE clause. Not all of those will necessarily be updated, as some may already contain the desired values.

Table 4-5. Protocol capability bits (continued)

Bit macro symbol	Hex value	Description
CLIENT_LONG_FLAG	0x0004	This flag will be set for all modern clients. Some old clients expect to receive only 1 byte of flags in the field definition record, while the newer ones expect 2 bytes. If this flag is cleared, the client is old and wants only 1 byte for field flags. This flag will also be set by the modern server to indicate that it is capable of sending the field definition in the new format with 2 bytes for field flags. Old servers (pre-3.23) will not report having this capability.
CLIENT_CONNECT_WITH_DB	0x0008	This flag is also set for all modern clients and servers. It indicates that the initial default database can be specified during authentication.
CLIENT_NO_SCHEMA	0x0010	If set, the client is asking the server to consider the syntax *db_name.table_name.col_name* an error. This syntax is normally accepted.
CLIENT_COMPRESS	0x0020	When set, indicates that the client or the server is capable of using the compressed protocol.
CLIENT_ODBC	0x0040	Apparently was created to indicate that the client is an ODBC client. At this point, it does not appear to be used.
CLIENT_LOCAL_FILES	0x0080	When set, indicates that the client is capable of uploading local files with LOAD DATA LOCAL INFILE.

CLIENT_IGNORE_SPACE	0x0100	When set, communicates to the server that the parser should ignore the space characters between identifiers and subsequent '.' or '(' characters. This flag enables syntax such as:
		
		`db_name .table_name`
		
		or
		
		`length (str)`
		
		which would normally be illegal.

CLIENT_PROTOCOL_41	0x0200	When set, indicates that the client or the server is capable of using the new protocol that was introduced in version 4.1.
CLIENT_INTERACTIVE	0x0400	When set, the client is communicating to the server that it is accepting commands directly from a human. For the server, this means that a different inactivity timeout value should be applied. The server has two settings: `wait_timout` and `interactive_timeout`. The former is for regular clients, while the latter is for the interactive ones. This distinction was created to deal with applications using buggy persistent connection pools that would lose track of established connections without closing them first, keep creating new ones, and eventually overflow the server `max_connections` limit. The workaround was to set `wait_timeout` to a low value that would disconnect the lost connections sooner. This, unfortunately, had a side effect of disconnecting interactive clients too soon, which was solved by giving them a separate timeout.

Table 4-5. Protocol capability bits (continued)

Bit macro symbol	Hex value	Description
CLIENT_SSL	0x0800	When set, indicates the capability of the client or the server to use SSL.
CLIENT_IGNORE_SIGPIPE	0x1000	Used internally in the client code in versions 3.23 and 4.0. SIGPIPE is a Unix signal sent to a process when the socket or the pipe it is writing to has already been closed by the peer. However, a thread in a threaded application on some platforms may get a SIGPIPE signal spuriously under some circumstances. Versions 3.23 and 4.0 permit the client programmer to choose whether SIGPIPE should be ignored. Version 4.1 just blocks it during the client initialization and does not worry about the issue from that point on.
CLIENT_TRANSACTIONS	0x2000	When set in the packet coming from the server, indicates that the server supports transactions and is capable of reporting transaction status. When present in the client packet, indicates that the client is aware of servers that support transactions.
CLIENT_RESERVED	0x4000	Not used.
CLIENT_SECURE_CONNECTION	0x8000	When set, indicates that the client or the server can authenticate using the new SHA1 method introduced in 4.1.
CLIENT_MULTI_STATEMENTS	0x10000	When set, indicates that the client can send more than one statement in one query, for example: `res = mysql_query(con,"SELECT a FROM t1 WHERE id =1; SELECT b FROM t1 WHERE id=3");`
CLIENT_MULTI_RESULTS	0x20000	When set, indicates that the client can receive results from multiple queries in the same statement.
CLIENT_REMEMBER_OPTIONS	0x80000000	Internal flag used inside the client routines. Never sent to the server.

Command Packet

Once the authentication is complete, the client begins sending commands to the server using command packets. The body of a command packet is documented in Table 4-6.

Table 4-6. Format of client command packet

Offset in the body	Length	Description
0	1	Command code.
1	For the noncompressed packet, total packet length from the header − 1. For the compressed packet, the compressed body length − 1.	The argument of the command, if present.

The command codes are contained in enum `server_command`, defined in *include/mysql_com.h*. The command-handling logic can be found in the `switch` statement of `dispatch_command( )` in *sql/sql_parse.cc*.

Table 4-7 documents different types of commands with their codes and arguments.

Table 4-7. Client commands

Command code enum value	Code numeric value	Argument description	Command description
COM_SLEEP	0	No argument.	Never sent by a client. Reserved for internal use.
COM_QUIT	1	No argument.	Tells the server to end the session. Issued by the client API call `mysql_close( )`.
COM_INIT_DB	2	A string containing the name of the database.	Tells the server to change the default database for the session to the one specified by the argument. Issued by the client API call `mysql_select_db( )`.
COM_QUERY	3	A string containing the query.	Tells the server to run the query. Issued by the client API call `mysql_query( )`.
COM_FIELD_LIST	4	A string containing the name of the table.	Tells the server to return a list of fields for the specified table. This is an obsolete command still supported on the server for compatibility with old clients. Newer clients use the `SHOW FIELDS` query.
COM_CREATE_DB	5	A string containing the name of the database.	Tells the server to create a database with the specified name. This is an obsolete command still supported on the server for compatibility with old clients. Newer clients use the `CREATE DATABASE` query.
COM_DROP_DB	6	A string containing the name of the database.	Tells the server to drop the database with the specified name. This is an obsolete command still supported on the server for compatibility with old clients. Newer clients use the `DROP DATABASE` query.

Table 4-7. Client commands (continued)

Command code enum value	Code numeric value	Argument description	Command description
COM_REFRESH	7	A byte containing the bit mask of reloading operations.	Tells the server to refresh the table cache, rotate the logs, re-read the access control tables, clear the host name lookup cache, reset the status variables to 0, clear the replication master logs, or reset the replication slave depending on the options in the bit mask. Issued by the client API call mysql_refresh( ).
COM_SHUTDOWN	8	No argument.	Tells the server to shut down. Issued by the client API call mysql_shutdown( ).
COM_STATISTICS	9	No argument.	Tells the server to send back a string containing a brief status report. Issued by the client API call mysql_stat( ).
COM_PROCESS_INFO	10	No argument.	Tells the server to send back a report on the status of all running threads. This is an obsolete command still supported on the server for compatibility with old clients. Newer clients use the SHOW PROCESSLIST query.
COM_CONNECT	11	No argument.	Never sent by a client. Used for internal purposes.
COM_PROCESS_KILL	12	A 4-byte integer with the low byte first containing the MySQL ID of the thread to be terminated.	Tells the server to terminate the thread identified by the argument. Issued by the client API call mysql_kill( ). This is an obsolete command still supported on the server for compatibility with old clients. Newer clients use the KILL query.
COM_DEBUG	13	No argument.	Tells the server to dump some debugging information into its error log. Issued by the client API call mysql_dump_debug_info( ).
COM_PING	14	No argument.	Tells the server to respond with an OK packet. If the server is alive and reachable, it will. Issued by the client API call mysql_ping( ).

Table 4-7. Client commands (continued)

Command code enum value	Code numeric value	Argument description	Command description
COM_TIME	15	No argument.	Never sent by a client. Used for internal purposes.
COM_DELAYED_ INSERT	16	No argument.	Never sent by a client. Used for internal purposes.
COM_CHANGE_USER	17	A byte sequence in the following format: zero-terminated user name, encrypted password, zero-terminated default database name.	Tells the server the client wants to change the user associated with this session. Issued by the client API call mysql_ change_user( ).
COM_BINLOG_DUMP	18	A byte sequence in the following format: 4-byte integer for the offset, 2-byte integer for the flags, 4-byte integer for the slave server ID, and a string for the log name. All integers are formatted with the low byte first.	Tells the server to send a continuous feed of the replication master log events starting at the specified offset in the specified log. Used by the replication slave, and in the *mysqlbinlog* command-line utility.
COM_TABLE_DUMP	19	A byte sequence in the following format: 1 byte for database name length, database name, 1 byte for table name length, table name.	Tells the server to send the table definition and data to the client in raw format. Used when a replication slave receives a LOAD DATA FROM MASTER query.
COM_CONNECT_OUT	20	No argument.	Never sent by a client. Used for internal purposes.
COM_REGISTER_ SLAVE	21	A byte sequence in the following format: a 4-byte integer for the server ID, then a sequence of 1 byte-length prefixed strings in the following order: slave host name, slave user to connect as, slave user password. Then a 2-byte slave user port, 4-byte replication recovery rank, and another 4-byte field that is currently unused. All integers have the low byte first.	Tells the replication master server to register the slave using the information supplied in the argument. This command is a remnant of the started fail-safe replication project. It was introduced in the early version 4.0, but not much has changed since. It is possible that this command might get removed in the future versions.
COM_PREPARE	22	A string containing the statement.	Tells the server to prepare the statement specified by the argument. Issued by the client API call mysql_stmt_prepare( ). New in version 4.1.
COM_EXECUTE	23	A byte sequence in the following format: 4-byte statement ID, 1 byte for flags, and 4-byte iteration count. All integers have the low byte first.	Tells the server to execute the statement referenced by the statement ID. Issued by the client API call mysql_stmt_ execute( ). New in version 4.1.

Table 4-7. Client commands (continued)

Command code enum value	Code numeric value	Argument description	Command description
COM_LONG_DATA	24	A byte sequence in the following format: 4 byte statement ID, 2 byte parameter number, parameter string. Both integers have the low byte first.	Tells the server the packet contains the data for one bound parameter in a prepared statement. Used to avoid unnecessary copying of a large amount of data when the value of the bound parameter is very long. Issued by the client API call `mysql_stmt_send_long_data( )`. New in version 4.1.
COM_CLOSE_STMT	25	4-byte statement ID with the low byte first.	Tells the server to close the prepared statement specified by the statement ID. Issued by the client API call `mysql_stmt_close( )`. New in version 4.1.
COM_RESET_STMT	26	4-byte statement ID with the low byte first.	Tells the server to discard the current parameter values in the prepared statement specified by the statement ID that may have been set with `COM_LONG_DATA`. Issued by the client API call `mysql_stmt_reset( )`. New in version 4.1.
COM_SET_OPTION	27	2-byte code for the option, low byte first.	Tells the server to enable or disable the option specified by the code. At this point, seems to be used only to enable or disable the support of multiple statements in one query string. Issued by the client API call `mysql_set_server_option( )`. New in version 4.1.
COM_END	28	No argument.	Never sent by a client. Used for internal purposes.

When MySQL developers add a new command, to keep the backward compatibility for the older clients, all new commands are added immediately before COM_END in the enum server_command. Adding it anywhere else would alter the numeric codes of the commands and thus break all of the commands after the point of the insertion in older clients. This requirement allows us to easily track the history of features to a certain extent. For example, we can tell that prepared statements were added after replication because COM_PREPARE follows COM_BINLOG_DUMP.

Server Responses

Once the server receives a command, it processes it and sends one or more response packets. Several types of responses are discussed in this section.

Data Field

Data fields are critical components in many of the server response packets. A data field consists of a length specifier sequence followed by the actual data value. The length specifier sequence can be understood by studying the definition of net_store_length( ) from *sql/pack.c*:

```
char *
net_store_length(char *pkg, ulonglong length)
{
  uchar *packet=(uchar*) pkg;
  if (length < (ulonglong) LL(251))
  {
    *packet=(uchar) length;
    return (char*) packet+1;
  }
  /* 251 is reserved for NULL */
  if (length < (ulonglong) LL(65536))
  {
    *packet++=252;
    int2store(packet,(uint) length);
    return (char*) packet+2;
  }
  if (length < (ulonglong) LL(16777216))
  {
    *packet++=253;
    int3store(packet,(ulong) length);
    return (char*) packet+3;
  }
  *packet++=254;
  int8store(packet,length);
  return (char*) packet+8;
}
```

As you can see, if the value of length does not exceed 251 (i.e., if it can fit into 1 byte without a conflict with the reserved values), the code just stores it in a byte. If it is 251 and higher but fits into 2 bytes, the code prefixes it with the value of 252 and then writes it out in the following 2 bytes. If 2 bytes is not enough, but 4 would do, the code uses 253 for the code, and then occupies the next 4 bytes with the length value. If 4 bytes is not enough, the code uses 254 for the code, and stores it in 8 bytes. It must be noted that all length values following the code are stored with the low byte first.

One may ask why the 1 byte length is limited to 251, when the first reserved value in the net_store_length( ) is 252. The code 251 has a special meaning. It indicates that there is no length value or data following the code, and the value of the field is the SQL NULL.

Why such a complexity? Most of the time the data field is fairly short, and, especially if a query returns a lot of records and/or selects a lot of columns, there could be many of them in the response. Wasting even a byte per field in this situation would add up to a large overhead. The probability of a field length being greater than 250 is relatively low, but even in that case, wasting a byte is barely noticeable since the server is already sending at least 253 bytes: at least 2 for the length, and at least 251 for the field value.

Immediately after the length sequences is the actual data value, which is converted to a string representation.

In the pre-4.1 versions, the standard server API call for storing a data field in a buffer is net_store_data( ), which exists in several variants, one for each possible data argument type. The net_store_data( ) family is found in *sql/net_pkg.cc* in those older version. Versions 4.1 and higher use Protocol::store( ), which in the case of the simple protocol, just wraps around net_store_data( ). Both are implemented in *sql/protocol.cc*.

Note that in version 4.1, when returning the data for prepared statements fields and when the data value is not a string, the data is sent in the raw binary format with the low byte first without a length specifier.

OK Packet

An OK packet is sent to indicate that the server successfully completed the command. It is sent in response to the following commands:

- COM_PING
- COM_QUERY if the query does not need to return a result set; for example, INSERT, UPDATE, or ALTER TABLE
- COM_REFRESH
- COM_REGISTER_SLAVE

This type of packet is appropriate for commands that do not return a result set. Its format, however, permits sending some extra status information, such as the number of modified records, the value of the automatically generated primary key, or a custom status message in a string format. The structure of the packet body is documented in Table 4-8.

Table 4-8. Format of server's OK packet

Offset in the body	Length	Description
0	1	A byte with the value of 0, indicating that the packet has no fields.
1	rows_len	The number of records that the query has changed in the field length format described in the "Data Field" section, earlier in this chapter. Its length varies depending on the value. I will refer to its length as rows_len to express the subsequent offsets.

Table 4-8. Format of server's OK packet (continued)

Offset in the body	Length	Description
1 + rows_len	id_len	The value of the generated auto-increment ID for the primary key. Set to 0 if not applicable in the context. The value is stored in the field length format of a data field. I will refer to the length of this value as id_len.
1 + rows_len + id_len	2	Server status bit mask, low byte first. For details on different values, see the macros starting with STATUS_ in *include/mysql_com.h*. In the protocol of version 4.0 and earlier, the status field is present only if it is a nonzero value. In the protocol of version 4.1 and later, it is reported unconditionally.
3 + rows_len + id_len	2	Present only in the protocol of version 4.1 and later. Contains the number of warnings the last command has generated. For example, if the command was COM_QUERY with LOAD DATA INFILE, and some of the fields or lines could not be properly imported, a number of warnings will be generated. The number is stored with the low byte first.
5 + rows_len + id_len in version 4.1 and later protocol., 1 +rows_len + id_len or 3 +rows_len + id_len in the older protocol, depending on whether the server status bit mask was included.	msg_len	An optional field for the status message if one is present in the standard data field format with the field length followed by field value, which in this case is a character string.

To send an OK packet from inside the server, you must call send_ok( ). In version 4.1 and later, the function is declared in *sql/protocol.h*, and defined in *sql/protocol.cc*. In the earlier versions, it is declared in *sql/mysql_priv.h* and defined in *sql/net_pkg.cc*.

Error Packet

When something goes wrong with the processing of a command, the server responds with an error packet. The format is documented in Table 4-9.

Table 4-9. Format of server's error packet

Offset in the body	Length	Description
0	1	A byte containing 255. The client will always treat a response packet starting with a byte containing 255 as an error message.
1	2	The error code. Low byte first. The field will not be included if the server is talking to a very ancient pre-3.23 client, and the subsequent offsets should be adjusted accordingly in that case.
3	2	Character '#' followed by the byte containing the value of the ODBC/JDBC SQL state. Present only in version 4.1 and later.
5 in version 4.1 and later, 3 in 4.0 and earlier	Varies	Zero-terminated text of the error message.

To send an error packet from inside the server, call send_error( ), which is defined in *sql/protocol.cc* in version 4.1 and later, and in *sql/net_pkg.cc* in version 4.0 and earlier.

EOF Packet

The end-of-file (EOF) packet is used to communicate a number of messages:

- End-of-field information data in a result set
- End-of-row data in a result set
- Server acknowledgment of COM_SHUTDOWN
- Server reporting success in response to COM_SET_OPTION and COM_DEBUG
- Request for the old-style credentials during authentication

The body of an EOF packet always starts with a byte containing decimal 254. In the pre-4.1 era, there was nothing else in the body in addition to this byte. Version 4.1 added another 4 bytes of status fields with the potential of going up to 7 bytes. The format of the version 4.1 EOF body is outlined in Table 4-10.

Table 4-10. Format of server's EOF packet

Offset in the body	Length	Description
0	1	Byte with the decimal 254
1	2	Number of warnings
3	2	Server status bit mask

The reason for the 7 byte limit in the status bytes area is that the decimal 254 byte followed by an 8 byte string at the beginning of a packet body can have a different meaning: it can specify the number of fields in a result set using the field length format described in the "Data Field" section, earlier in this chapter.

To send an EOF packet, the server uses send_eof( ), which is defined in *sql/protocol.cc* in 4.1 and later, and in *sql/net_pkg.cc* in the earlier versions.

Result Set Packets

A large number of queries produce a result set. Some examples are SELECT, SHOW, CHECK, REPAIR, and EXPLAIN. Any time the expected information from a query is more than a simple status report, a result set is returned.

The result set consists of a sequence of packets. First, the server sends information about the fields with a call to Protocol::send_fields( ) in *sql/protocol.cc* in version 4.1 and later. In the older versions, the function is called send_fields( ) and is found in *sql/net_pkg.cc*. This stage produces the following sequence of packets:

- A packet with the body consisting of the standard field-length specifier sequence. However, this time, the meaning of the number is different. It indicates the number of fields in the result set.
- A group of field description packets (see the upcoming explanation for the format description), one for each field, in the field order of the result set.
- A terminating EOF packet.

The format of the field description packet body is shown in Tables 4-11 and 4-12. Table 4-11 shows the format for versions 4.0 and earlier, while Table 4-12 shows the format for versions 4.1 and later. Because most of the packet elements have variable lengths, the offsets are dependent on the content of the previous fields. I will, therefore, omit the offset column in the format descriptions. Finally, Table 4-13 explains the different field option flags.

Table 4-11. Format of server's result set sequence, versions 4.0 and earlier

Length	Description
Varies	Table name of the field in the data field format. If the table was aliased in the query, contains the name of the alias.
Varies	Column name of the field in the data field format. If the column was aliased in the query, contains the name of the alias.
4	Data field-formatted value of field length, low byte first.
2	Data field-formatted field-type code according to enum field_types in *include/mysql_com.h*.
1	Decimal value 3, meaning the next 3 bytes contain data. The idea is to make the sequence look like a standard data field.
2	Bit mask of field option flags (low byte first). See Table 4-12 for the explanation of the bits.
1	Decimal point precision of the field.
Varies	Optional element. If present, contains the default value of the field in the standard field data format.

Table 4-12. Format of server's result set sequence, versions 4.1 and later

Length	Description
4	Data field (see the section "Data Field," earlier in this chapter) containing the ASCII string def.
Varies	Database name of the field in the data field format.
Varies	Table name of the field in the data field format. If the table was aliased in the query, contains the name of the alias.
Varies	Table name of the field in the data field format. If the table was aliased in the query, contains the original name of the table.
Varies	Column name of the field in the data field format. If the column was aliased in the query, contains the name of the alias.
Varies	Column name of the field in the data field format. If the column was aliased in the query, contains the original name of the table.
1	Byte containing decimal 12, meaning that 12 bytes of data follow. The idea is to make the sequence look like a standard data field.

Length	Description
2	Character set code of the field (low byte first).
4	Field length (low byte first).
1	Type code of the field according to enum field_types in *include/mysql_com.h*.
2	Bit mask of field option flags (low byte first). See Table 4-13 for the explanation of the bits.
1	Decimal-point precision of field values.
2	Reserved.
Varies	Optional element. If present, contains the default value of the field in the standard field data format.

Table 4-13. Option flags in server's result set packets

Bit macro	Hexadecimal bit value	Description
NOT_NULL_FLAG	0x0001	The field value cannot be NULL (it is declared with the NOT NULL attribute).
PRI_KEY_FLAG	0x0002	The field is a part of the primary key.
UNIQUE_KEY_FLAG	0x0004	The field is a part of a unique key.
MULTIPLE_KEY_ FLAG	0x0008	The field is a part of some non-unique key.
BLOB_FLAG	0x0010	The field is a BLOB or TEXT.
UNSIGNED_FLAG	0x0020	The field was declared with the UNSIGNED attribute, which has the same meaning as the unsigned keyword in C.
ZEROFILL_FLAG	0x0040	The field has been declared with the ZEROFILL attribute, which tells the server to pad the numeric types with leading zeros in the output to fit the specified field length.
BINARY_FLAG	0x0080	The field has been declared with the BINARY attribute, which tells the server to compare strings byte-for-byte in a case-sensitive manner.
ENUM_FLAG	0x0100	The field is an ENUM.
AUTO_INCREMENT_ FLAG	0x0200	The field has been declared with the AUTO_INCREMENT attribute, which enables the automatic generation of primary key values when a new record is inserted.
TIMESTAMP_FLAG	0x0400	The field is a timestamp.
SET_FLAG	0x0800	The field is a SET.
NUM_FLAG	0x8000	Used with cursors in version 4.1 to indicate that the field is numeric.

Following the field definition sequence of packets, the server sends the actual rows of data, one packet per row. Each row data packet consists of a sequence of values stored in the standard field data format. When reporting the result of a regular query (sent with COM_QUERY), the field data is converted to the string format. When using a prepared statement (COM_PREPARE), the field data is sent in its native format with the low byte first.

After all of the data rows have been sent, the packet sequence is terminated with an EOF packet.

CHAPTER 5
Configuration Variables

Much can be learned about the internal workings of MySQL server by studying its configuration variables. In some cases, the very existence of a variable with a certain name tells a story. For example, key_buffer_size reveals that MySQL uses a key cache. query_cache_size suggests that the server can cache the results of a query to avoid unnecessary work when it is run repeatedly without any modifications to the tables that it references. innodb_flush_log_at_trx_commit suggests that the InnoDB storage engine supports transactions, and may optionally not write out its transaction log to disk on every commit. slave_compressed_protocol reveals that MySQL supports replication with a slave that can request that the data transfer be compressed.

Other option names are perhaps not as self-explanatory, but you will learn a lot by asking yourself why that option exists, and studying the source to find out how the different settings affect the behavior.

MySQL has over 200 different options. Every one of them tells a story. Some reveal the presence of a feature. Some show the richness of MySQL optimization algorithms. Some demonstrate MySQL's ability to self-administer. Some are there because some platform-specific bug needed to be tracked down or worked around at some point. Others exist just to allow the user to choose a file or a directory used for some internal operation, but their very existence permits us to take a peek at what MySQL is doing behind the scenes. Due to the space constraints, we cannot hear all of those stories, so we'll focus on the most interesting ones.

Configuration Variables Tutorial

To compensate for the lack of coverage for many configuration variables in this chapter, this section contains a brief "nuts-and-bolts" tutorial on how option parsing works. This will enable you to track down unfamiliar options in the source, as well as add your own.

Configuration File and Command-Line Options

`mysqld` can receive configuration variable settings on the command line, or it can read them from configuration files. There can be multiple configuration files, and their contents can be merged with the command-line configuration options.

The first file to be examined is */etc/my.cnf*. By default, other locations are also searched after a successful or unsuccessful attempt to load */etc/my.cnf* in the given order: first *my.cnf* in the directory specified by a compiled-in macro DATADIR, and then *.my.cnf* (note the initial period) in the home directory of the real (rather than effective) user that started *mysqld*. Note that the loading attempts in this sequence continue regardless of whether the previous attempt succeeded or failed. Thus, several configuration files could be potentially combined.

To find out which configuration files *mysqld* is loading on Linux, you can run the following shell command:

```
$ strace -e stat64 mysqld --print-defaults > /dev/null
```

which will produce an output similar to this:

```
stat64("/etc/my.cnf", {st_mode=S_IFREG|0644, st_size=2025, ...}) = 0
stat64("/usr/var/my.cnf", 0xbfffdcbc)   = -1 ENOENT (No such file or directory)
stat64("/home/sasha/.my.cnf", 0xbfffdcbc) = -1 ENOENT (No such file or directory)
upeek: ptrace(PTRACE_PEEKUSER, ... ): Input/output error
```

The error message from *strace* about ptrace( ) on the last line can be safely ignored. The important parts of the output are the traced calls to stat64( ). The first argument in each of those calls is the name of the configuration file that *mysqld* is trying to load. Here the files are */etc/my.cnf*, */usr/var/my.cnf*, and */home/sasha/.my.cnf*, in that order. You can see that the first file exists, while the other two do not.

Another way to get the same information is to run:

```
$ mysqld --verbose --help | head -15
```

which produces something like this:

```
/reiser-data/oreilly/mysql-5.1.11/sql/mysqld  Ver 5.1.11-beta-log for pc-linux-gnu on
i686 (Source distribution)
Copyright (C) 2000 MySQL AB, by Monty and others
This software comes with ABSOLUTELY NO WARRANTY. This is free software,
and you are welcome to modify and redistribute it under the GPL license

Starts the MySQL database server

Usage: /usr/bin/mysqld [OPTIONS]

Default options are read from the following files in the given order:
/etc/my.cnf ~/.my.cnf /usr/var/my.cnf
The following groups are read: mysqld server mysqld-5.1
The following options may be given as the first argument:
--print-defaults        Print the program argument list and exit
--no-defaults           Don't read default options from any options file
```

The message, among other things, tells us that it is going to check */etc/my.cnf, ~/.my.cnf,* and */usr/etc/my.cnf* in that order.

The loading of the configuration file can be disabled with the command-line argument *--no-defaults*. If used, it must be the first argument. Alternative configuration files can be specified with *--defaults-file* and *--defaults-extra-file*. When *--defaults-file* is given, the compiled-in configuration files sequence is skipped, and the specified file is loaded instead. If *--defaults-extra-file* is given, the specified file is loaded after the compiled-in configuration files sequence has been loaded. Note that just like *--no-defaults*, *--defaults-file* and *--defaults-extra-file* must come first in the argument list, or you will get an error about an unknown option. As a consequence, the two options cannot be used together.

What happens when several conflicting configuration option sources are combined? A good way to understand what happens and why is to examine what *mysqld* does behind the scenes to process the configuration options. One of the first things main( ) in *sql/mysqld.cc* does is call init_common_variables( ), also from *sql/mysqld.cc*, which in turn calls load_defaults( ) from *mysys/default.c*. load_defaults( ) is responsible for loading all of the configuration files that are available. You may notice that load_defaults( ) receives as arguments &argv, the array of command-line arguments, and &argc, the number of command-line arguments. It does this so that it can insert the configuration file options into the list and make it look to the command-line argument processing code as if those options have been specified on the command line. It is important to note that the arguments from the configuration files get inserted into the list before the regular command-line arguments in the order that the files are processed.

The command-line arguments are processed later on with a call to get_options( ) from *sql/mysqld.cc*, which transfers control to handle_options( ) from *mysys/my_getopt.c*. handle_options( ) in turn begins to process the merged list of arguments in order starting from the first one. What happens if the same variable in that list is set more than once? From the logic of the argument processing, we can see that the setting that appears last in the list will be the one that will actually take effect.

There is one exception to the previous rule. For security purposes, the *--user* option is not allowed to be reset with a subsequent option value in the processing chain.

Therefore, we can observe that in the case of conflicting settings with some exceptions, the command-line arguments have the highest precedence. After that, it is *.my.cnf* in the home directory of the real user, *my.cnf* in the compiled-in DATADIR, and last of all */etc/my.cnf*.

Although *mysqld* provides many options to load the configuration, the recommended way is to use only */etc/my.cnf* and make sure that other configuration files *mysqld* is interested in do not exist, as well as that no command-line arguments are given.

The configuration file follows the format informally defined as follows:

```
[section_name]
option_name=option_value#comment
option_name=option_value
#comment
option_with_no_argument
```

There can be several sections, each often used by a program with the same name. Thus, *mysqld* looks for the section labeled mysqld. There can be only one option per line. Comments can be put on their own lines or at the end of an option line, and start with #. For the numeric option values, K, M, or G suffixes can be used to indicate kilobytes, megabytes, or gigabytes. The equivalent lowercase suffixes are also allowed. Single or double quotes are allowed around the arguments. The following example illustrates these rules:

```
[mysqld]
key-buffer-size=128M
# make sure we log queries that do not use keys
log-long-format
long-query-time='3' # anything longer than this is too long
max-connections=300
socket="/var/lib/mysql/mysql.sock"
datadir=/var/lib/mysql
```

Historically, the server configuration parameters have been divided into two groups: options and variables. In version 3.23, numeric variables had to be set with the set-variable option. For example, the 3.23 equivalent of:

```
max-connections=300
```

would have been:

```
set-variable= max_connections=300.
```

True to its commitment to backward compatibility, later versions of MySQL still support the 3.23 style syntax for setting variables. However, a rewrite of the configuration parameter processing code in 4.0 has eliminated the distinction.

Internals of the Configuration Option Parsing

The configuration variables are defined by struct my_option my_long_options[] from *sql/mysqld.cc*, while struct my_option is defined in *include/my_getopt.h*. Table 5-1 lists its members in the order they are defined in the structure. Table 5-2 lists the variable type codes used in the var_type member, and Table 5-3 lists the argument type codes used in the arg_type member.

Table 5-1. Members of struct my_option

Definition	Description
`const char *name`	Option name as it appears in the configuration file. On the command line, the option name is prefixed with a double hyphen: `--`.
`int id`	A unique integer code for the option. If the code fits within the printable ACSII character range, it is also used for the short (prefixed by a single hyphen) form of the command-line option. For example, if the value is the ASCII code for b, this option can be specified with *-b* on the command line.
`const char *comment`	A brief documentation of the option that appears in the output of *mysqld --help*.
`gptr *value`	A pointer to the memory location that will store the value of the option once it is parsed. The type of the variable pointed at should be specified by the appropriate value of the `var_type` member. If the option accepts no arguments, should be set to 0.
`gptr *u_max_value`	A pointer to the memory location that will store the maximum possible value of the option. Usually points to a member of a `max_system_variables` structure, which results in its initialization.
`const char **str_values`	At this point, does not appear to be used anywhere in the code. Apparently was intended to point to an array of possible string values for the option. Set it to 0 if you are adding your own option.
`ulong var_type`	Variable type code. For possible values and their meanings, see Table 5-2. The pre-processor macros containing the values are defined in *include/my_getopt.h*.
`enum get_opt_arg_type arg_type`	Argument type code. For possible values, see Table 5-3. `enum get_opt_arg_type` is defined in *include/my_getopt.h*.
`longlong def_value`	Default value.
`longlong min_value`	Minimum value. If a lower value is specified, the actual value of the option is set to the minimum value.
`longlong max_value`	Maximum value. If a higher value is specified, the actual value of the option is set to the maximum value.
`longlong sub_size`	The value to subtract from the option before storing it in the variable associated with the option.
`long block_size`	The option value will be adjusted to be a multiple of this parameter.
`int app_type`	Apparently reserved for future use. Safe to set to 0.

Table 5-2. Variable type codes allowed in the var_type field

Macro	Decimal value	Description
GET_NO_ARG	1	There is no variable to worry about because the option accepts no argument.
GET_BOOL	2	The variable is of type `my_bool`.
GET_INT	3	The variable is of type `int`.
GET_UINT	4	The variable is of type `uint`.
GET_LONG	5	The variable is of type `long`.
GET_ULONG	6	The variable is of type `ulong`.
GET_LL	7	The variable is of type `longlong`.

Table 5-2. *Variable type codes allowed in the var_type field (continued)*

Macro	Decimal value	Description
GET_ULL	8	The variable is of type `ulonglong`.
GET_STR	9	The variable is of type `char*`. When the corresponding option is parsed, the variable will be pointed to the location containing the option value. In other words, it points to somewhere in the middle of one of the members of the `argv` array. No memory is allocated.
GET_STR_ALLOC	10	The variable is of type `char*`. If the initial value is not 0, the option parsing code assumes that the pointer has been allocated earlier with `my_malloc()` and will free it with a call to `my_free()`. Otherwise the pointer is allocated with `my_malloc()`. Thus, the value of the option can end up either in a predefined location allocated by the caller, or in a location allocated by the options parser .
GET_DISABLED	11	The option is understood by the option parser but is disabled. If used, the parsing is aborted and an error code is returned.
GET_ASK_ADDR	128	This value is ORed with other values. If enabled, the address for the variable will be provided by a special function `mysql_getopt_value()` from *sql/mysqld.cc*. This is useful for option arguments in the style of *namespace.arg_name*; e.g., `keycache1.key_buffer_size`. The `mysql_getopt_value()` method receives the value of the *namespace* part as an argument, and is able to supply the correct storage address based on this information. Currently, this syntax is used to support configuration of multiple key caches in MyISAM tables, but could be used for other things in the future.

Table 5-3. *Argument type codes allowed in the arg_type field*

Value	Description
NO_ARG	The option does not accept an argument. It is an error to provide one. This type is usually used for Boolean flags.
OPT_ARG	The option may accept an argument, but it is not an error to not provide one. In that case the value of the variable will be set to its default value. This type is usually used for options that tell MySQL to log something, and may optionally specify the location of the log, or for options that enable a feature that has several different modes of operations, with one being a very reasonable default, and others being somewhat obscure.
REQUIRED_ARG	The option requires the user to provide an argument. If no argument is supplied, an error is reported. This type is usually used for numeric variables, or for other options where it does not make sense to just name the option and expect the server to supply a reasonable default.

Each member of `my_long_options` corresponds to a configuration option. The option parsing happens in `get_option()` in *sql/mysqld.cc*, which is just a wrapper around `handle_options()` from *mysys/my_getopt.c*. If processing an option is as simple as just initializing a variable, it is sufficient to provide an appropriate address and a variable type in the definition of the corresponding member of the `my_long_options` array. In some cases, a more complex initialization is required. In these cases the `get_one_option()` callback from *sql/mysqld.cc* is used. This function is called for each option by `handle_options()` after the value of the option has been initialized.

Example of Adding a New Configuration Option

Let us consider an example of adding a simple new configuration option. On occasion, when trying to start *mysqld*, a problem may arise. A stale instance of *mysqld* might be running and using the resources that the new instance will try to acquire. This is going to cause an error. We will add an option, kill-old-mysqld, that kills an old instance of *mysqld* if such is present. The code shown in this section is available from this book's web site, as listed in the preface.

For this example, I assume that you have gone through the steps in Chapter 2, and have a source tree where you have previously had a successful build.

First, we open *sql/mysqld.cc* in a text editor. Then we find the initialization of my_long_options and add the following entry somewhere in the array (it is a good idea to put it in alphabetical order by option names, but anywhere else would work):

```
{"kill-old-mysqld", OPT_KILL_OLD_MYSQLD,
"Kill old instance of mysqld on startup",
(gptr*) &opt_kill_old_mysqld, (gptr*) &opt_kill_old_mysqld, 0,GET_BOOL, NO_ARG,
0, 0, 0, 0, 0, 0},
```

Note that we are now referencing a nonexistent value OPT_KILL_OLD_MYSQLD and a variable opt_kill_old_mysqld, which also does not exist. Let's quickly fix these issues. Find enum options_mysqld in the same file, and add OPT_KILL_OLD_MYSQLD to it (conventionally, new options are frequently added at the end, but anywhere else would work). Then we add a global variable with the following definition:

```
my_bool opt_kill_old_mysqld = 0;
```

The location of it is not relevant in terms of code functionality, but it is a good idea to follow established conventions. You can search for my_bool opt_skip_slave_start and place it in that general area.

Now the option is recognized by the parser, and the variable gets initialized. Our next step is to actually do something when that option is present. In main( ), after the call to init_common_variables( ), place the following piece of code:

```
if (opt_kill_old_mysqld)
    kill_old_mysqld();
```

Now we need to declare and define kill_old_myslqd( ). First, place the following declaration somewhere at the top of the file (a good place would be right after the static void mysql_init_variables(void) line):

```
static void kill_old_mysqld(void);
```

Then put the following definition somewhere in the file (may just as well be after the part where mysql_init_variables( ) is defined):

```
static void kill_old_mysqld(void)
{
  File fd = -1;
```

```c
  /* pid value can have no more than 20 digits,
     and we need one extra byte for the new line character
   */

  char buf[21];
  char* p;
  long pid;

  /* return if we cannot open the file */
  if ((fd= my_open(pidfile_name,O_RDONLY,MYF(0))) < 0)
    return;

  /* Populate the buffer. For the sake of simplicity
     we do not deal
     with the case of a partial read, and leave it
     as an exercise for
     the meticulous reader.
   */
  if (my_read(fd, buf, sizeof(buf), MYF(0)) <= 0)
    goto err;

  /* boundary for strchr() */
  buf[sizeof(buf) - 1]= 0;

  /* find the end of line and put a \0 terminator instead */
  if (!(p= strchr(buf,'\n')))
    goto err;
  *p= 0;

  if (!(pid= strtol(buf,0,10)))
    goto err;

  /* Support for Windows is left as an exercise for
     the reader */
#ifndef __WIN__
  /* A crude kill method with no checks.
     A more refined method is left
     as an exercise for the reader.
   */
  kill(pid, SIGTERM);
  sleep(5);
  kill(pid, SIGKILL);
  sleep(2);
#endif

  /* Cleanup. Should be executed in all cases,
     success or error
   */
err:
  if (fd >= 0)
    my_close(fd,MYF(0));
}
```

Because we have modified only sql/mysqld.cc, it is sufficient to run *make* only in the *sql* directory. If you made the modifications with no typos, it will produce a new *mysqld* binary with the support for the new option.

You may have noticed from the comments in the source that, to keep this example simple, I have left a lot of dirty work as an exercise for the reader. Hopefully, this will help you appreciate the challenges of the MySQL development team. Due to its requirements for portability and robustness, even simple additions to the code base involve a lot of error checking and handling, and a lot of portability workarounds. There is a long road from "it works for me" to "it is ready for production release."

Interesting Aspects of Specific Configuration Variables

Now that you understand the general handling of configuration variables, this section presents the stories of particular variables that affect *mysqld* significantly.

big-tables

The MySQL optimizer tries as hard as it can to avoid using a temporary table when resolving a query. However, in some cases this grim task just has to be done. Then, if at all possible, it will try to use an in-memory temporary table. Unfortunately, the size of the table cannot always be estimated in advance. Sometimes in the process of populating the table, the maximum in-memory table size limit is reached (the limit is controlled by the tmp_table_size setting). When this happens, the temporary table needs to be converted to a disk type (i.e., MyISAM). This means re-creating the table and repopulating it with the rows collected in the in-memory table up to this point.

For a typical MySQL usage, the need to convert an in-memory table to disk is a rare occurrence. However, there are applications that run into this situation a lot. If you know in advance that the temporary result is going to be more than can be stored in memory, the big-tables option comes in handy. It tells the server to not even bother creating an in-memory table, and to start with a disk-based table right away.

When enabled, big-tables can still be overridden with the SQL_SMALL_RESULT query option for one particular query. Alternatively, when big-tables is disabled, SQL_BIG_RESULT option can be used to force the optimizer to start out with a disk-based table.

For further study of this option, look for create_tmp_table( ) in *sql/sql_select.cc*. Just like many others in this file, this is a very large function. Once you have found the start of the definition, you will probably need to use the search function of your editor again. This time look for OPTION_BIG_TABLES.

concurrent-insert

A frequent complaint about MyISAM tables, especially back in the early days of 3.23, was that the use of table locks (as opposed to only row or page locks) caused serious performance degradation due to unnecessarily high lock contention. This issue gained a good amount of publicity in the open source community when the popular development site SourceForge (*http://sourceforge.net*) discovered with its own benchmark that MySQL did not scale very well with its application, and migrated to PostgreSQL. Several other users observed similar results. The degradation in performance under high load was believed to be caused by the lock contention.

Indeed, there was good reason to believe so. While read locks are shared, the write lock is exclusive. If one thread is updating just one record, every other thread that wants to read or write to some other record must enter the queue to wait for the lock. This means you have to suspend it, and there is a context switch. If this happens enough, pretty soon all your CPU is doing is switching between threads instead of doing the work.

The assumption turned out to be incorrect, at least to a large extent. The problem was attributed to the inability of LinuxThreads to deal efficiently with frequently acquired and released mutexes, something MySQL server had to do a lot of. After a patch was applied to LinuxThreads, the benchmarks that performed a heavy mix of reads and writes scaled just fine as long as both types of queries were properly optimized.

In the meantime, however, a partial workaround was added. While the general case for a minimal conflict type of lock would have been fairly difficult, in one special case the lock contention could be minimized with only a few changes to the code. When a record is inserted into the table, the MyISAM storage engine first tries to find a previously deleted record whose space is large enough for the new record, and overwrites that space with the new record. However, if there are no records marked as deleted, the record is written at the end of the datafile. In the latter case, it turned out not to be so difficult to allow the INSERT and the SELECT operations to proceed concurrently.

When this option is enabled, the MyISAM storage engine attempts to use this optimization whenever possible.

To learn more about the concurrent insert, study these files in the *myisam* directory:

mi_open.c
mi_extra.c
mi_write.c
mi_range.c
mi_rkey.c
mi_rnext.c
mi_rnext_same.c
mi_rprev.c
mi_rsame.c

and search for concurrent_insert.

core-file

Debugging a threaded program can be quite a bit of a challenge. It is even more challenging when a crash happens, but no core file is produced. Sometimes you need that core file badly, as the crash cannot be duplicated in a debugger. And some platforms are not particularly anxious to generate a core file when threads are used.

In the unfortunate event of a crash, this option will engage the full power of the voodoo black magic known as MySQL in order to coax the uncooperative kernel to write out a core file. The magic is implemented in write_core( ) in *sql/stacktrace.c*.

default-storage-engine

In the past, this option was known as default-table-type, which is still supported. As MySQL AB made the transition from being a small company just trying to make a good database to a bigger entity trying to make an impression in the corporate world, it was discovered that IT managers respond to the term "storage engine" much better than "table type," which is perhaps a more intuitive term for a MySQL hacker.

Due to its development history and Monty's insight, MySQL ended up with a very powerful architecture that abstracts the storage engine from the parser and optimizer enough to allow multiple storage engines.

One type of storage engine, MEMORY, stores tables only in memory. MyISAM provides persistent storage and a number of fancy features such as full-text search and spatial indexing, but does not have transactions or row-level locks. InnoDB provides transactions and row-level locks, but it is slower on some operations than MyISAM and requires more disk space. Depending on the need of your application, you can pick the right type of storage engine on a per-table basis.

The storage engine can be specified when creating a table. If omitted, the one specified by default-storage-engine is used. It can also be changed for existing tables with the ALTER TABLE command. The default value of default-storage-engine is MyISAM.

To study the storage engines, take a look at:

sql/handler.h
sql/handler.cc
sql/ha_myisam.h
sql/ha_myisam.cc
sql/ha_innodb.h
sql/ha_innodb.cc
sql/ha_heap.h
sql/ha_heap.cc
Other files matching the patterns *sql/ha_*.cc* and *sql/ha_*.h*

delay-key-write

This option was added in the early days of 3.23 to optimize the queries that update keys (INSERT, UPDATE, and DELETE) in MyISAM tables. Normally, the server flushes the changed key blocks out of the MyISAM key cache at the end of every query. This could cause severe performance degradation in some cases.

One approach to this performance problem is to delay the key block flushing. When the key writes are delayed, the changed blocks are not flushed out at the end of a query. The flushing happens later under one the following circumstances:

- All of the tables are removed from the table cache with FLUSH TABLES.
- The table is removed from the table cache with FLUSH TABLE.
- The table cache is flushed during server shutdown.
- The table is displaced from the table cache with a new table.
- The changed key blocks are displaced from the key cache with new blocks.

If delay-key-write is set to ON, only the tables with the DELAY_KEY_WRITE=1 setting are handled this way. When the setting is ALL, all of the MyISAM key writes are delayed regardless of the table options. When set to OFF, delayed key writes do not happen regardless of the table options.

The advantage of using this option is the performance gain. The disadvantage is a higher risk of table corruption should a crash happen.

For further study of this option, find the start of mi_lock_database( ) definition in *myisam/mi_locking.c*, and look for the call to flush_key_blocks( ). You may also want to study the flush_key_blocks( ) itself in *mysys/mf_keycache.c*.

ft_stopword_file

MyISAM tables support full-text keys, which allow the storage engine to look up records quickly by words in the middle of character strings. In contrast, a regular B-tree index can only be used to look up records based on the entire value or at least a prefix of the key.

The full-text search capabilities are highly customizable. This option represents one of the many full-text search configuration options. During full-text indexing, in order to improve the quality of the index, some frequently used words are ignored. For example, if the text column contains regular English sentences, there is little value to indexing the word the, as it will appear in an overwhelming majority of the records. Such words are called *stop words*.

By default, MySQL uses a built-in list of stop words defined by the ft_precompiled_ stopwords array in *myisam/ft_static.c*. It works very well if the text you are indexing is a collection of standard English sentences, but it will likely be unsuitable if used for other languages or if the collection does not contain regular text. You can create your own stop word list and specify it with this option. Note that if you change the stop word list, it is necessary to reindex the existing tables, which can be done with REPAIR TABLE tbl_name QUICK.

To learn more about how full-text indexing works, take a look at:

myisam/ft_boolean_search.c
myisam/ft_eval.c
myisam/ft_nlq_search.c
myisam/ft_parser.c
myisam/ft_static.c
myisam/ft_stem.c
myisam/ft_stopwords.c
myisam/ft_update.c

innodb_buffer_pool_size

This buffer setting is one of the most important InnoDB variables. It controls how much memory is used to cache both InnoDB table data and indices. Note that InnoDB differs from MyISAM in the way the table data is cached. MyISAM caches only the keys, and simply hopes the OS will do a good job caching the data. InnoDB does not put any faith in the OS and takes the matter of caching the data into its own hands.

To learn more about how the InnoDB buffering works, start by taking a look at buf_pool_init( ), buf_page_create( ), and buf_page_get_gen( ) in *innobase/buf/buf0buf.c*. Also take a look at the macro wrappers for buf_page_get_gen( ) in *innobase/include/buf0buf.h*, particularly buf_page_get( ), which is used most frequently in the code. The same file also contains an extensive explanation of the buffering internals.

innodb_flush_log_at_trx_commit

InnoDB by design has much more stringent data safety requirements than MyISAM. It tries very hard to make sure that the data is still consistent with the absolute minimum loss even if you turn the power off in the middle of a transaction. However, a fine balance must be achieved between performance and data safety, and each application has its own standards.

InnoDB maintains a transaction log that is used for recovery during server startup. The recovery is attempted regardless of whether there was a crash or not. In the case of a crash, the log has pending transactions to redo. If there was no crash, no pending transactions are found in the log, so there is nothing to be done.

We can see, therefore, that the integrity of the transaction log is crucial in the recovery process. One way to ensure its integrity is to flush it to disk every time a transaction is committed. This allows us to recover every transaction that gets committed in the case of a crash. However, if the application performs short transactions frequently, this becomes a performance killer. Each log flush implies at least one disk write, and even with modern disks you can only do so many of them per second, although InnoDB can group commits to overcome this limitation to a certain extent.

This problem can be addressed by slightly reducing the stringency of the data safety requirements, and flushing the log to disk only once per second. With this approach, under the assumption of intact disk I/O (something we can expect from properly functioning hardware and operating system), our data is still consistent but could be up to one second old after the recovery. For many applications this is a negligible risk and is worth the hundred-fold or so improvement in performance that comes from a dramatic reduction in disk writes.

When `innodb_flush_log_at_trx_commit` is set to 0, the log buffer is written out to the logfile once per second, and the flush-to-disk operation is performed on the file descriptor, but nothing is done during a transaction commit. When this value is 1, during each transaction commit the log buffer is written out to the logfile, and the flush-to-disk operation is performed on the file descriptor. When set to 2, during each commit the log buffer is written out to the file descriptor, but the flush-to-disk operation is not performed on it. However, the flushing on the file descriptor takes place once per second.

I must note that the once-per-second flushing is not 100 percent guaranteed due to the process scheduling issues (for example, we might not get the CPU right at the time when we would like to flush), but an attempt is made, and except for the cases of extreme CPU overload, the actual intervals are very close to one second. When the server gets the CPU, it will check whether it has been a second since the last flush, and do another if it is time.

For further study of this option, take a look at `srv_master_thread( )` in *innobase/srv/srv0srv.c* (look for calls to the `log_buffer_flush_to_disk( )` function) and `trx_commit_off_kernel( )` in *innobase/trx/trx0trx.c* (look for calls to the `log_write_up_to( )` function).

innodb_file_per_table

MyISAM tables, since the very beginning, have had the advantage of easy backup and copying on a per-table basis without any involvement on the part of the server. This is possible because a MyISAM table is stored in three files: *table_name.frm* for the table definition, *table_name.MYD* for the data, and *table_name.MYI* for the keys.

When InnoDB was introduced into MySQL, many users missed the convenience of table manipulation on the file system level. Initially InnoDB tables could reside only in the tablespace file or raw device. However, version 4.1.1 added the ability to place each table in its own file.

When enabled, `innodb_file_per_table` causes new tables to have their index and data stored in a separate file, *table_name.ibd*. Nevertheless, this does not give the user the freedom to manipulate those files like MyISAM. As of this writing, InnoDB still stores a lot of meta information in its global tablespace, which makes such manipulations impossible, although work is in progress to facilitate those operations and make it possible to copy *.ibd* files from one server instance to another.

At this point, `innodb_file_per_table` only helps with backing up and restoring individual tables on the same server, and even that requires some tricks. The backup must be taken either when the server is down, or after all transactions have been committed and no new ones have started. To restore, you first run `ALTER TABLE tbl_name DISCARD TABLESPACE`, then copy the *.ibd* file into the appropriate database directory, and then run `ALTER TABLE tbl_name IMPORT TABLESPACE`.

Note that this option is of type `NO_ARG`. This means that it does not take a regular non-Boolean argument. If present, it is on; if absent, it is off. It can, however, optionally take a Boolean argument of 1 or 0.

For more details on how this option works, study `dict_build_table_def_step( )` in *innobase/dict/dict0crea.c*. Look for the `srv_file_per_table` variable.

innodb_lock_wait_timeout

Unlike the MyISAM storage engine, which supports only table locks, InnoDB can lock individual records, which is known as *row level locking*. This can bring great performance benefits for a wide variety of applications, but it unfortunately also introduces a problem: potential deadlocks. Let's say, for example, that thread 1 acquires an exclusive lock on record A. In the meantime, thread 2 acquires an exclusive lock on record B. Thread 1 then, while still holding the lock on A, attempts to acquire a lock on B, but has to wait for thread 2 to release it. In the meantime, thread 2 is trying to lock record A while still holding the lock on B. Thus neither one can progress, and we have a deadlock condition.

While it is possible to use an algorithm that avoids potential deadlocks, such a strategy can very easily cause severe performance degradation. InnoDB approaches the problem from a different angle. Normally deadlocks are very rare, especially if the application was written with some awareness of the problem. Therefore, instead of preventing them, InnoDB just lets them happen, but it periodically runs a lock detection monitor that frees the deadlock "prisoner" threads and allows them to return and report to the client that they have been aborted because they've been waiting for their lock longer than the value of this option.

Note that the deadlock monitoring thread does not actually examine the sequence of the locks each thread is holding to figure out the existence of a logical database deadlock. Rather, it assumes that if a certain thread has exceeded the time limit in waiting for a lock that it requested, it is probably logically deadlocked. Even if it is not, it doesn't matter—the user would appreciate getting an error message rather than waiting indefinitely while nothing productive is being accomplished.

The deadlock detection thread is implemented in `srv_lock_timeout_and_monitor_thread( )` in *innobase/srv/srv0srv.c*.

innodb_force_recovery

In a perfect world, this option would never be needed in a trasnactional database. But, unfortunately, some very unexpected things happen. Even a perfectly implemented transactional system with a perfect logic still depends on the assumption that it will read back from the disk exactly what it wrote to it last time. Any computer professional who has been around knows that this assumption is sometimes not true for a number of reasons: hardware failure, operating system bugs, user errors, etc. Additionally, InnoDB itself, although exceptionally robust, might still have a bug. The bottom line: there are times when the tablespace gets corrupted so badly that the standard recovery algorithm fails.

Again, from the purely theoretical point of view, corruption would force us to say that whatever we have on disk in place of our old tablespace is just a bunch of random data. Fortunately, in most practical situations there exists a better answer. Usually, the fatal corruption destroys only a couple of pages, while the rest of the data is intact. It is therefore possible, perhaps by way of a semi-educated guess at times, to recover most of the lost data.

This option tells InnoDB how hard to try to recover the lost data. 0 means not to go beyond the standard recovery algorithm, while 6 means to bring the database up at all costs and then try hard to run the queries without crashing. If the value of this option is greater than 0, no queries that update the tables are allowed. The user is expected to dump the tables salvaging the data, and then re-create a clean tablespace and repopulate it.

To learn more about what happens when you force a recovery, search for the variable srv_force_recovery in the following files:

innobase/buf/buf0buf.c
innobase/dict/dict0dict.c
innobase/fil/fil0fil.c
innobase/ibuf/ibuf0ibuf.c
innobase/log/log0recv.c
innobase/row/row0mysql.c
innobase/row/row0sel.c
innobase/srv/srv0srv.c
innobase/srv/srv0start.c
innobase/trx/trx0sys.c
innobase/trx/trx0undo.c

init-file

This option runs a set of SQL commands from the specified file on server startup. One of the possible uses is to load the data from disk-based tables into in-memory (i.e., MEMORY) tables for faster access.

init-file can also be used to verify the integrity of certain data, perform a cleanup, ensure that the important tables exist, or do something else of that nature. For example, you could put SET GLOBAL var=value or LOAD INDEX INTO CACHE into it.

To learn more about this option, study read_init_file( ) and bootstrap( ) in *sql/mysqld.cc*, as well as handle_bootstrap( ) in *sql/sql_parse.cc*.

key_buffer_size

MyISAM storage engine caches table keys. This option controls the size of the MyISAM key cache. Note that there is no option to set the data cache in MyISAM. Unlike InnoDB, MyISAM hopes that the operating system will do a good job caching, which does happen very often on Linux.

To learn more about how the MyISAM key cache works, take a look at *mysys/mf_keycache.c*.

language

This option specifies the path to the directory containing the error message file *errmsg.sys*. Different directories contain files in different languages, thus the name of the option.

I find this option interesting for a couple of reasons. Unlike many applications of MySQL's degree of complexity—which often do not run without a suite of configuration files, shared libraries, and other paraphernalia—the *mysqld* binary is not nearly as capricious when you copy it to another system and try to run it. However, there is one external file it will absolutely not run without: *errmsg.sys*. When you are trying to run some quick and dirty test on a system with a particular binary without having to install all of the MySQL files, you can copy *mysqld* and *errmsg.sys* to some directory, e.g., */tmp/mysql* and execute something like this to start the server:

```
/tmp/mysql/mysqld --skip-grant --skip-net \
--datadir=/tmp/mysql --socket=/tmp/mysql/mysql.sock \
--language=/tmp/mysql &
```

Thus, language has the honor of being one of the options needed to start a lean, inconspicuous "parachuted into the enemy camp" MySQL server.

Another distinction of this option and its associated MySQL functionality is that it serves as a creative language-learning tool. By starting MySQL with different language options, you can read error messages in different languages, which helps you build some basic technical vocabulary or at least acquire a collection of silly phrases to entertain unsuspecting natives. Back in the days of 3.23 when MySQL had only 190 error messages, I jokingly proposed to my colleagues a book title, *Learn Swedish in 190 Days Through MySQL Error Messages*. As of this writing, the number is up to

301. As MySQL continues to increase in functionality, the proposed book is becoming less and less marketable due to the increase in the number of error messages, and therefore, the days one would need to learn Swedish.

The server error-message numbers are defined in *include/mysqld_error.h*. The numbering starts from 1,000. For each code, there is a corresponding message in the sequential order of numeric codes in *sql/share/language_name/errmsg.txt*. The build process creates *errmsg.sys* from *errmsg.txt* using a utility called *comp_err*, which is a part of the source tree. The source of *comp_err* is in *extra/comp_err.c*.

In version 5.0 the error message maintenance was simplified, and all of the error-message data is now contained in one file, *errmsg.txt*.

To learn more about how MySQL deals with error messages, take a look at init_errmessage( ) from *sql/derror.cc*, and at the ER( ) macro from *sql/unireg.h*.

log

This option enables the general activity log, which records every command. Sometimes MySQL developers call it the *query log*. It is very helpful for debugging clients, but on the other hand, the log grows very fast on active servers, and therefore the option should be used with care.

To learn more about it, take a look at the MYSQL_LOG class in *sql/sql_class.h* and *sql/log.cc*. The actual logging for this type of log happens in the function:

```
MYSQL_LOG::write(THD *,enum enum_server_command ,const char*,...)
```

Note that the logging code was refactored in version 5.1. For versions 5.1 and later, additional log classes were added and moved to *sql/log.h*. The method that writes to the general log has also changed its signature to:

```
bool MYSQL_LOG::write(time_t event_time, const char *user_host, uint user_host_len,
int thread_id, const char *command_type, uint command_type_len,  const char *sql_
text, uint sql_text_len)
```

log-bin

This option enables the update log in binary format (thus *-bin* in the name). It is primarily used for replication on a replication master, but it can also be used for incremental backup. The logging happens on the logical level; i.e., queries along with some meta information are being logged. This option was introduced in version 3.23 during the development of replication.

For a quick introduction to how the binary logging works, take a look at MYSQL_LOG::write(Log_event*). However, the details of the format of the log are discussed in Chapter 12.

log-isam

This option keeps track of the low-level MyISAM storage engine operations, such as opening and closing tables, writing or reading the records, index file status queries and updates, and other functions. The log can be viewed with the `myisamlog` command-line utility, whose source can be found in *myisam/myisamlog.c*.

The logging functions are implemented in *myisam/mi_log.c*. The log itself and the output of `myisamlog` are discussed in greater detail in Chapter 10.

This option has existed since the very early days of MySQL (in pre-3.23 it logged ISAM activity, as the MyISAM storage engine did not yet exist). It has been helpful in debugging MyISAM problems on numerous occasions, and is a great tool for learning about MyISAM.

log-slow-queries

This option enables the logging of queries that the optimizer believes are less than optimal. There are two criteria: execution time (controlled by the `long_query_time` option) and key use.

If you ask a MySQL expert to help you troubleshoot a performance problem, probably the first thing he will tell you to do is to enable `log-slow-queries` along with `log-queries-not-using-indexes` (`log-long-format` for versions older than 4.1), and examine it to account for every query that hits that log.

The logging is implemented using the standard MySQL log class in *sql/log.cc*. However, for a budding MySQL hacker perhaps the most interesting part of the source associated with this option is the following segment out of *sql/sql_parse.cc*:

```
if ((ulong) (thd->start_time - thd->time_after_lock) >
      thd->variables.long_query_time ||
      ((thd->server_status &
        (SERVER_QUERY_NO_INDEX_USED | SERVER_QUERY_NO_GOOD_INDEX_USED)) &&
        (specialflag & SPECIAL_LOG_QUERIES_NOT_USING_INDEXES)))
  {
    long_query_count++;
    mysql_slow_log.write(thd, thd->query, thd->query_length, start_of_query);
  }
```

As you can see, this code fragment controls the decision on which queries get logged. If your system runs a lot of queries that are raising false alarms (or perhaps you have your own definition of slow), you might find it beneficial to play with this area of code. One simple test you could add is to check whether `thd->examined_row_count` is above a certain threshold.

max_allowed_packet

MySQL network communication code was written under the assumption that queries are always reasonably short, and therefore can be sent to and processed by the server in one chunk, which is called a *packet* in MySQL terminology. The server allocates the memory for a temporary buffer to store the packet, and it requests enough to fit it entirely. This architecture requires a precaution to avoid having the server run out of memory—a cap on the size of the packet, which this option accomplishes.

The code of interest in relation to this option is found in *sql/net_serv.cc*. Take a look at my_net_read( ), then follow the call to my_real_read( ) and pay particular attention to net_realloc( ).

This variable also limits the length of a result of many string functions. See *sql/field.cc* and *sql/item_strfunc.cc* for details.

max_connections

Each new client connection consumes a certain amount of system resources. Many operating systems do not fare well when the resources are limited. This applies particularly to memory. This option puts a cap on the number of maximum connections the server is willing to take. The idea is to have the MySQL server throttle itself down before it hijacks the system in case of some unexpected load spike.

The code relating to this option is fairly simple and is located at the start of create_new_thread( ) in *sql/mysqld.cc*.

max_heap_table_size

A *heap table* is MySQL jargon for an in-memory table. The name comes from the fact that it is allocated from the program's heap. In-memory tables are very fast. However, they require a precaution—they can be quite easily populated to the point of having the system run out of memory. This option puts a cap on how big each in-memory table can get.

Note that this option will not keep a malicious user from performing a denial-of-service attack; she can create a large number of in-memory tables of the allowed size, overrunning the memory that way.

To study the implementation of the option, first examine ha_heap::create( ) in *sql/ha_heap.cc* and follow it to heap_create( ) in *heap/hp_create.c*. Then start in ha_heap::write_row( ) in *sql/ha_heap.cc* and follow it to heap_write( ) in *heap/hp_write.c*. Follow it to next_free_record_pos( ) in the same file. The following block does the magic:

```
if (info->records > info->max_records && info->max_records)
    {
      my_errno=HA_ERR_RECORD_FILE_FULL;
      DBUG_RETURN(NULL);
    }
```

max_join_size

This is another option designed primarily to keep buggy applications and inexperienced users from taking the server down. It tells the optimizer to abort the queries that it believes would require it to examine more than the given number of record combinations.

On the code level, the magic happens in the following block inside JOIN::optimize( ) in *sql/sql_select.cc*:

```
if (!(thd->options & OPTION_BIG_SELECTS) &&
    best_read > (double) thd->variables.max_join_size &&
    !(select_options & SELECT_DESCRIBE))
  {                                        /* purecov: inspected */
    my_message(ER_TOO_BIG_SELECT, ER(ER_TOO_BIG_SELECT), MYF(0));
    error= 1;                              /* purecov: inspected */
    DBUG_RETURN(1);
  }
```

max_sort_length

The MySQL record-sorting algorithm (knows as *filesort*) uses fixed-size key values for sorting. This requires memory allocations in proportion to the maximum possible size of a given key. If sorting were to be done using the full length of a blob or text column, it could require enormous amounts of memory allocation, since those columns could potentially be as big as 4 GB (for a LONGBLOB). To solve the problem, MySQL puts a limit on the length of the key prefix it will use for sorting. The trade off is that the sort results are correct only to the prefix values.

This variable imposes a limit on the length of the sort key prefix. Originally, this cut-off point for the BLOB sort key was 1,024. However, arbitrary magic numbers are bad, so it was made to be a parameter, which is controlled by this option.

On the code level, the turning point is in the following lines inside sortlength( ) in *sql/filesort.cc*:

```
if (sortorder->field->type( ) == FIELD_TYPE_BLOB)
    sortorder->length= thd->variables.max_sort_length;
```

myisam-recover

This option enables the automatic repair of corrupted MyISAM tables as soon as the MyISAM storage engine discovers the corruption. Normally corruptions should never happen. However, power can fail, the operating system may crash or have a bug in the I/O code, and MySQL itself may crash or have a bug in the MyISAM storage engine. While the MyISAM tables lack the robustness of InnoDB for recovery from such crashes, most of the time even the most severe problems can be overcome with a table repair, often losing no more than just one record.

With this option disabled, the repair would have to be done using the REPAIR TABLE command (online), or the *myisamchk* utility (offline). The advantage of enabling it is fairly obvious. Suppose that, in the middle of the night, a small table somehow gets corrupted. It is very nice not to get awakened by your pager telling you that your web application is down when all you have to do to fix it is a manual repair. The disadvantage is that this option could potentially trigger a large CPU- and I/O-intensive repair without your knowledge, making things a lot worse for the end user during that time.

The code related to this option, although conceptually very simple, is perhaps a bit difficult to follow. The storage engine class (a subclass of handler) can optionally define the bool auto_repair( ) method. The default implementation returns false; however, bool ha_myisam::auto_repair( ) returns true if myisam_recover_opt is not 0. openfrm( ) in *sql/table.cc* attempts to open the table. On failure, it checks whether the storage engine reported that the table is corrupted, and then, if auto_repair( ) returns true, sets the crashed flag in its TABLE* argument, which is the table descriptor. When openfrm( ) returns to its caller open_unireg_entry( ) in *sql/sql_base.cc*, the crashed flag is checked, and a repair is attempted if it is set.

A good practical exercise for a budding MySQL hacker is to change bool ha_myisam:: auto_repair( ) in *sql/ha_myisam.h* so that it reports the auto repair capabilities only for the tables that are named with a separate configuration option.

query_cache_type

MySQL has a fairly unique feature: it can cache results of queries. One may ask why in the world an application would run the same query over and over on the data that has not changed. However, MySQL users reported on average about a 60 percent improvement in performance in their applications after this feature appeared for the first time in version 4.0.

This option sets the caching strategy. The possible values are 0 for no cache, 1 to cache all queries except the ones with the SQL_NO_CACHE flag, and 2 to cache only the ones with the SQL_CACHE flag.

This is one of the many options that control the behavior of the query cache. To learn about how the query cache works, study *sql/sql_cache.cc*.

read_buffer_size

Although the MyISAM storage engine does not cache data rows in general, a read-ahead buffer is used when performing sequential scans. This option controls its size.

On the code level, two sections are worth studying in connection with this option. The first one is from init_read_record( ) in *sql/records.cc*:

```
info->read_record=rr_sequential;
    table->file->ha_rnd_init(1);
    /* We can use record cache if we don't update dynamic length tables */
    if (!table->no_cache &&
       (use_record_cache > 0 ||
        (int) table->reginfo.lock_type <= (int) TL_READ_HIGH_PRIORITY ||
        !(table->db_options_in_use & HA_OPTION_PACK_RECORD) ||
        (use_record_cache < 0 &&
         !(table->file->table_flags() & HA_NOT_DELETE_WITH_CACHE))))
      VOID(table->file->extra_opt(HA_EXTRA_CACHE,
                                  thd->variables.read_buff_size));
```

As we follow the call to handler::extra_opt() in the case of MyISAM table, we eventually end up in mi_extra() from *myisam/mi_extra.c*. The buffer allocation happens in the following section:

```
cache_size= (extra_arg ? *(ulong*) extra_arg :
                    my_default_record_cache_size);
      if (!(init_io_cache(&info->rec_cache,info->dfile,
                          (uint) min(info->state->data_file_length+1,
                                     cache_size),
                          READ_CACHE,0L,(pbool) (info->lock_type != F_UNLCK),
                          MYF(share->write_flag & MY_WAIT_IF_FULL))))
      {
        info->opt_flag|=READ_CACHE_USED;
        info->update&= ~HA_STATE_ROW_CHANGED;
      }
```

relay-log

This option rarely needs to be set because the default value is usually acceptable. However, it was included because its presence and name illuminated the internal workings of the MySQL replication.

MySQL replication uses a master/slave paradigm. The master logs its updates. The slave stays connected to the master and continuously reads the contents of the master update log, known in MySQL jargon as the *binary log*. The slave then applies the updates it reads from the master to its copy of the data, and thus is able to stay in sync.

In the 3.23 version, there was only one slave thread that applied the updates immediately. This worked fine when the slave was able to keep up with the master. However, there were situations when the slave fell behind a lot. Were the master to experience a fatal unrecoverable crash, the slave would never get the data it had not yet replicated. To address this problem, the slave algorithm was reworked in version 4.0. The slave now has two threads: one for network I/O, and the other for applying the SQL updates. The I/O thread reads the updates from the master and appends them to the so-called relay log. The SQL thread in turn reads the contents of the relay log, and applies them to the slave data.

Learning more about this option really means understanding how the replication is implemented on the slave. To get started, take a look at handle_slave_sql( ) and handle_slave_io( ) in *sql/slave.cc*. Note that both are declared with the pthread_ handler_decl( ) macro, and might be easy to miss on a casual examination. The replication is discussed in greater detail in Chapter 12.

server-id

This option assigns a numeric ID to the server to be identified among its replication peers on the network. The need for it arose from the following situation. Suppose server A is a slave of server B, which in turn is a slave of server C, which is a slave of server A. An update happens on server A. B picks it up from the binary log of A, applies it and logs it to its own binary log. C picks it up from the binary log of B, applies it, and again logs it to its own binary log. Then A sees it in the binary log of C. It should not apply it. There has to be some way to tell A that the update it sees in the binary log of C originated from A, and therefore should be ignored.

The solution was to assign each server participating in replication a unique 32-bit ID, similar in concept to an IP address. Each binary log event is tagged with the ID of the server that originated it. When a slave applies a binary log event received from another server, it logs it with whatever server ID was in the log event record rather than its own. If it sees that the event has its own ID, it does not apply it (unless replicate-same-server-id option is enabled). This breaks potentially infinite update loops in a circular replication topology.

To learn more about this option, search for server_id in *sql/log_event.h*, *sql/log_ event.cc*, and *sql/slave.cc*.

skip-grant-tables

This option tells the server to start without loading the access privilege tables. This means two things. First, they do not need to exist. Second, since they are not used, the server will positively authenticate any set of credentials from any host that can establish a connection to the server.

This option is particularly useful when you have lost the MySQL root user password. You can start the server with skip-grant-tables, connect to it, use SQL statements to manually edit the privilege tables, and then either issue FLUSH PRIVILEGES or just restart the server.

For security reasons, it is recommended that you also use skip-networking in conjunction with skip-grant-tables. Otherwise, anybody on the network who can get to your MySQL port will have unlimited access to your server. If you take this security precaution, FLUSH PRIVILEGES is not enough to put the server into its normal mode, and a restart with regular options is required to enable network connections.

This option is also useful when you want to deploy a minimum installation of the server. By eliminating the need for privilege tables, you are able to run an instance of MySQL server with only two files: *mysqld* and *errmsg.sys*.

The handling of this option in the source code is fairly simple, as you would expect. If it is set, on initialization `acl_init()` from *sql/sql_acl.cc* is called with the second argument set to 1, which makes it skip reading the privilege tables. Additionally, `grant_init()` from *sql/sql_acl.cc* is not called at all, which leaves the `initialized` flag (a static variable in *sql/sql_acl.cc*) set to 0. `acl_getroot()`, which is the entry point for user authentication lookup, short-circuits and returns 0 (success), setting all the bits in the access mask `thd->master_access`. This enables the client to have unrestricted access to the server functionality.

skip-stack-trace

No matter how hard you try to avoid them, crashes happen. Having proper debugging information is critical to making sure the same type of crash does not happen again. MySQL users have had a difficult time collecting such information. An effort has been made to help them create meaningful bug reports.

On an x86 or Alpha Linux, the MySQL server binary is capable of unwinding its own stack and printing the stack trace when it receives a fatal signal such as SIGSEGV. In addition, the postmortem diagnostic message includes the query that was executing as well as the settings of the variables that are most likely to cause a crash. Although reliable in most cases, the reported values should always be taken with at least a small grain of salt. If the server crashed already, the memory could very well be seriously corrupted, making the reported data absolutely bogus.

This report has been helpful on many occasions in catching a wide range of bugs, including the ones that only happened in some production environments and could not be duplicated otherwise.

By default, the stack tracing takes place when a fatal signal is received; however, sometimes it is not desirable (e.g., if you are trying to debug the crash in a debugger). This option turns off this post-crash self-diagnostic.

The stack tracing code can be found in *sql/stacktrace.c*. The entry point is `print_stacktrace()`.

slave-skip-errors

The slave replication algorithm was originally designed to stop replicating if an error was encountered when the replicated query failed on the slave. Indeed, if it succeeded on the master, and the slave has the same data as the master did when it succeeded, there is no reason for it to fail. If it does, you would ideally want to stop replicating and have the DBA check things out manually to verify the integrity of the data.

This approach, however, proved undesirable in many situations. In practice, most applications that use MySQL have a high degree of record isolation. In other words, although a table may contain millions of records, if one record is incorrect or gone altogether, the problem can be fixed manually or even simply ignored. In those situations, it is more important for the replication to progress in a timely manner than for the data on the slave to always be a perfect replica of the master. And if this is a priority, errors such as a duplicate key error can be simply ignored as the replication continues.

This option tells the slave server which error codes it should ignore. The error codes to ignore can be specified in a comma-delimited list, or one could just use the keyword all to ignore all errors.

To see how this option works, take a look at Query_log_event::exec_event( ) and ignored_error_code( ) in *sql/log_event.cc*.

When records need to be sorted, MySQL uses an algorithm that is known as *filesort* in MySQL jargon. The record set is broken into chunks, and each chunk is sorted with a radix sort. If there is more than one chunk, each sorted chunk is written out to a temporary file while being merged with the already sorted collection. This way, we can get the best of both worlds: the speed of a radix sort and the ability to sort large collections of records.

sort_buffer_size

This option indirectly controls the size of the chunk sorted in memory with the radix sort by specifying how much memory the radix sort is allowed to use.

To learn more about the filesort algorithm and its implementation, take a look at *sql/filesort.cc*.

sql-mode

Despite ANSI SQL being a standard, when run with defaults most databases (including MySQL) end up speaking it with a bit of an accent, and what is worse, not being tolerant of the accents spoken by other databases. This may present a problem when porting applications.

This option is an *accent adjuster*. By setting it to different values, you can tell MySQL that a REAL is an alias for FLOAT instead of DOUBLE; a space is allowed between the database and table names; || means string concatenation rather logical OR; and other tweaks needed to port an application from some other database to MySQL without changes in its code.

There are a lot of places in the code that are affected by the use of this option. Some things to do to become familiar with how it works:

- Examine the `sql_mode_names` variable definition in *sql/mysqld.cc*.
- Look at `fix_sql_mode( )` in *sql/set_var.cc*.
- Search for `sql_mode` in *sql/sql_yacc.yy*, *sql/sql_show.cc*, *sql/sql_parse.cc*, and *sql/sql_lex.cc*.

table_cache

`table_cache` is one of the core parts of the MySQL code. It caches table descriptors, which greatly increases the speed of the queries. Each time a table is referenced in query, the table cache may already have the needed descriptor, and the expensive operation of initializing one does not need to be done.

This option controls how many table descriptors (not tables!) can be cached at the same time. You can view the contents of the table cache with the SHOW OPEN TABLES command.

To learn more about the table cache, take a look at `open_table( )` in *sql/sql_base.cc* and follow its execution.

temp-pool

This option exists specifically to work around a design flaw in the Linux kernel (at least in version 2.4). When a process repeatedly creates and removes files with unique names, the kernel ends up allocating large amounts of memory that it never releases. MySQL may on occasion need to create a temporary file to resolve a query. On a large site with a lot of traffic and a wide diversity of queries, this may take place frequently enough to cause serious problems. For most users, it did not until MySQL was put to use on one very loaded site with a number of frequently executing, sophisticated queries. MySQL developers responded with a workaround by adding an option to limit the possibilities for the name of the temporary table to a smaller set of names.

To see how this option works, take a look at the beginning of `create_tmp_table( )` in *sql/select.cc*.

transaction-isolation

This option was primarily the result of the introduction of InnoDB into the MySQL code base. When two or more different transactions occur in parallel, there are several different models or sets of rules for what a read operation should return when some data was written by another transaction but not yet committed. This set of rules is known by the term of *transaction isolation level*.

Many transactional engines, including InnoDB, give the user an option to select a desired transaction isolation level for a given transaction. This option allows you to set a global transaction isolation level for the whole server.

To learn more about how this option works, study `row_sel_get_clust_rec_for_mysql( )` in *innobase/row/row0sel.c*.

## CHAPTER 6

Thread-Based Request Handling

When implementing a server, a programmer is faced with a dilemma as to whether to use threads or processes to handle requests. Both have advantages and disadvantages. From its very inception, MySQL has used threads. In this chapter we discuss the rationale, strengths and weaknesses, and implementation of thread-based request handling in the MySQL server.

Threads Versus Processes

Perhaps the most important difference between a process and a thread is that a child thread shares the heap (global program data) with the parent, while a child process does not. This has a number of implications when you are deciding which model to use.

Advantages of Using Threads

Threads have been implemented in programming libraries and operating systems industry-wide for the following reasons:

- Reduced memory utilization. The memory overhead of creating another thread is limited to the stack plus some bookkeeping memory needed by the thread manager.

- No advanced techniques required to access server-global data. If the data could possibly be modified by another concurrently running thread, all that needs to be done is to protect the relevant section with a mutual exclusion lock or *mutex* (described later in this chapter). In the absence of such a possibility, the global data is accessed as if there were no threads to worry about.

- Creating a thread takes much less time than creating a process because there is no need to copy the heap segment, which could be very large.

- The kernel spends less time in the scheduler on context switches between threads than between processes. This leaves more CPU time for the heavily loaded server to do its job.

Disadvantages of Using Threads

Despite the importance of threads in modern computing, they are known to have drawbacks:

- Programming mistakes are very expensive. If one thread crashes, it brings the whole server down. One rogue thread can corrupt the global data, causing other threads to malfunction.

- Programming mistakes are easy to make. A programmer must think constantly about the possibility of some other thread doing things to cause trouble, and how to avoid it. An extra-defensive programming approach is required.

- Threaded servers are notorious for synchronization bugs that are nearly impossible to duplicate in testing but happen at a very wrong time in production. The high probability of such bugs is a result of having a shared address space, which brings on a much higher degree of thread interaction.

- Mutex contention at some point can get out of hand. If too many threads try to acquire the same mutex at the same time, this may result in excessive context switching, with lots of CPU time spent in the kernel scheduler and very little left to do the job.

- 32-bit systems are limited to 4 GB address space per process. Since all threads share the same address space, the whole server is theoretically limited to 4 GB of RAM even when there is a lot more physical RAM available. In practice the address space starts getting very crowded at a much smaller limit, somewhere around 1.5 GB on x86 Linux.

- The crowded 32-bit address space presents another problem. Each thread needs some room for its stack. When a stack is allocated, even if the thread does not use the majority of the allocated space, the address space of the server has to be reserved for it. Each new stack reduces potential room for the heap. Thus, even though there might be plenty of physical memory, it may not possible to have large buffers, to have a lot of concurrent threads, and to give each thread plenty of room for its stack at the same time.

Advantages of Using Forked Processes

The drawbacks of threads correspond to the strengths of using multiple processes instead:

- Programming mistakes are not so fatal. Although a definite possibility, it is not as easy for a rogue forked-server process to disrupt the whole server.

- Programming mistakes are much less likely. Most of the time, the programmer only needs to think of one thread of execution, undisturbed by possible concurrent intruders.

- Much fewer phantom bugs. If a bug happens once, it is usually fairly easy to duplicate it. With its own address space for each forked process, there is not much interaction between them.

- On a 32-bit system, the issue of running out of address space is usually not as acute.

Disadvantages of Using Forked Processes

To wrap up our overview, I'll list the problems with multiple processes, which mirror the advantages of threads:

- Memory utilization is suboptimal. Possibly large memory segments are copied unnecessarily when a child is forked.

- Special techniques are required to share data between processes. This makes it cumbersome to access the data global to the server.

- Creating a process requires more overhead in the kernel than creating a thread. One big performance hit is the need to copy the data segment of the parent process. Linux, however, cheats in this area by implementing what is called *copy-on-write*. The actual copy of a parent process page does not take place until the child or the parent modifies that page. Until then, both use the same page.

- Context switches between processes are more time-consuming than between threads because the kernel needs to switch the pages, file descriptor tables, and other extra context info. Less time is left for the server to do the actual work.

In summary, a threaded server is ideal when a lot of data needs to be shared between the connection handlers, and when the programming skills are not lacking. When it came down to deciding which model was the right one for MySQL, the choice was clear. A database server needs to have lots of shared buffers, and other shared data.

As far as the programming skills were concerned, they were not lacking at all. Just as a good rider becomes one with the horse, Monty had become one with the computer. It pained him to see system resources wasted. He felt confident enough to be able to write virtually bug-free code, deal with the concurrency issues presented by threads, and even work with a small stack. What an exciting challenge! Needless to say, he chose threads.

Implementation of Request Handling

The server listens in the main thread for connections. For each connection, it allocates a thread to handle it. Depending on the server configuration settings and current status, the thread may be either created anew or dispatched from the thread cache. The client issues requests, and the server satisfies them until the client sends a session-terminating command (COM_QUIT) or until the session ends abnormally. Upon terminating the client session, depending on the server configuration settings and status, the thread may either terminate or enter the thread cache to wait for another request dispatch.

Structures, Variables, Classes, and API

Perhaps the most important class for threads is THD, which is a class for thread descriptors. Nearly every one of the server functions inside the parser and optimizer accepts a THD object as an argument, and it usually comes first in the parameter list. The THD class is discussed in detail in Chapter 3.

Whenever a thread is created, its descriptor is put into a global thread list I_List<THD> threads. (I_List<> is a class template for linked lists; see *sql/sql_list.h* and *sql/sql_list.cc*.) The list is mainly used for three purposes:

- To provide the data for the SHOW PROCESSLIST command
- To locate the target thread when executing the KILL command
- To signal all threads to terminate during shutdown

Another list of I_List<THD> plays an important role: thread_cache. It is actually used in a rather unexpected manner: as a means of passing a THD object instantiated by the main thread to the thread waiting in the thread cache that is being dispatched to handle the current request. For details, see create_new_thread( ), start_cached_thread( ), and end_thread( ) in *sql/mysqld.cc*.

All operations related to creating, terminating, or keeping track of threads are protected by a mutex LOCK_thread_count. Three POSIX threads condition variables are used in conjunction with threads. COND_thread_count helps with synchronization during shutdown to make sure all threads have finished their work and exited before the main thread terminates. COND_thread_cache is broadcast when the main thread decides to wake up a cached thread and dispatch it to handle the current client session. COND_flush_thread_cache is used by the cached threads to signal that they are about to exit during shutdown or when processing SIGHUP.

In addition, a number of global status variables are used in relation to threads. They are summarized in Table 6-1.

Table 6-1. Global variables related to threads

Variable definition	Description
int abort_loop	A flag to signal to all threads that it is time to clean up and exit. The server never forces a thread to exit preemptively because doing so without giving it a chance to clean up could cause serious data corruption. Rather, each thread is coded to pay attention to the environment and exit when asked.
int cached_thread_count	A status variable to keep track of the number of threads that have terminated and are waiting to be dispatched to handle new requests. Can be viewed in the output of SHOW STATUS under Threads_connected.
int kill_cached_threads	A flag indicating that all cached threads should exit. The cached threads are waiting on COND_thread_cache in end_thread( ). They exit if they see that this flag is set.

Table 6-1. Global variables related to threads (continued)

Variable definition	Description
int max_connections	A server configuration variable setting a limit on the maximum number of non-administrative client connections the server is willing to accept. Once this limit is reached, one additional administrative connection is allowed to give the DBA a chance to fix the crisis caused by reaching this limit.
	The purpose of this limit is to allow the server to put brakes on itself before it takes the system down by utilizing too many resources.
	The limit is controlled by the configuration variable max_connections, with the default value of 100.
int max_used_connections	A status variable keeping track of the maximum number of concurrent connections the server has experienced since it was started. Its value can be viewed in the output of SHOW STATUS under Max_used_connections.
int query_id	A variable used for generating unique query ID numbers. Each time a query is sent to the server, it is assigned the current value of this variable, following which the variable is incremented by 1.
int thread_cache_size	A server configuration variable specifying the maximum number of threads in the thread cache. If set to 0 (the default), the thread caching is disabled. Controlled by the configuration variable thread_cache_size.
int thread_count	A status variable to keep track of how many threads exist at the moment. Can be viewed in the output of SHOW STATUS under Threads_cached.
int thread_created	A status variable to keep track of how many threads were created since the start of the server. Can be viewed in the output of SHOW STATUS under Threads_created.
int thread_id	A variable used for generating unique thread ID numbers. Each time a thread is started, it is assigned the current value of this variable, following which the variable is incremented by 1. Can be viewed in the output of SHOW STATUS under Connections.
int thread_running	A status variable to keep track of the number of threads that are currently answering a query. Incremented by 1 at the start of dispatch_command( ) in *sql/sql_parse.cc*, and decremented by 1 toward the end of it. Can be viewed in the output of SHOW STATUS under Threads_running.

Execution Walk-Through

The standard select()/accept( ) request dispatching loop is found in handle_connections_sockets( ) in *sql/mysqld.cc*. After a fairly sophisticated combination of tests of what could possibly go wrong in accept( ) on a wide variety of platforms, we finally get to the following code segment:

```
if (!(thd= new THD))
{
  (void) shutdown(new_sock,2);
  VOID(closesocket(new_sock));
  continue;
}
```

This creates an instance of THD. After some additional THD object manipulation, the execution descends into create_new_thread( ) in the same file, *sql/mysqld.cc*. A few more checks and initializations, and we reach the conditional that determines how the request handling thread is obtained. There are two possibilities: use a cached thread or create a new one.

With the thread caching enabled, an old thread simply goes to sleep instead of exiting when it is done serving client requests. When a new client connects, instead of just creating a new thread, the server first checks to see whether it has any sleeping threads in the cache. If it does, it wakes one of them up, passing the THD instance as an argument.

Although caching threads could give a boost in performance on a heavily loaded system, the original motivation for the feature was to debug a timing problem on Linux on an Alpha system.

Alternatively, if the thread caching is disabled or there are no cached threads available, a new thread has to be created to handle the request.

The decision is made in the following test:

```
if (cached_thread_count > wake_thread)
{
  start_cached_thread(thd);
}
```

start_cached_thread( ) from *sql/mysqld.cc* wakes a thread that is currently not serving requests, if such a thread exists. The condition cached_thread_count > wake_thread guarantees the existence of a sleeping thread, so the function is never called if no cached threads are sleeping. This also covers the case when the thread cache has been disabled.

If the test for cached thread availability comes out negative, the code turns to the else part, where the job of spawning a new thread gets done in the following line:

```
if ((error=pthread_create(&thd->real_id,&connection_attrib,
                          handle_one_connection,
                          (void*) thd)))
```

The new thread starts off in handle_one_connection( ) from *sql/sql_parse.cc*.

handle_one_connection( ), after some checks and initializations, gets down to business:

```
while (!net->error && net->vio != 0 && !thd->killed)
{
  if (do_command(thd))
      break;
}
```

Commands are accepted and processed as long as no loop exit condition is encountered. Possible exit conditions are:

* A network error.
* The thread is killed with the KILL command by the database administrator, or by the server itself during the shutdown.

- The client sends a `COM_QUIT` request telling the server it is done with the session, in which case `do_command( )` from *sql/sql_parse.cc* returns a nonzero value.

- `do_command( )` returns a nonzero value for some other reason. Currently, the only other possibility is if the replication master decides to abort the feed of updates requested by a slave (or a client pretending to be a slave) through `COM_BINLOG_DUMP`.

Afterward, `handle_one_connection( )` enters the thread termination/cleanup stage. The key element of this code segment is the call to `end_thread( )` from *sql/mysqld.cc*.

`end_thread( )` starts with some additional cleanup but then hits the interesting part: the possibility of putting the currently executing thread into the thread cache. The decision is made by testing the following conditional:

```
if (put_in_cache && cached_thread_count < thread_cache_size &&
    ! abort_loop && !kill_cached_threads)
```

If `end_thread( )` decides to cache this thread, the following loop is executed:

```
while (!abort_loop && ! wake_thread && ! kill_cached_threads)
    (void) pthread_cond_wait(&COND_thread_cache, &LOCK_thread_count);
```

The loop waits until it is awakened by `start_cached_thread( )`, the `SIGHUP` signal handler, or the shutdown routine. The code can tell that the signal to arise came from `start_cached_thread( )` by the nonzero setting of `wake_thread`. In such an event, it picks up the `THD` object passed by `start_cached_thread( )` from the thread_cache list, and then returns (note the `DBUG_VOID_RETURN` macro) to `handle_one_connection( )` to start serving the new client.

If the thread does not get the chance of going into the thread cache, its fate is to terminate through `pthread_exit( )`.

Thread Programming Issues

MySQL faces many of the same complications as other programs that depend on threads.

Standard C Library Calls

When writing code that can be concurrently executed by several threads, functions from external libraries must be called with extra care. There is always a chance that the called code uses a global variable, writes to a shared file descriptor, or uses some other shared resource without ensuring mutual exclusion. If this is the case, we must protect the call by a mutex.

While exercising caution, MySQL must also avoid unnecessary protection, or it will experience a decrease in performance. For example, it is reasonable to expect `malloc( )` to be thread-safe. Other potentially non-thread-safe functions such as `gethostbyname( )` often have thread-safe counterparts. The MySQL build configuration scripts test whether these are available and use them whenever possible. If the appropriate thread-safe counterpart is not detected, the protective mutex is enabled as the last resort.

Overall, MySQL saves itself a lot of thread-safety worries by implementing many standard C library equivalents in the portability wrapper in *mysys* and in the string library under *strings*. Even when C library calls are made eventually, they happen through a wrapper in most cases. If a call on some system unexpectedly turns out to lack thread safety, the problem can be easily fixed by adding a protective mutex to the wrapper.

Mutually Exclusive Locks (Mutexes)

In a threaded server, several threads may access shared data. If they do so, each thread must make sure the access is mutually exclusive. This is accomplished through mutually exclusive locks, otherwise known as mutexes.

As the application's degree of complexity increases, you face a dilemma as to how many mutexes to use, and which ones should protect what data. On one end of the spectrum, you could have a separate mutex for each variable. This has the advantage of reducing the mutex contention to the minimum, but it has a few problems. What happens if you need to access a group of variables atomically? You have to acquire a mutex for each individual variable. If you do so, you must make sure to always acquire them in the same order to avoid deadlocks. The frequent calls to pthread_mutex_lock() and pthread_mutex_unlock() would cause a performance degradation, and the programmer would be very likely to make a mistake in the order of calls and cause a deadlock.

On the other end of the spectrum is having a single mutex for everything. This makes it very simple for the programmer—get the lock when accessing a global variable, and release it when done. Unfortunately, this approach has a very negative impact on performance. Many threads would be unnecessarily made to wait while one was accessing some variable that the others did not need to have protected.

The solution is in some balanced grouping of the global variables and in having a mutex for each group. This is what is done in MySQL to solve this problem.

Table 6-2 contains a list of global mutexes in MySQL, with descriptions of the respective groups of variables they protect.

Table 6-2. Global mutexes

Mutex name	Mutex description
LOCK_Acl	Initialized but not used currently in the code. May be removed in the future.
LOCK_active_mi	Protects the active_mi pointer, which points to the active replication slave descriptor. At this point, the protection is redundant because the active_mi value never gets changed concurrently. However, the protection will become necessary when multi-master support is added.
LOCK_bytes_received	Protects the bytes_received status variable, which keeps track of how many bytes the server has received from all of its clients since it was started. Unused in versions 5.0 and higher.

Table 6-2. Global mutexes (continued)

Mutex name	Mutex description
LOCK_bytes_sent	Protects the `bytes_received` status variable, which keeps track of how many bytes the server has received from all of its clients since it was started. Unused in versions 5.0 and higher.
LOCK_crypt	Protects the calls to the Unix C library call `crypt()`, which is not thread-safe.
LOCK_delayed_create	Protects the variables and structures involved in the creation of a thread to handle delayed inserts. Delayed inserts return to the client immediately even if the table is locked, in which case they are processed in the background by a delayed insert thread.
LOCK_delayed_insert	Protects `I_List<delayed_insert> delayed_threads`, a list of delayed insert threads.
LOCK_delayed_status	Protects the status variables that keep track of delayed insert operations.
LOCK_error_log	Protects writes to the error log.
LOCK_gethostbyname_r	Protects calls to `gethostbyname()` inside `my_gethostbyname_r()` in *mysys/my_gethostbyname.c* on systems that do not have a native C library call `gethostbyname_r()`.
LOCK_global_system_variables	Protects operations to modify global configuration variables from a client thread.
LOCK_localtime_r	Protects the call to `localtime()` inside `localtime_r()` in *mysys/my_pthread.c* on systems that do not have a native C library call `localtime_r()`.
LOCK_manager	Protects the data structures used by the manager thread, which currently is responsible for periodically flushing the tables (if `flush_time` setting is not 0), and the cleanup of Berkeley DB logs.
LOCK_mapped_file	Protects the data structures and variables used in operations with memory-mapped files. Currently there exists internal support for this functionality, but it does not appear to be used anywhere in the code.
LOCK_open	Protects the data structures and variables relevant to the table cache, and opening and closing tables.
LOCK_rpl_status	Protects the variable `rpl_status`, which was intended to be used in the failsafe automatic recovery replication. At this point, this is mostly dead code.
LOCK_status	Protects the variables displayed in the output of SHOW STATUS.
LOCK_thread_count	Protects the variables and data structures involved in the creation or destruction of threads.
LOCK_uuid_generator	Protects the variables and data structures used in the UUID() SQL function.
THR_LOCK_charset	Protects the variables and data structures relevant to character set operations.
THR_LOCK_heap	Protects the variables and data structures relevant to the in-memory (MEMORY) storage engine.
THR_LOCK_isam	Protects the variables and data structures relevant to the ISAM storage engine.
THR_LOCK_lock	Protects the variables and data structures relevant to the table lock manager.
THR_LOCK_malloc	Protects the variables and data structures relevant to the `malloc()` family call wrappers. Mostly used with the debugging mode version of `malloc()` (see *mysys/safemalloc.c*).
THR_LOCK_myisam	Protects the variables and data structures relevant to the MyISAM storage engine.

Table 6-2. Global mutexes (continued)

Mutex name	Mutex description
THR_LOCK_net	Currently used to protect the call to inet_ntoa( ) in my_inet_ntoa( ) from *mysys/my_net.c*.
THR_LOCK_open	Protects the variables and data structures that keep track of open files.

In addition to global mutexes, there are a number of class/structure encapsulated mutexes used to protect portions of that particular structure or class. There are also a couple of file scope global (static) mutexes in the *mysys* library.

Read-Write Locks

A mutually exclusive lock is not always the best solution to protect concurrency-sensitive operations. Imagine a situation when a certain variable is modified by only one thread and only infrequently, but it is read by many others often. If we were to use a mutex, most of the time one reader would end up waiting for the other to finish reading even though it could have just executed concurrently.

There is another type of lock that is more suitable for this situation: a *read-write lock*. Read locks can be shared, while write locks are exclusive. Thus, multiple readers can proceed concurrently as long as there is no writer.

Clearly, a read-write lock is able to do everything a mutex can, and more. Why not use the read-write locks all the time? As the saying goes, there is no free lunch, and it applies very well in this case. The extra functionality comes at the cost of greater implementation complexity. As a result, read-write locks require more CPU cycles even when the lock is obtained immediately.

Thus, in choosing the type of lock to use, one must consider the probability of first-try failure to acquire it, as well as how it will be reduced by changing from a mutex to a read-write lock. For example, if the typical use involves 1 failure for every 1,000 attempts, a read-write lock helps with concurrency once for every 999 times it wastes the CPU. Even if changing to a read-write lock reduces the probability of failure to a virtual zero, it is still not worth it.

However, if the probability of first-try failure is only 1 time out of 10, perhaps the 9 times of extra CPU cycles trying the read-write lock can be offset by the fact that on the 10th time we actually get the lock and do not have to wait as long as we would have if it were a mutex. On the other hand, if using the read-write lock in this particular case does not significantly reduce the probability of first-try failure, the CPU overhead might still not be worth it.

Most MySQL critical regions are fairly short, which leads to a low probability of the first-try failure. Thus, in most cases a mutex is preferred to a read-write lock. However, there are a few cases where a read-write lock is used. Table 6-3 summarizes the read-write locks in MySQL.

Table 6-3. Read-write locks used by MySQL

Read-write lock name	Read-write lock description
LOCK_grant	Protects variables and data structures dealing with the access control.
LOCK_sys_init_connect	Protects the system variable descriptor sys_init_connect against modifications while the commands it stores are being executed. The sys_init_connect system variable descriptor stores the commands to be executed every time a new client connects as specified by the init-connect configuration setting.
LOCK_sys_init_slave	Protects the system variable descriptor sys_init_slave against modifications while the commands it stores are being executed. The sys_init_slave system variable descriptor stores the commands to be executed on the master every time a slave connects to the master as specified by the init-slave configuration setting.

Synchronization

A threaded application is often faced with the problem of thread synchronization. One thread needs to know that the other has reached a certain state. POSIX threads provides a mechanism to accomplish this: *condition variables*. A thread waiting for a condition can call pthread_cond_wait( ), passing it the condition variable and the mutex used in the given context. The call must also be protected by the same mutex. A thread that believes it has reached the given condition may either signal it with pthread_cond_signal( ) or broadcast it with pthread_cond_broadcast( ). The signal or the broadcast must also be protected by the same mutex that the waiting thread uses with pthread_cond_wait( ). A signaled condition wakes up only one thread that is waiting for it, while a broadcast one wakes up all waiting threads.

MySQL uses several POSIX condition variables. They are summarized in Table 6-4.

Table 6-4. Condition variables used by MySQL

Condition variable name	Condition variable description
COND_flush_thread_cache	Signaled by end_thread( ) in *sql/mysqld.cc* during the purging of the thread cache to communicate to flush_thread_cache( ) (also in *sql/mysqld.cc*) that a thread has exited. This gives flush_thread_cache( ) a chance to wake up and check whether there are any more threads left to terminate. Used with the mutex LOCK_thread_count.
COND_manager	Signaled to force the manager thread (see *sql/sql_manager.cc*) to wake up and perform the scheduled set of maintenance tasks. Currently there are only two possible tasks: clean up Berkeley DB logs and flush the tables. Used with the mutex LOCK_manager.
COND_refresh	Signaled when the data in the table cache has been updated. Used with the mutex LOCK_open.
COND_thread_count	Signaled when a thread is created or destroyed. Used with the mutex LOCK_thread_count.
COND_thread_cache	Signaled to wake up a thread waiting in the thread cache. Used with the mutex LOCK_thread_count.

In addition to these condition variables, a number of structures and classes use local conditions for synchronization of operations on that class or structure. There also exist a couple of file scope global (static) condition variables inside the *mysys* library.

Preemption

The term *preemption* means interrupting a thread to give the CPU some other task. MySQL generally uses the "responsible citizen" approach to preemption. The preempting thread sets the appropriate flags, telling the thread being preempted that it needs to clean up and terminate or yield. At that point, it becomes the responsibility of the thread being preempted to notice the message and comply.

Most of the time this approach works very well, but there is one exception. If the thread being preempted is stuck performing a blocking I/O, it will not have a chance to check the preempting message flags. To address the problem, MySQL uses a technique known in MySQL developer terminology as the *thread alarm*.

A thread that is about to enter blocking I/O makes a request to receive an alarm signal after a timeout period with a call to thr_alarm( ). If the I/O completes before the timeout, the alarm is canceled with end_thr_alarm( ). The alarm signal on most systems interrupts the blocking I/O, thus allowing the thread that is potentially being preempted to check the flags and the error code from the I/O and to take the appropriate action. The action is usually to clean up and exit the I/O loop if preempted, or else retry the I/O.

Both thr_alarm( ) and end_thr_alarm( ) take an alarm descriptor argument that must be initialized with a call to init_thr_alarm( ) prior to its first use. The thread alarm routines are implemented in *mysys/thr_alarm.c*.

## CHAPTER 7

The Storage Engine Interface

MySQL provides a layer of abstraction that permits different storage engines to access their tables using the same API. In the past, this interface was called the *table handler*. More recently, the term *storage engine* was introduced. In the current terminology, *storage engine* refers to the code that actually stores and retrieves the data, while *table handler* refers to the interface between the storage engine and the MySQL optimizer.

The abstract interface greatly facilitates the task of adding another storage engine to MySQL. It was created during the transition from version 3.22 to version 3.23, and it was instrumental in the quick integration of the InnoDB storage engine, which brought in robust transactional capabilities, multi-versioning, and row-level locks. It can be used for integrating custom storage engines, which permits you to quickly develop an SQL interface to just about anything that knows how to read and write records.

The interface is implemented through an abstract class named handler, which provides methods for basic operations such as opening and closing a table, sequentially scanning through the records, retrieving records based on the value of a key, storing a record, and deleting a record. Each storage engine implements a subclass of handler, implementing the interface methods to translate the handler operations into the low-level storage/retrieval API calls of that particular storage engine. Starting in version 5.0, the handlerton structure was added to allow storage engines to provide their own hooks for performing operations that do not necessarily involve one-table instances such as initialization, transaction commit, savepoint, and rollback.

In this chapter we will examine the handler class and the handlerton structure, and then provide—as a modestly-sized example you can study—a simple storage engine for reading comma-delimited files.

The handler Class

The handler class is defined in *sql/handler.h* and implemented in *sql/handler.cc*. Note that it is a subclass of Sql_alloc (defined in *sql/sql_list.h*). Sql_alloc is a class with no members that merely overrides the new and delete operators so that new allocates memory from the memory pool associated with the connection, while delete does nothing. Indeed, it does not need to, as all the memory in the memory pool is freed at once with a call to free_root( ) from *mysys/my_alloc.c* during the cleanup stage after executing a statement.

An instance of handler is created for each table descriptor. Note that it is possible to have several table descriptors for the same table, and therefore just as many instances of handler in the same server. The new index_merge join method in version 5.0 added an interesting twist. In the past, the multiple handler instances for the same table resulted only from having several copies of the table descriptor in the table cache, and thus one handler instance per descriptor. Now, with the addition of index_merge, additional handler instances may be created during optimization.

The data members of handler are documented in Table 7-1. The methods of handler are documented in Table 7-2.

Table 7-1. handler data members

Member definition	Member description
struct st_table *table	Table descriptor associated with the given instance of handler.
byte *ref	Stores the value of the current record reference. The record reference is an internal, unique record identifier for the given table. For this field, MyISAM uses the offset of the record in the datafile. InnoDB uses the value of the primary key formatted in a special way. MEMORY uses a pointer to the start of the record. The length of the value is stored in the ref_length member.
byte *dupp_ref	Additional "register" to store the reference to a record that caused a unique key conflict when inserting a new record.
ulonglong data_file_length	Length of the datafile, for engines that use one. The ones that do not use a datafile "wing it" by storing in this variable the combined length of all of the records plus the holes where newly inserted records could be put. This value is used in the output of SHOW TABLE STATUS.
ulonglong max_data_file_length	Maximum possible length of the datafile referred to by the data_file_length member. Appears in the output of SHOW TABLE STATUS.
ulonglong index_file_length	Length of the index file, for engines that use one. The ones that do not use an index file put here the approximate amount of memory or disk space used for storing the indexes for this table. Appears in the output of SHOW TABLE STATUS.
ulonglong max_index_file_length	Maximum possible length of the index file. Currently, only MyISAM and ISAM handlers set this value.

Table 7-1. handler data members (continued)

Member definition	Member description
`ulonglong delete_length`	The number of allocated but unused bytes. In MyISAM, the amount of space occupied by records that have been marked as deleted. Appears in the output of SHOW TABLE STATUS.
`ulonglong auto_increment_value`	The value that will be assigned to the autoincrement column on the next insert that does not specify a value for that column if no `INSERT_ID` was set. This value can be set with an `AUTO_INCREMENT` clause during table creation or with `ALTER TABLE`.
`ha_rows records`	The number of records in the table. InnoDB provides just an estimate, due to the complications caused by multi-versioning. Appears in the output of SHOW TABLE STATUS.
`ha_rows deleted`	The number of records in the table that are marked as deleted.
`ulong raid_chunksize`	Associated with the RAID feature for MyISAM tables. Removed in 5.1.
`ulong mean_rec_length`	Average length of a record. Appears in the output of SHOW TABLE STATUS.
`time_t create_time`	Table creation time. Appears in the output of SHOW TABLE STATUS.
`time_t check_time`	Last time the table was checked with CHECK TABLE. Appears in the output of SHOW TABLE STATUS.
`time_t update_time`	Last time the table was updated. Appears in the output of SHOW TABLE STATUS.
`key_range save_end_range`	A storage variable used in the `handler::read_range_first()` member method.
`key_range *end_range`	A storage variable used in a number of member methods associated with reading records based on the value of a key range.
`KEY_PART_INFO *range_key_part`	A storage variable used in the `read_range_first()` member method.
`int key_compare_result_on_equal`	A storage variable used in the `read_range_first()` and `compare_key()` member methods. Contains the result `compare_key()` should return if the actual value of the key turns out to be equal to the one it is being compared against. Depending on the mode of traversing the key range, the optimizer may find it more convenient to think that an equal value is the same as a lesser or a greater value, and make such a request in `read_range_first()`. For example, when searching for a range key < *const*, `compare_key()` returns a "greater than" result even for key values that are equal to *const*. This simplifies the boundary checks on the upper level.
`bool eq_range`	A storage variable used in the `read_range_first()` and `read_range_next()` member methods. Set to true if the start and the end of the range have the same value.

Table 7-1. handler data members (continued)

Member definition	Member description
uint errkey	Contains the number of the last key on which an error occurred. Frequently the error is the attempt to create a duplicate key value of a unique key.
uint sortkey	The key number, if one exists, according to which the records have been physically ordered. If such a key does not exist, set to 255. Currently unused.
uint key_used_on_scan	The key number, if one exists, that was last used to scan the records. If no such key exists, set to MAX_KEY.
uint active_index	The number of the currently selected key. If none is selected, set to MAX_KEY.
uint ref_length	The length of the value stored in the ref member.
uint block_size	The size of the key block used for this table.
uint raid_type	Associated with the RAID feature for MyISAM tables. Removed in 5.1.
uint raid_chunks	Associated with the RAID feature for MyISAM tables. Removed in 5.1.
FT_INFO *ft_handler	Full-text key operations descriptor. Currently applicable only in MyISAM tables.
enum {NONE=0, INDEX, RND} inited	Indicates whether the handler object has been initialized to read a key (INDEX), to scan the table (RND), or not at all (NONE). A call to ha_init_index( ) sets this value to INDEX, while a call to ha_init_rnd( ) sets it to RND. The cleanup and resetting the value to NONE is performed by ha_end_index( ) and ha_end_rnd( ), respectively.
bool auto_increment_column_changed	Set by update_auto_increment( ) to indicate whether the last operation resulted in a change to the autoincrement column value.
bool implicit_emptied	Set in by the MEMORY handler to indicate that the in-memory table got emptied during server restart. This information is needed for proper replication logging.

The methods of handler are documented in Table 7-2.

Table 7-2. handler methods

Method definition	Method description
int ha_open (const char *name, int mode, int test_if_locked)	Opens the table specified by the name argument. This argument is the path to the *.frm* file containing the definition of the table, with the *.frm* extension stripped off. For example, if the table's *.frm* file is *./test/t1.frm*, the argument string is *./test/t1*. The remaining arguments are passed to open( ) and are interpreted by the specific storage engine. Returns 0 on success, or a nonzero error code on failure.
void update_auto_increment( )	Determines the autoincrement value to be inserted and stores it in the autoincrement field descriptor.

Table 7-2. handler methods (continued)

Method definition	Method description
`virtual void print_error` `(int error, myf errflag)`	Prints an error message to the error log. This method has a generic implementation that deals with the most common errors. If an unknown error code is encountered, the message is looked up via `get_error_message( )`. The `error` argument is the error code. The `errflag` argument is passed to `my_error( )` from `mysys/my_error.c` and is usually 0.
`virtual bool get_error_message` `(int error, String *buf)`	Locates the storage-engine-specific error message in case it is not known to `print_error( )`. The `error` argument is the error code. The `buf` argument is the address of the `String` buffer that stores the resulting message. Returns `true` if the error in the storage engine was temporary. Returns `false` otherwise.
`uint get_dup_key(int error)`	Returns the number of the key associated with the last duplicate key error. If the argument contains an error code not connected with a duplicate key error, returns `(uint)-1`.
`void change_table_ptr(TABLE *table_arg)`	Sets the `table` member to the value supplied by the argument.
`virtual double scan_time( )`	Returns an estimated number of block read operations needed to scan the entire table.
`virtual double read_time` `(uint index, uint ranges, ha_rows rows)`	Returns an estimated number of block read operations it would take to read `rows` number of rows from `ranges` number of ranges using the key number `index`.
`virtual const key_map *keys_to_use_for_` `scanning( )`	Normally, the MySQL optimizer scans the table without using keys, as the full scan of a plain datafile is faster than traversing a B-tree index. However, some storage engines may organize their data in such a way that it is beneficial to traverse a key in the case of a full table scan. This method returns a key map with bits set for the keys that can be used for scanning the table.
`virtual bool has_transactions( )`	Returns `true` if the storage engine supports transactions. The default implementation returns `false`. Not virtual since 5.1.
`virtual uint extra_rec_buf_length( )`	`openfrm( )` from *sql/table.cc* allocates a temporary record buffer to store the current record in the table descriptor. The size of the buffer is the logical length of the record, plus possibly some extra reserved length for the purposes specific to the storage engine. This method returns the value of this extra length.
`virtual ha_rows estimate_rows_upper_bound( )`	Returns the maximum number of records that could be examined when scanning the table.
`virtual const char *index_type` `(uint key_number)`	Returns a pointer to a textual description of the index specified by the argument.
`int ha_index_init(uint idx)`	Initializes the storage engine to perform operations on the key specified by the argument. Returns 0 on success, and a nonzero value on failure.

Table 7-2. handler methods (continued)

Method definition	Method description
int ha_index_end( )	Performs cleanup after the key operations in the storage engine. Must be called after ha_index_init( ). Returns 0 on success, and a nonzero value on failure.
int ha_rnd_init(bool scan)	Initializes the storage engine for position-based record reads. The argument specifies whether a full table scan is going to be performed. Returns 0 on success, and a nonzero value on failure.
int ha_rnd_end( )	Cleans up after position-based reads. Must be called after ha_rnd_init( ). Returns 0 on success, and a nonzero value on failure.
int ha_index_or_rnd_end( )	Calls either ha_index_end( ) or ha_rnd_end( ) depending on which initialization took place previously. Returns 0 on success, and a nonzero value on failure.
uint get_index(void) const	Returns the number of the currently selected index.
virtual int open(const char *name, int mode, uint test_if_locked)=0	Does the real work to open the table (as opposed to ha_open( ), which is just a wrapper). The name argument is the path to the *.frm* file, with the extension stripped off. The remaining arguments contain flags that specify what to initialize and what to do if the table files are locked. The flags are mostly meaningful to the MyISAM storage engine. Returns 0 on success, or a nonzero error code on failure. Note that this method is pure virtual and must be implemented in a subclass.
virtual int close(void)=0	Closes the table, performing the necessary cleanup. Must be called after open( ). Returns 0 on success, or a nonzero error code on failure. Note that this method is pure virtual, and must be implemented in a subclass.
virtual int write_row(byte * buf)	Inserts into the table the record pointed to by the argument. This call is the bottom of the execution stack shared by all storage engines when handling an INSERT query. Note that the method has a default implementation returning HA_ERR_WRONG_COMMAND. Thus, failure to implement it results in all INSERT queries returning an error.
virtual int update_row(const byte * old_data, byte * new_data)	Updates the record pointed to by old_data to have the contents pointed to by new_data. This call is the bottom of the execution stack shared by all storage engines when handling an UPDATE query. Note that the method has a default implementation that returns HA_ERR_WRONG_COMMAND. Thus, failure to implement it results in all UPDATE queries returning an error.
virtual int delete_row(const byte * buf)	Deletes from the table the record pointed to by the argument. This call is the bottom of the execution stack shared by all storage engines when handling a DELETE query. The method has a default implementation that returns HA_ERR_WRONG_COMMAND.

Table 7-2. handler methods (continued)

Method definition	Method description
`virtual int index_read(byte * buf, const byte * key,uint key_len, enum ha_rkey_ function find_flag)`	Positions the key cursor according to the values of `key` and `key_len` on the first key, and reads the record into `buf` if a match exists. The matching is performed according to the lookup method specified by `find_flag`. The operation is performed with the currently active index. `enum ha_rkey_ function` is defined in *include/my_base.h*. Returns 0 on success, or a nonzero error code on failure. The method has a default implementation that returns `HA_ERR_WRONG_ COMMAND`.
`virtual int index_read_idx(byte * buf, uint index, const byte * key,uint key_len, enum ha_rkey_function find_flag)`	Same as `index_read( )` except that the key specified by the index argument is made active first.
`virtual int index_next(byte * buf)`	Reads the next record from the active index into the buffer specified by the argument, and advances the active key cursor. Returns 0 on success, and a nonzero error code on failure. The method has a default implementation that returns `HA_ ERR_WRONG_COMMAND`.
`virtual int index_prev(byte * buf)`	Reads the previous record from the active index into the buffer specified by the argument, and moves back the active key cursor. Returns 0 on success, and a nonzero error code on failure. The method has a default implementation that returns `HA_ERR_WRONG_COMMAND`.
`virtual int index_first(byte * buf)`	Reads the first record from the active index into the buffer specified by the argument, and positions the active key cursor immediately after it. Returns 0 on success, and a nonzero error code on failure. The method has a default implementation that returns `HA_ERR_WRONG_COMMAND`.
`virtual int index_last(byte * buf)`	Reads the last record from the active index into the buffer specified by the argument, and positions the active key cursor immediately before it. Returns 0 on success, and a nonzero error code on failure. The method has a default implementation that returns `HA_ERR_WRONG_COMMAND`.
`virtual int index_next_same (byte *buf, const byte *key, uint keylen)`	Starting from the currently active record, reads the next record that has the same key value as the previously read record into the buffer pointed to by `buf`. Because some storage engines do not store the value of the last read key, the `key` and `keylen` arguments are used to remind them. On success, the active key cursor is advanced, and 0 is returned. On failure, a nonzero error code is returned. The method has a default implementation that returns `HA_ERR_WRONG_ COMMAND`.
`virtual int index_read_last (byte * buf, const byte * key, uint key_len)`	Reads into `buf` the record found through the last key value matching the values of `key` and `key_len`, and positions the cursor immediately before that record. On success, returns 0. On failure, a nonzero error code is returned. The method has a default implementation that returns `HA_ERR_WRONG_ COMMAND`.

Table 7-2. handler methods (continued)

Method definition	Method description

`virtual int read_range_first`
`(const key_range *start_key,`
`const key_range *end_key,`
`bool eq_range, bool sorted)`
	Reads the first record from the range specified by the `start_key` and `end_key` arguments into the `table->record[0]` buffer. The range boundaries are saved to be used by `read_range_next( )`. The `eq_range` argument indicates whether the start and the end of the range have the same value. This information can certainly be obtained by examining `start_key` and `end_key`, but the caller has often done it already, and some CPU cycles can be saved if this information is passed down. The `sorted` argument tells whether the caller expects to receive the records in the key order. The `key_range` type is defined in *include/my_base.h*. The method returns 0 on success, and a nonzero error code on failure. The method has a default implementation that calls `index_first( )` to read the first value if `start_key` is 0, or `index_read( )` otherwise to read the first matching key value for the start of the range. `compare_key( )` is used to test whether the read key is still in the range. Currently, only the NDB cluster engine (see *sql/ha_ndbcluster.cc*) reimplements this method.

`virtual int read_range_next( )`	Reads the next record from the current range into the `table->record[0]` buffer. Returns 0 on success, and a non-zero error code on failure. In the method's default implementation, if `eq_range` (remembered from the `read_range_first( )` call) is set to `true`, `index_next_same( )` is called to position the index cursor on the next key value that is equal to the previous one. Otherwise, `index_next( )` is called to move to the next key value, followed by a call to `compare_key( )` to check whether that value is within the range. Currently, only the NDB cluster engine (see *sql/ha_ndbcluster.cc*) reimplements this method.
`int compare_key(key_range *range)`	Compares the key of the current record (in `table->record[0]`) with the value of the key range limit specified by the argument. Returns 0 if the values are the same or the value of `range` is 0; returns -1 if the current record key is less than the range limit; and returns 1 if the current record key is greater than the range limit.
`virtual int ft_init( )`	Re-initializes the storage engine for full-text key operations. Can be called when MySQL needs to repeat full-text search many times; e.g., in a join. Currently meaningful only in MyISAM. Returns 0 on success, and a nonzero error code otherwise. The default implementation returns `HA_ERR_WRONG_COMMAND`.

Table 7-2. handler methods (continued)

Method definition	Method description

`virtual FT_INFO *ft_init_ext`
`(uint flags,uint inx, const byte *key,`
`uint keylen)`
	Initializes the full-text engine for a search. Currently meaningful only in MyISAM. The `flags` argument specifies the search mode, the `inx` argument is the number of the index, and the `key` and `keylen` arguments supply the key to search. Starting in 5.0, the last two arguments have been replaced with `String*`. Returns a pointer to a full-text search descriptor on success, and `NULL` on error. The default implementation simply returns `NULL`.

`virtual int ft_read(byte *buf)`	Reads the next record on the currently active full-text key into the buffer pointed to by the argument. Currently meaningful only in MyISAM. Returns 0 on success, and a nonzero error code on error. The default implementation returns `HA_ERR_WRONG_COMMAND`.
`virtual int rnd_next(byte *buf)=0`	Reads the next record during a sequential table scan into the buffer pointed to by `buf`, advancing the sequential scan cursor. Returns 0 on success, and a nonzero error code on error. Note that the method is pure virtual and must be implemented in the subclass.
`virtual int rnd_pos` `(byte * buf, byte *pos)=0`	Reads a record specified by `pos` into `buf`. The interpretation of `pos` is up to the storage engine. MyISAM uses the datafile offset of the record. InnoDB uses the primary key value. MEMORY uses the memory address of the record. Returns 0 on success, and a nonzero error code on failure. Note that the method is pure virtual and must be implemented in the subclass.
`virtual int read_first_row` `(byte *buf, uint primary_key)`	Retrieves one arbitrarily chosen record from the table and places it into the buffer pointed to by the `buf` argument. The `primary_key` argument affects the method by which the record is chosen. Currently, the default implementation uses two methods for choosing this record. The first one scans the table and returns the first record not marked as deleted, whereas the other method picks the first record in the key with the number of the `primary_key` argument. The first method is used if there are fewer than 10 records marked as deleted, or if the `primary_key` argument is greater than or equal to `MAX_KEY`. Otherwise the second method is chosen. No storage engine reimplements this method at this point. Returns 0 on success, and a nonzero error code on failure.
`virtual int restart_rnd_next` `(byte *buf, byte *pos)`	Currently meaningful only in MyISAM, where this method is an alias for `rnd_pos( )`. The default implementation returns `HA_ERR_WRONG_COMMAND`. At this time, the method is called only once, by the code that removes duplicates from the result set when processing `SELECT DISTINCT` on a temporary table. It is possible that this method will be renamed or eliminated in the future.

Table 7-2. handler methods (continued)

Method definition	Method description
`virtual int rnd_same(byte *buf, uint inx)`	Rereads the current record into `buf`, possibly using the key number `idx` if its value is greater than or equal to 0. Returns 0 on success and a nonzero error code on error. Currently this method is never called, and no storage engine implements it. The default implementation returns `HA_ERR_WRONG_COMMAND`. However, the MEMORY and MyISAM engines have the hooks to provide the implementations of this method in *heap/hp_rsame.c* and *myisam/mi_rsame.c*.
`virtual ha_rows records_in_range(uint inx, key_range *min_key, key_range *max_key)`	Returns an estimated number of records matching the key values limited by `min_key` and `max_key` in the key number `inx`. The default implementation returns 10. The worst thing that can happen if a bogus value is returned is that the optimizer will prefer a less optimal key or choose not to use a key at all.
`virtual void position(const byte *record)=0`	Stores the unique reference value to the current record in the `ref` member. For MyISAM tables, this value is the position of the record in the datafile; thus the name of the method. Some storage engines may not remember the unique reference value of the last record, and may need to look at the actual record, which is supplied by the argument. Note that the method is pure virtual and must be implemented in the subclass.
`virtual void info(uint flag)=0`	Updates the values of various statistical variables of this object based on the value of the argument. Note that the method is pure virtual and must be implemented in the subclass.
`virtual int extra (enum ha_extra_function operation)`	Gives hints to the storage engines to use some special optimizations. For example, if the argument is `HA_EXTRA_KEYREAD`, read operations on a key may retrieve only those parts of the record that are included in the key. Returns 0 on success and a nonzero error code otherwise. The default implementation just returns 0, as hints are safe to ignore.
`virtual int extra_opt(enum ha_extra_function operation, ulong cache_size)`	Similar to `extra( )` except that it allows the caller to pass an argument to the requested operation (`cache_size`). Mainly used for controlling cache sizes for various types of I/O.
`virtual int reset( )`	Wrapper around `handler:extra(HA_EXTRA_RESET)`. Frees the resources allocated by earlier `extra( )` calls, and resets the operational modes of the storage engine to the defaults.
`virtual int external_lock (THD *thd, int lock_type)=0`	MySQL calls this method once at the beginning of every statement for every table used in the statement. MyISAM just locks the key file via the operating system if the external locking option is enabled, thus the historical name of the option. Transactional storage engines use it as a hook for starting a transaction and performing other initializations if necessary. Returns 0 on success, and a nonzero error code on error. Note that the method is pure virtual and must be implemented in a subclass.

Table 7-2. handler methods (continued)

Method definition	Method description
`virtual void unlock_row( )`	Called during UPDATE or DELETE for each row that did not match the WHERE clause to remove unnecessary row locks. Used by InnoDB to clear the locks on the rows read in the semiconsistent read mode (read last committed version if the current version is locked by another transaction).
`virtual int start_stmt(THD *thd)`	Called at the beginning of a transaction initiated via LOCK TABLES, giving a transactional storage engine a chance to register the start of a transaction. Returns 0 on success, and a nonzero error code on error. The default implementation does nothing and reports success.
`virtual int delete_all_rows( )`	Deletes all rows at once from the table. This is an optional optimization. If not supported, the table is cleared via multiple calls to `delete_row( )`. Returns 0 on success, and a nonzero error code on error. The default implementation returns HA_ERR_WRONG_COMMAND.
`virtual longlong get_auto_increment( )`	Returns the next value of the autoincrement key. Interestingly enough, although this method has a fairly complex default implementation, most existing storage engines re-implement it.
`virtual int check` `(THD* thd, HA_CHECK_OPT* check_opt)`	Checks the table for structural errors. Called when the CHECK TABLE command is issued. The thd argument is the current thread descriptor. The check_opt argument points to a structure describing the options for the operation. Returns 0 on success and a nonzero error code on failure. The default implementation returns HA_ADMIN_NOT_IMPLEMENTED.
`virtual int restore` `(THD* thd, HA_CHECK_OPT* check_opt)`	Recreates the index file from the .frm and datafiles. Currently implemented only in MyISAM. Returns 0 on success and a nonzero error code on failure. The default implementation returns HA_ADMIN_NOT_IMPLEMENTED. This method will be removed in 5.2.
`virtual int repair` `(THD* thd, HA_CHECK_OPT* check_opt)`	Repairs a corrupted table. Called when REPAIR TABLE is issued. Returns 0 on success and a nonzero error code on failure. The default implementation returns HA_ADMIN_NOT_IMPLEMENTED.
`virtual int optimize` `(THD* thd, HA_CHECK_OPT* check_opt)`	Restructures the table to be in the most optimal form for a typical query. Called when OPTIMIZE TABLE is issued. Returns 0 on success and a nonzero error code on failure. The default implementation returns HA_ADMIN_NOT_IMPLEMENTED.
`virtual int analyze` `(THD* thd, HA_CHECK_OPT* check_opt)`	Updates the index statistics used by the optimizer. Called when ANALYZE TABLE is issued. Returns 0 on success and a nonzero error code on failure. The default implementation returns HA_ADMIN_NOT_IMPLEMENTED.

Table 7-2. handler methods (continued)

Method definition	Method description
`virtual int assign_to_keycache (THD* thd, HA_CHECK_OPT* check_opt)`	Assigns the keys of this table to the key cache specified inside the `check_opt` structure. Called when `CACHE INDEX` command is issued. Returns 0 on success and a nonzero error code on failure. The default implementation returns `HA_ ADMIN_NOT_IMPLEMENTED`.
`virtual int preload_keys (THD* thd, HA_CHECK_OPT* check_opt)`	Loads the keys of this table into the cache specified inside the `check_opt` structure. Called when `CACHE INDEX` is issued. Returns 0 on success and a nonzero error code on failure. The default implementation returns `HA_ADMIN_NOT_ IMPLEMENTED`.
`virtual bool check_and_repair(THD *thd)`	Checks the table for corruption and repairs it if necessary. Returns 0 on success and 1 on error. The default implementation just returns 1.
`virtual int dump(THD* thd, int fd = -1)`	Writes the table data in the format particular to the storage engine to the file handle specified by `fd`. If `fd` is less than 0, the data is written to the network connection associated with `thd`. The dump format must be understood by `net_read_ dump( )`. The method is used for `LOAD DATA FROM MASTER`. Currently implemented only in MyISAM. Returns 0 on success, and a nonzero error code on error. The default implementation returns `HA_ERR_WRONG_COMMAND`. This method will be removed in 5.2.
`virtual int disable_indexes(uint mode)`	Disables the use of keys in the table. Called when `DISABLE KEYS` is issued. Often used before a large sequence of updates while holding a lock on the table. The default implementation returns `HA_ERR_WRONG_COMMAND`.
`virtual int enable_indexes(uint mode)`	Re-enables the use of keys in the table. Called when `ENABLE KEYS` command is issued. The default implementation returns `HA_ERR_WRONG_COMMAND`.
`virtual int indexes_are_disabled(void)`	Returns 1 if indexes in this table have been disabled, and 0 otherwise.
`virtual void start_bulk_insert (ha_rows rows)`	Instructs the storage engine to enable the bulk insert optimization. MySQL calls it before inserting a large number of rows into the table. MyISAM optimizes bulk inserts by caching key values in memory and inserting them into the B-tree index in key order. The default implementation does nothing.
`virtual int end_bulk_insert( )`	Called at the end of a bulk insert batch. Returns 0 on success, and a nonzero error code otherwise. The default implementation just returns 0.
`virtual int discard_or_import_ tablespace(my_bool discard)`	A method used by InnoDB to perform operations on a table space allocated for this table. Discarding prepares the table space for an import from the backup. Importing restores the data from the backup after the table space file to be restored has been copied into its designated location. Called when executing `ALTER TABLE ... DISCARD TABLESPACE` or `ALTER TABLE ... IMPORT TABLESPACE`. Returns 0 on success, and a nonzero error code on error. The default implementation returns `HA_ERR_WRONG_COMMAND`.

Table 7-2. handler methods (continued)

Method definition	Method description
`virtual int net_read_dump(NET* net)`	Reads the table data from the network connection specified by the argument and stores it in such a way that a call to `repair( )` is sufficient to bring the table into a consistent state. Returns 0 on success, and a nonzero error code on error. The default implementation returns HA_ERR_WRONG_COMMAND. Will be removed in 5.2.
`virtual char *update_table_comment (const char * comment)`	Used in SHOW TABLES to display some extra information about the table in the Comment column. Returns a pointer to the string containing the updated comment value. Note that if it returns a value different from the argument, the caller assumes the new pointer was allocated with `my_malloc( )`, and will free it with `my_free( )` after use. InnoDB is the only engine that provides its own implementation. The default implementation just returns the value of the argument.
`virtual void append_create_info (String *packet)`	Appends extra information specific to the storage engine to the String object specified by the argument. Used for generating the output of SHOW CREATE TABLE. The default implementation does nothing.
`virtual char* get_foreign_key_create_info( )`	Returns a pointer to the string containing the part of the CREATE TABLE statement that creates the foreign keys. Used for generating the output of SHOW CREATE TABLE. The default implementation returns 0.
`virtual uint referenced_by_foreign_key( )`	Returns 1 if the table associated with this object is referenced by some foreign key, and 0 otherwise. The default implementation returns 0.
`virtual void init_table_handle_for_ HANDLER( )`	Prepares the table for subsequent HANLDER commands. HANDLER commands provide a low-level interface to some storage engine operations through SQL. The default implementation does nothing.
`virtual void free_foreign_key_create_ info(char* str)`	Frees the pointer returned by `get_foreign_key_ create_info( )` if needed. The default implementation does nothing.
`virtual const char *table_type( ) const =0`	Returns a pointer to the string containing the name of the storage engine. Note that this method is pure virtual and must be implemented in the subclass.
`virtual const char **bas_ext( ) const =0`	Returns an array of character string pointers to file extensions of the files in which this storage engine stores the data and keys. The last element of the array is 0. Note that this method is pure virtual and must be implemented in the subclass.
`virtual ulong table_flags(void) const =0`	Returns a bit mask of capabilities of this storage engine. The capabilities are defined in *sql/handler.h*. Note that this method is pure virtual and must be implemented in the subclass.
`virtual ulong index_flags (uint idx, uint part, bool all_parts) const =0`	Returns a bit mask of capabilities of the key or its part specified by the arguments. The capabilities are defined in *sql/handler.h*. Note that this method is pure virtual and must be implemented in the subclass.

Table 7-2. handler methods (continued)

Method definition	Method description
`virtual ulong index_ddl_flags` `(KEY *wanted_index) const`	Returns a bit mask of capabilities for the given key with respect to creating or dropping that key. The default implementation returns DDL_SUPPORT, which means that a storage engine supports the index of a given definition, but cannot add it to the existing table (MySQL will create a new table with this index and copy the data over).
`virtual int add_index(TABLE *table_arg,` `KEY *key_info, uint num_of_keys)`	Adds the collection of keys to the table. The second argument is the start of the key definition array, while the third is its size. Returns 0 on success, and a nonzero error code on error. The default implementation returns HA_ERR_WRONG_COMMAND.
`virtual int drop_index(TABLE *table_arg,` `uint *key_num, uint num_of_keys)`	Drops the keys from the table specified by the arguments. Returns 0 on success, and a nonzero error code on error. The default implementation returns HA_ERR_WRONG_COMMAND.
`uint max_record_length() const`	Returns the maximum possible record length. The limit is either what the storage engine itself supports, or the limit imposed by the core code, whichever is less.
`uint max_keys() const`	Returns the maximum possible number of keys per table. The limit is either what the storage engine itself supports, or the limit imposed by the core code, whichever is less.
`uint max_key_parts() const`	Returns the maximum possible number of columns or column prefixes that a key can contain. The limit is either what the storage engine itself supports, or the limit imposed by the core code, whichever is less.
`uint max_key_length() const`	Returns the maximum possible length of a key. The limit is either what the storage engine itself supports, or the limit imposed by the core code, whichever is less.
`uint max_key_part_length() const`	Returns the maximum possible length of a key part. The limit is either what the storage engine itself supports, or the limit imposed by the core code, whichever is less.
`virtual uint max_supported_record_length()` `const`	Returns the limit on the length of a record imposed by this storage engine.
`virtual uint max_supported_keys() const`	Returns the limit on the number of keys imposed by this storage engine.
`virtual uint max_supported_key_parts()` `const`	Returns the limit on the number of key parts imposed by this storage engine.
`virtual uint max_supported_key_length()` `const`	Returns the limit on the key length imposed by this storage engine.
`virtual uint max_supported_key_part_` `length() const`	Returns the limit on the key part length imposed by this storage engine.
`virtual uint min_record_length` `(uint options) const`	Returns the lower limit on the length of a record imposed by this storage engine. The default implementation returns 1.

Table 7-2. handler methods (continued)

Method definition	Method description
`virtual bool low_byte_first() const`	Returns 1 if the native byte order of the records for this storage engine is little-endian; otherwise 0. The default implementation returns 1.
`virtual uint checksum() const`	Returns a live checksum for this table. The default implementation returns 0.
`virtual bool is_crashed() const`	Returns 1 if the table has been marked as crashed. This can happen if `CHECK TABLE` or just a regular read/write operation discovers a problem. The table then effectively gets taken offline by being marked as crashed. A successful run of `REPAIR TABLE` removes the mark.
`virtual bool auto_repair() const`	Returns 1 if the storage engine supports autorepairing corrupted tables. Currently only MyISAM has this capability.
`virtual int rename_table` `(const char *from, const char *to)`	Moves the table specified by `from` to the path specified by `to`. The arguments are paths to the table definition files with the *.frm* extension removed. The default implementation iterates through all the possible extensions returned by `bas_ext()` and renames the matching files. Returns 0 on success, and a nonzero error code on error.
`virtual int delete_table(const char *name)`	Deletes the table specified by `name`. The argument is the path to the table definition file with the *.frm* extension removed. The default implementation iterates through all the possible extensions returned by `bas_ext()` and deletes the matching files. Returns 0 on success, and a nonzero error code on error.
`virtual int create(const char *name,` `TABLE *form, HA_CREATE_INFO *info)=0`	Creates a table specified by `name` using the table descriptor `form` and the creation information descriptor `info`. Returns 0 on success, and a nonzero error code on error. Note that this method is pure virtual and must be implemented in the subclass.
`virtual uint lock_count(void) const`	Returns the number of regular lock descriptor blocks required to store the lock descriptor for this table. In most situations only one lock descriptor block is needed, with `MERGE` tables being the exception. A `MERGE` table needs one block per component table. The default implementation returns 1.
`virtual THR_LOCK_DATA **store_lock` `(THD *thd, THR_LOCK_DATA **to, enum` `thr_lock_type lock_type)=0`	Stores the location of the lock descriptor associated with this table at the address indicated by `to`. The other arguments supply the values of the current thread descriptor and the type of the lock in case the storage engine wants to know these values for its internal purposes. The main purpose of this method is to allow the storage engine to modify the lock before it gets stored. Row-level locking storage engines use it to prevent the table lock manager from putting an excessive lock on the table. Returns the value of `to` on success, and 0 on failure. Note that this method is pure virtual, and must be implemented in the subclass.

Table 7-2. handler methods (continued)

Method definition	Method description
`virtual uint8 table_cache_type()`	Returns the bit mask of options relevant for query caching. The default implementation returns `HA_CACHE_TBL_NONTRANSACT`, which permits caching regardless of whether there is a transaction in progress. Returning `HA_CACHE_TBL_TRANSACT` permits caching as long as the table is not involved in any active transactions. `HA_CACHE_TBL_ASKTRANSACT` means that query cache will ask the storage engine about every table, whether it can be cached. The storage engine may then use its transaction visibility rules to decide.
`virtual const COND *cond_push (const COND *cond)`	Used by storage engines capable of filtering out records that do not match a portion of the `WHERE` clause. Originally created for the NDB storage engine, which may store the records on remote nodes and can benefit from processing portions of the `WHERE` clause internally. The requested part of the `WHERE` clause represented by the argument is pushed onto the expression stack of this storage engine instance. Returns a new expression tree that the caller would have to evaluate to decide whether the record indeed matched the `WHERE` clause. If the filtering is fully completed inside the storage engine, returns `NULL`. The default implementation immediately returns the argument without doing anything else.
`virtual void cond_pop()`	Removes the top condition off the top of the storage engine condition stack. The default implementation does nothing.
`virtual void try_semi_consistent_read (bool flag)`	Used for communicating to the storage engine that it is acceptable to read the last committed version of a record if the current version is locked by another transaction. This is used by InnoDB to avoid unnecessary locks during `UPDATE` and `DELETE` queries.
`virtual bool was_semi_consistent_read()`	Returns `true` when the storage engine tells the optimizer not to update the last read record because it did not read the current version.

handlerton

Up until version 4.1, subclassing the `handler` class was the only method for a storage engine to connect to and interact with the core code. If the optimizer needed to do something with the storage engine, it would call a virtual method of `handler` for the current table. However, as the process of integrating various storage engines moved forward, it became apparent that interfacing through the handler methods alone was inadequate. Thus, a concept of a `handlerton` was created.

A handlerton is a C structure consisting mostly of callback function pointers. It is defined in *sql/handler.h*. The callbacks are invoked to handle certain events involving the given storage engine. For example, when a transaction is committed, a save point takes place, or a connection is closed, some special action may be required, in which case the `handlerton` will have the pointer to the appropriate callback. Table 7-3 documents the members of the `handlerton` structure.

Table 7-3. Members of the handlerton structure

Definition	Descripton
`const int interface_version`	Handlerton interface version number, which should be set to `MYSQL_HANDLERTON_INTERFACE_VERSION`.
`const char *name`	The name of the storage engine.
`SHOW_COMP_OPTION state`	Needed for the proper output of the Support column in the output of SHOW STORAGE ENGINES. Should normally be set to `SHOW_OPTION_YES`.
`const char *comment`	The value of the Comment column in the output of SHOW STORAGE ENGINES.
`enum legacy_db_type db_type`	Used in the *.frm* file to determine the storage engine type for the associated table.
`bool (*init)()`	The function to initialize the storage engine.
`uint slot`	For internal use by MySQL. Should be set to 0 initially.
`uint savepoint_offset`	Contains the offset to the savepoint storage area. Should be set initially to the size of the savepoint structure.
`int (*close_connection)(THD *thd)`	The function to perform storage-engine-specific cleanup when a connection is closed.
`int (*savepoint_set)(THD *thd, void *sv)`	The function to handle a savepoint.
`int (*savepoint_rollback)` `(THD *thd, void *sv)`	The function to handle ROLLBACK TO SAVEPOINT.
`int (*savepoint_release)` `(THD *thd, void *sv)`	The function to handle RELEASE SAVEPOINT.
`int (*commit)(THD *thd, bool all)`	The function to handle COMMIT.
`int (*rollback)(THD *thd, bool all)`	The function to handle ROLLBACK.
`int (*prepare)(THD *thd, bool all)`	The function to handle XA PREPARE.
`int (*recover)(XID *xid_list, uint len)`	The function to handle XA RECOVER.
`int (*commit_by_xid)(XID *xid)`	The function to handle XA COMMIT.
`int (*rollback_by_xid)(XID *xid)`	The function to handle XA ROLLBACK.
`void *(*create_cursor_read_view)()`	The function to open a cursor.
`void (*set_cursor_read_view)(void *)`	The function to fetch from a cursor.
`void (*close_cursor_read_view)(void *)`	The function to close a cursor.
`handler *(*create)(TABLE_SHARE *table)`	The function to create a table.
`void (*drop_database)(char* path)`	The function to drop a database.
`int (*panic)(enum ha_panic_function flag)`	The function to handle an emergency shutdown.
`int (*start_consistent_snapshot)(THD *thd)`	The function to handle START TRANSACTION WITH CONSISTENT SNAPSHOT.
`bool (*flush_logs)()`	The function to handle FLUSH LOGS.
`bool (*show_status)(THD *thd, stat_print_` `fn *print, enum ha_stat_type stat)`	The function to handle SHOW ENGINE STATUS.
`uint (*partition_flags)()`	The function that returns a set of flags indicating the capabilities of the storage engine to deal with table data partitioned across different filesystems.

Table 7-3. Members of the handlerton structure (continued)

Definition	Descripton
`uint (*alter_table_flags)(uint flags)`	The function that returns a set of flags indicating the different capabilities of the storage engine in the ALTER TABLE operation.
`int (*alter_tablespace)` `(THD *thd, st_alter_tablespace *ts_info)`	The function to handle ALTER TABLESPACE.

`int (*fill_files_table)(THD *thd,`
`struct st_table_list *tables,`
`class Item *cond)`
	The function to supply the data for SELECT * FROM information_schema.files.

`uint32 flags`	Bit mask of storage engine capabilities.
`int (*binlog_func)(THD *thd, enum_binlog_` `func fn, void *arg)`	The function to handle replication log operations.

`void (*binlog_log_query)(THD *thd,`
`enum_binlog_command binlog_command,`
`const char *query, uint query_length,`
`const char *db, const char *table_name)`
	The function to be called every time a query is written to the replication log.

`int (*release_temporary_latches)(THD *thd)`	A special callback created for InnoDB to avoid a deadlock when sending records to a client.

Adding a Custom Storage Engine to MySQL

There are a number of reasons for adding a custom storage engine to MySQL:

- You have a legacy, proprietary database and want to give it an SQL/ODBC interface.
- You have some very specific requirements in the areas of performance or data security that are not being met by any of the existing storage engines.
- You have created a low-level data storage and retrieval module that you believe will rule the world, but you do not want to (or are not able to) write an SQL optimizer to go with it.
- Your proprietary SQL optimizer does not meet your needs, and you want a better one for your storage engine.
- You just want to learn more about MySQL internals.

Let us illustrate with an example. Our storage engine will provide a read-only SQL interface to comma-separated value (CSV) text files. In version 4.1 and earlier, storage engine integration requires a lot of source modifications. It has become much cleaner in version 5.1. If you are writing a custom storage engine, depending on your needs, you may choose to lean toward a more mature code base (4.1), or go with what (at the time of this writing) is the bleeding edge (5.1). I will provide instructions for versions 4.1 and 5.1. For the sake of brevity, I will not provide instructions for other versions of MySQL. Those who need to integrate their storage engine into other versions are advised to search (case-insensitive) for the string "blackhole" in the source tree of the given version, and follow the patterns of the blackhole storage engine.

Integration Instructions for Version 4.1

The instructions in this section were created using the source of MySQL 4.1.11, but they should work fine on later 4.1 versions. We assume that you already have downloaded and unpacked the MySQL source distribution.

1. Copy the *ha_csv_4_1.cc* and *ha_csv4_1.h* files from the examples on the book's web site into the *sql/* directory. Name them *ha_csv.cc* and *ha_csv.h*, respectively. If you do not have Internet access, you can copy them from Examples 7-1 and 7-2. They provide the definition and the implementation of our storage engine class.

2. In *sql/Makefile.am*, add *ha_csv.h* to the noinst_HEADERS variable and *ha_csv.cc* to mysqld_SOURCES. This is necessary to include those files in the compilation framework.

3. To update the Makefiles, run the following set of commands at the top of the MySQL source tree:

    ```
    $ autoconf
    $ automake
    $ ./configure --prefix=/usr
    ```

4. Now you need to make a few changes to the core code to make it aware of the presence of a new storage engine. Add the following line to other include directives at the top of *sql/handler.cc*:

    ```
    #include "ha_csv.h"
    ```

5. Still in *sql/handler.cc*, extend the array sys_table_types[] with the following member (any position except the very last element in the array is fine):

    ```
    {"OREILLY_CSV", &have_yes,
        "Example CSV Engine - Understanding MySQL Internals",
        DB_TYPE_OREILLY_CSV}
    ```

6. In *sql/handler.cc*, extend the switch statement in get_new_handler( ) with the following code:

    ```
    case DB_TYPE_OREILLY_CSV:
        return new ha_csv(table);
    ```

7. In *sql/handler.h*, add a new member DB_TYPE_OREILLY_CSV to the enum db_type. Any position is fine except the last one.

8. Run *make* in the top directory. When the build is finished, you will have a binary in *sql/mysqld* that has support for your new storage engine.

Example 7-1. The ha_csv.h storage engine header file for MySQL 4.1

```
/* Tell GCC  this is a header file */
#ifdef USE_PRAGMA_INTERFACE
#pragma interface
#endif

/* The CSV lines could be big. Read them in blocks of 512. */
#define CSV_READ_BLOCK_SIZE   512

/*
  Following the tradition of other storage engines, we put all of the
  low-level information under a separate structure.
 */
struct CSV_INFO
{
  char fname[FN_REFLEN+1];
  int fd;
} ;

/* Now define the handler class. */
class ha_csv: public handler
{
protected:
  /* Low-level storage engine data. */
  CSV_INFO* file;

  /* Lock structures for the table lock manager. */
  THR_LOCK_DATA lock;
  THR_LOCK thr_lock;

  /* Table scan cursor.*/
  my_off_t pos;

  /* Buffer for reading CSV line blocks. */
  char read_buf[CSV_READ_BLOCK_SIZE];

  /* Buffer for parsing the field values. */
  String field_buf;

  /* See the comment in the implementation file. */
  int fetch_line(byte* buf);

  /* Initializes the storage engine object for a sequential scan. */
  int rnd_init(bool scan)
  {
    pos = 0;
    records = 0;
    return 0;
  }
public:
 /* Constructor. */
 ha_csv(TABLE* table): handler(table), file(0) {}
```

Example 7-1. The ha_csv.h storage engine header file for MySQL 4.1 (continued)

```
/* Destructor. */
~ha_csv( ) {}

/* See the comments in the implementation file for the methods below. */
int open(const char *name, int mode, uint test_if_locked);
int close(void);
int rnd_next(byte *buf);
int rnd_pos(byte * buf, byte *pos);
void position(const byte *record);
void info(uint flags);
int external_lock(THD *thd, int lock_type);
const char **bas_ext( ) const;
ulong table_flags(void) const;
ulong index_flags(uint idx, uint part, bool all_parts) const;
int create(const char *name, TABLE *form, HA_CREATE_INFO *info);
THR_LOCK_DATA **store_lock(THD *thd,
                           THR_LOCK_DATA **to,
                           enum thr_lock_type lock_type);

/*
  Returns the storage engine type string used in the output of
  SHOW TABLE STATUS
*/
const char *table_type( ) const { return "OREILLY_CSV"; }

};
```

Example 7-2. The ha_csv.cc storage engine implementation for MySQL 4.1

```
/* Tell GCC we are in the implementation source file. */
#ifdef USE_PRAGMA_IMPLEMENTATION
#pragma implementation
#endif

/* Main include file in the sql/ directory. */
#include "mysql_priv.h"

/* Our own header file for this storage engine. */
#include "ha_csv.h"

/* Used by ha_csv::bas_ext( ). */
static const char* csv_ext[]= {".csv",0};

/* Called when the table is opened. */
int ha_csv::open(const char *name, int mode, uint test_if_locked)
{
  /* Initialize the lock structures used by the lock manager. */
  thr_lock_init(&thr_lock);
  thr_lock_data_init(&thr_lock,&lock,NULL);

  /* Allocate memory for the datafile descriptor. */
  file= (CSV_INFO*)my_malloc(sizeof(CSV_INFO),MYF(MY_WME));
```

```
  if (!file)
    return 1;

  /* Translate the name of the name into the datafile name. */
  fn_format(file->fname, name, "", ".csv",
    MY_REPLACE_EXT|MY_UNPACK_FILENAME);

  /*
    Open the file, and save the file handle id in the datafile
    descriptor structure.
   */
  if ((file->fd = my_open(file->fname,mode,MYF(0))) < 0)
  {
    int error = my_errno;
    close();
    return error;
  }

  /* Read operations start from the beginning of the file. */
  pos = 0;
  return 0;
}

/* Called when the table is closed. */
int ha_csv::close(void)
{
  /*
    Clean up the lock structures, close the file handle, and
    deallocate the datafile descriptor memory.
   */
  thr_lock_delete(&thr_lock);
  if (file)
  {
    if (file->fd >= 0)
      my_close(file->fd, MYF(0));
    my_free((gptr)file,MYF(0));
    file = 0;
  }
  return 0;
}

/*
  Read the line from the current position into the
  caller-provided record buffer.
 */
int ha_csv::fetch_line(byte* buf)
{
  /*
    Keep track of the current offset in the file as we read
    portions of the line into a buffer.
    Start at the current read cursor position.
   */
```

```
my_off_t cur_pos = pos;

/*
   We will use this to iterate through the array of
   table field pointers to store the parsed data in the right
   place and the right format.
 */
Field** field = table->field;

/*
   Used in parsing to remember the previous character. The impossible
   value of 256 indicates that the last character either did not exist
   (we are on the first one), or its value is irrelevant.
*/
int last_c = 256;

/* Set to 1 if we are inside a quoted string. */
int in_quote = 0;

/* How many bytes we have seen so far in this line. */
uint bytes_parsed = 0;

/* Loop break flag. */
int line_read_done = 0;

/* Truncate the field value buffer. */
field_buf.length(0);

/* Attempt to read a whole line. */
for (;!line_read_done;)
{
  /* Read a block into a local buffer and deal with errors. */
  char buf[CSV_READ_BLOCK_SIZE];
  uint bytes_read = my_pread(file->fd,buf,sizeof(buf),cur_pos,MYF(MY_WME));
  if (bytes_read == MY_FILE_ERROR)
    return HA_ERR_END_OF_FILE;
  if (!bytes_read)
    return HA_ERR_END_OF_FILE;

  /*
     If we reach this point, the read was successful. Start parsing the
     data we have read.
  */
  char* p = buf;
  char* buf_end = buf + bytes_read;

  /* For each byte in the buffer. */
  for (;p < buf_end;)
  {
    char c = *p;
    int end_of_line = 0;
```

Example 7-2. The ha_csv.cc storage engine implementation for MySQL 4.1 (continued)

```
int end_of_field = 0;
int char_escaped = 0;

switch (c)
{
  /*
    A double-quote marks the start or the end of a quoted string
    unless it has been escaped.
  */
  case '"':
    if (last_c == '"' || last_c == '\\')
    {
      field_buf.append(c);
      char_escaped = 1;

      /*
        When we see the first quote, in_quote will get flipped.
        A subsequent quote, however, tells us we are still inside the
        quoted string.
      */
      if (last_c == '"')
        in_quote = 1;
    }
    else
      in_quote = !in_quote;
    break;
  /*
    Treat the backslash as an escape character.
  */
  case '\\':
    if (last_c == '\\')
    {
      field_buf.append(c);
      char_escaped = 1;
    }
    break;

  /*
    Set the termination flags on end-of-line unless it is quoted.
  */
  case '\r':
  case '\n':
    if (in_quote)
    {
      field_buf.append(c);
    }
    else
    {
      end_of_line = 1;
      end_of_field = 1;
    }
    break;
```

```
    /* Comma signifies end-of-field unless quoted. */
    case ',':
      if (in_quote)
      {
        field_buf.append(c);
      }
      else
        end_of_field = 1;
      break;

    /*
      Regular charcters just get appended to the field
      value buffer.
    */
    default:
      field_buf.append(c);
      break;
  }

  /*
    If at the end a field, and a matching field exists in the table
    (it may not if the CSV file has extra fields), transfer the field
    value buffer contents into the corresponding Field object. This
    actually takes care of initializing the correct parts of the buffer
    argument passed to us by the caller. The internal convention of the
    optimizer dictates that the buffer pointers of the Field objects
    must already be set up to point at the correct areas of the buffer
    argument prior to calls to the data-retrieval methods of the handler
    class.
  */
  if (end_of_field && *field)
  {
    (*field)->store(field_buf.ptr(),field_buf.length( ),
      system_charset_info);
    field++;
    field_buf.length(0);
  }

  /*
    Special case - a character that was escaped itself should not be
    regarded as an escape character.
  */
  if (char_escaped)
    last_c = 256;
  else
    last_c = c;
  p++;

  /* Prepare for loop exit on end-of-line. */
  if (end_of_line)
  {
    if (c == '\r')
```

```
      p++;
    line_read_done = 1;
    in_quote = 0;
    break;
    }
  }

  /* Block read/parse cycle is complete - update the counters. */
  bytes_parsed += (p - buf);
  cur_pos += bytes_read;
}

/*
  Now we are done with the line read/parsing. We still have a number
  of small tasks left to complete the job.
*/

/* Initialize the NULL indicator flags in the record. */
memset(buf,0,table->null_bytes);

/*
  The parsed line may not have had the values of all of the fields.
  Set the remaining fields to their default values.
 */
for (;*field;field++)
{
  (*field)->set_default();
}

/* Move the cursor to the next record. */
pos += bytes_parsed;

/* Report success. */
return 0;
}

/* Called once for each record during a sequential table scan. */
int ha_csv::rnd_next(byte *buf)
{
  /*
    Increment the global statistics counter displayed by SHOW STATUS
    under Handler_read_rnd_next.
  */
  statistic_increment(ha_read_rnd_next_count,&LOCK_status);

  /* fetch_line() does the actual work. */
  int error = fetch_line(buf);

  /*
    On success, update our estimate for the total number of records in the
    table.
  */
```

```
  if (!error)
    records++;

  /* Return whatever code we got from fetch_line( ) to the caller. */
  return error;
}

/*
  Positions the scan cursor at the position specified by set_pos and
  read the record at that position. Used in GROUP BY and ORDER BY
  optimization when the "filesort" technique is applied.
*/
int ha_csv::rnd_pos(byte * buf, byte *set_pos)
{
  statistic_increment(ha_read_rnd_count,&LOCK_status);
  pos = ha_get_ptr(set_pos,ref_length);
  return fetch_line(buf);
}

/*
  Stores the "position" reference to the current record in the ref
  variable. At this point, this method is called in situations that are
  impossible for this storage engine, but this could change in the future.
 */
void ha_csv::position(const byte *record)
{
  ha_store_ptr(ref,ref_length,pos);
}

/* Updates the statistical variables in the handler object. */
void ha_csv::info(uint flags)
{
  /*
    The optimizer must never think that the table has fewer than
    two records unless this is indeed the case. Reporting a smaller number
    makes the optimizer assume it needs to read no more than one record from
    the table. Our storage engine doesn't always know the number of records,
    and in many cases cannot even make a good guess. To be safe and to keep
    things simple, we always report that we have at least 2 records.
  */
  if (records < 2)
    records = 2;

  /*
    The rest of the variables merely appear in SHOW TABLE STATUS output and
    do not affect the optimizer. For the purpose of this example they can
    be set to 0.
  */

  deleted = 0;
  errkey = 0;
  mean_rec_length = 0;
```

Example 7-2. The ha_csv.cc storage engine implementation for MySQL 4.1 (continued)

```
  data_file_length = 0;
  index_file_length = 0;
  max_data_file_length = 0;
  delete_length = 0;
  if (flags & HA_STATUS_AUTO)
    auto_increment_value = 1;
}


/*
  This is essentially a callback for the table lock manager, saying:
  "I am locking this table internally; please take care of the things
  specific to the storage engine that need to be done in conjunction with
  this lock." MyISAM needed to lock the files in this case in some
  configurations, thus the name external_lock(). In our case, there is
  nothing to do - we just report success.
*/
int ha_csv::external_lock(THD *thd, int lock_type)
{
  return 0;
}


/*
   Returns an array of all possible file extensions used by the storage
   engine.
*/
const char ** ha_csv::bas_ext( ) const
{
  return csv_ext;
}


/*
   We need this function to report that the records member cannot be used
   to optimize SELECT COUNT(*) without a WHERE clause. Note that the value
   records actually shows the correct count after a full scan, and can
   indeed be used to optimize SELECT COUNT(*). This is left as an exercise
   for the reader.
 */
ulong ha_csv::table_flags(void) const
{
  return HA_NOT_EXACT_COUNT;
}


/*
  Our storage engine does not support keys, so we report no special
  key capabilities.
*/
ulong ha_csv::index_flags(uint idx, uint part, bool all_parts) const
{
  return 0;
}

/* Nothing special to do on the storage engine level when the table
```

Example 7-2. The ha_csv.cc storage engine implementation for MySQL 4.1 (continued)

```
   is created. The .CSV file is placed externally into the data directory.
*/
int ha_csv::create(const char *name, TABLE *form, HA_CREATE_INFO *info)
{
  return 0;
}

/* This method is needed for the table lock manager to work right. */
THR_LOCK_DATA ** ha_csv::store_lock(THD *thd,
           THR_LOCK_DATA **to,
           enum thr_lock_type lock_type)
{
  if (lock_type != TL_IGNORE && lock.type == TL_UNLOCK)
    lock.type=lock_type;

  *to++ = &lock;
  return to;
}
```

Integration Instructions for Version 5.1

The following instructions were created using version 5.1.11. While it appears that the procedure of custom storage-engine integration should have stabilized at that point, it is still possible that some changes might be introduced into later 5.1 versions that would require modifications to these instructions. When in doubt, search for the string "blackhole" in the source and follow the pattern of the blackhole storage engine.

1. Create a directory *storage/oreilly-csv* in the source tree, and copy the files *ha_csv_5_1.h* and *ha_csv_5_1.cc* from the book's web site into that directory, naming them *ha_csv.h* and *ha_csv.cc* accordingly. If you do not have access to the Internet, use Examples 7-3 and 7-4.

2. Copy *Makefile.am* from the book's web site (or from Example 8-5) to *storage/oreilly-csv*.

3. Search for MYSQL_STORAGE_ENGINE in *configure.in* to find the section for plug-in macros. Add the following lines right after the blackhole plug-in section (or after some other plug-in section):

```
MYSQL_STORAGE_ENGINE(oreilly-csv,, [Example Storage Engine for Understanding
MySQL Internals],
    [Read-only access to CSV files])
MYSQL_PLUGIN_DIRECTORY(oreilly-csv, [storage/oreilly-csv])
MYSQL_PLUGIN_STATIC(oreilly-csv, [liboreillycsv.a])
```

4. Execute the following shell commands:

```
$ autoconf
$ automake
$ ./configure --prefix=/usr --with-plugins=oreilly-csv
$ make
```

Here are Examples 7-3, 7-4, and 7-5.

Example 7-3. The ha_csv.h storage engine header file for MySQL 5.1

```
/* Tell GCC  this is a header file */
#ifdef USE_PRAGMA_INTERFACE
#pragma interface
#endif

/* The CSV lines could be big. Read them in blocks of 512. */
#define CSV_READ_BLOCK_SIZE    512

/*
  Following the tradition of other storage engines, we put all of the
  low-level information under a separate structure.
 */
struct CSV_INFO
{
  char fname[FN_REFLEN+1];
  int fd;
} ;

/* Now define the handler class. */
class ha_csv: public handler
{
protected:
  /* Low-level storage engine data. */
  CSV_INFO* file;

  /* Lock structures for the table lock manager. */
  THR_LOCK_DATA lock;
  THR_LOCK thr_lock;

  /* Table scan cursor.*/
  my_off_t pos;

  /* Buffer for reading CSV line blocks. */
  char read_buf[CSV_READ_BLOCK_SIZE];

  /* Buffer for parsing the field values. */
  String field_buf;

  /* See the comment in the implementation file. */
  int fetch_line(byte* buf);

  /* Initializes the storage engine object for a sequential scan. */
  int rnd_init(bool scan)
  {
    pos = 0;
    records = 0;
    return 0;
  }
  int index_init(uint idx)
  {
```

```
    active_index=idx;
    return 0;
  }
public:
 /* Constructors. */
 ha_csv(TABLE_SHARE* table_arg);

 /* Destructor. */
 ~ha_csv( ) {}

 /* See the comments in the implementation file for the methods below. */
 int open(const char *name, int mode, uint test_if_locked);
 int close(void);
 int rnd_next(byte *buf);
 int rnd_pos(byte * buf, byte *pos);
 void position(const byte *record);
 void info(uint flags);
 int external_lock(THD *thd, int lock_type);
 const char **bas_ext( ) const;
 ulong table_flags(void) const;
 ulong index_flags(uint idx, uint part, bool all_parts) const;
 int create(const char *name, TABLE *form, HA_CREATE_INFO *info);
 THR_LOCK_DATA **store_lock(THD *thd,
                    THR_LOCK_DATA **to,
                    enum thr_lock_type lock_type);

 /*
   Returns the storage engine type string used in the output of
   SHOW TABLE STATUS
 */
 const char *table_type( ) const { return "OREILLY_CSV"; }

};
```

Example 7-4. The ha_csv.cc storage engine implementation for MySQL 5.1

```
/* Tell GCC we are in the implementation source file. */
#ifdef USE_PRAGMA_IMPLEMENTATION
#pragma implementation
#endif

#include "mysql_priv.h"
#include <mysql/plugin.h>

/* Our own header file for this storage engine. */
#include "ha_csv.h"

/* Used by ha_csv::bas_ext( ). */
static const char* csv_ext[]= {".csv",0};

/* A callback for the handlerton descriptor */
static handler *csv_create_handler(TABLE_SHARE *table);
```

Example 7-4. The ha_csv.cc storage engine implementation for MySQL 5.1 (continued)

```
/*
   Used in the plug-in as well as the handlerton descriptor. Corresponds
   to the name of the storage
   engine used in the ENGINE= syntax
 */
static const char csv_hton_name[]= "OREILLY_CSV";

/*
   Used in the plug-in descriptor. Corresponds to the comment that appears
   in the output of SHOW STORAGE ENGINES
*/
static const char csv_hton_comment[]=
  "Simple read-only CSV file storage engine";

handlerton csv_hton= {
  MYSQL_HANDLERTON_INTERFACE_VERSION,
  csv_hton_name,
  SHOW_OPTION_YES,
  csv_hton_comment,
  DB_TYPE_BLACKHOLE_DB,
  NULL,
  0,       /* slot */
  0,       /* savepoint size. */
  NULL,    /* close_connection */
  NULL,    /* savepoint */
  NULL,    /* rollback to savepoint */
  NULL,    /* release savepoint */
  NULL,    /* commit */
  NULL,    /* rollback */
  NULL,    /* prepare */
  NULL,    /* recover */
  NULL,    /* commit_by_xid */
  NULL,    /* rollback_by_xid */
  NULL,    /* create_cursor_read_view */
  NULL,    /* set_cursor_read_view */
  NULL,    /* close_cursor_read_view */
  csv_create_handler,    /* Create a new handler */
  NULL,    /* Drop a database */
  NULL,    /* Panic call */
  NULL,    /* Start Consistent Snapshot */
  NULL,    /* Flush logs */
  NULL,    /* Show status */
  NULL,    /* Partition flags */
  NULL,    /* Alter table flags */
  NULL,    /* Alter Tablespace */
  NULL,    /* Fill FILES table */
  HTON_CAN_RECREATE | HTON_ALTER_CANNOT_CREATE,
  NULL,    /* binlog_func */
  NULL,    /* binlog_log_query */
  NULL       /* release_temporary_latches */
};
```

Example 7-4. The ha_csv.cc storage engine implementation for MySQL 5.1 (continued)

```
/*
   A callback wrapper used for instatiating the handler object.
*/
static handler *csv_create_handler(TABLE_SHARE *table)
{
  return new ha_csv(table);
}

/* Constructor */
ha_csv::ha_csv(TABLE_SHARE *table_arg)
  :handler(&csv_hton, table_arg)
{}



/* Called when the table is opened. */
int ha_csv::open(const char *name, int mode, uint test_if_locked)
{
  /* Initialize the lock structures used by the lock manager. */
  thr_lock_init(&thr_lock);
  thr_lock_data_init(&thr_lock,&lock,NULL);

  /* Allocate memory for the data file descriptor. */
  file= (CSV_INFO*)my_malloc(sizeof(CSV_INFO),MYF(MY_WME));
  if (!file)
    return 1;

  /* Translate the name of the name into the datafile name. */
  fn_format(file->fname, name, "", ".csv",
    MY_REPLACE_EXT|MY_UNPACK_FILENAME);

  /*
     Open the file, and save the file handle id in the data
     file descriptor structure.
   */
  if ((file->fd = my_open(file->fname,mode,MYF(0))) < 0)
  {
    int error = my_errno;
    close();
    return error;
  }

  /* Read operations start from the beginning of the file. */
  pos = 0;
  return 0;
}

/* Called when the table is closed. */
int ha_csv::close(void)
{
```

Example 7-4. The ha_csv.cc storage engine implementation for MySQL 5.1 (continued)

```
  /*
     Clean up the lock structures, close the file handle, and
     deallocate the datafile descriptor memory.
   */
  thr_lock_delete(&thr_lock);
  if (file)
  {
    if (file->fd >= 0)
      my_close(file->fd, MYF(0));
    my_free((gptr)file,MYF(0));
    file = 0;
  }
  return 0;
}

/*
   Read the line from the current position into the
   caller-provided record buffer.
 */
int ha_csv::fetch_line(byte* buf)
{
  /*
     Keep track of the current offset in the file as we read
     portions of the line into a buffer.
     Start at the current read cursor position.
   */
  my_off_t cur_pos = pos;

  /*
     We will use this to iterate through the array of
     table field pointers to store the parsed data in the right
     place and the right format.
   */
  Field** field = table->field;

  /*
     Used in parsing to remember the previous character. The impossible
     value of 256 indicates that the last character either did not exist
     (we are on the first one), or its value is irrelevant.
   */
  int last_c = 256;

  /* Set to 1 if we are inside a quoted string. */
  int in_quote = 0;

  /* How many bytes we have seen so far in this line. */
  uint bytes_parsed = 0;

  /* Loop breaker flag. */
  int line_read_done = 0;
```

Example 7-4. The ha_csv.cc storage engine implementation for MySQL 5.1 (continued)

```
/* Truncate the field value buffer. */
field_buf.length(0);

/* Attempt to read a whole line. */
for (;!line_read_done;)
{
  /* Read a block into a local buffer and deal with errors. */
  char buf[CSV_READ_BLOCK_SIZE];
  uint bytes_read = my_pread(file->fd,buf,sizeof(buf),cur_pos,MYF(MY_WME));
  if (bytes_read == MY_FILE_ERROR)
    return HA_ERR_END_OF_FILE;
  if (!bytes_read)
    return HA_ERR_END_OF_FILE;

  /*
    If we reach this point, the read was successful. Start parsing the
    data we have read.
  */
  char* p = buf;
  char* buf_end = buf + bytes_read;

  /* For each byte in the buffer. */
  for (;p < buf_end;)
  {
    char c = *p;
    int end_of_line = 0;
    int end_of_field = 0;
    int char_escaped = 0;

    switch (c)
    {
      /*
        A double-quote marks the start or the end of a quoted string
        unless it has been escaped.
      */
      case '"':
        if (last_c == '"' || last_c == '\\')
        {
          field_buf.append(c);
          char_escaped = 1;

          /*
            When we see the first quote, in_quote will get flipped.
            A subsequent quote, however, tells us we are still inside the
            quoted string.
          */
          if (last_c == '"')
            in_quote = 1;
        }
        else
          in_quote = !in_quote;
        break;
```

Example 7-4. The ha_csv.cc storage engine implementation for MySQL 5.1 (continued)

```
      /*
        Treat the backslash as an escape character.
      */
      case '\\':
        if (last_c == '\\')
        {
          field_buf.append(c);
          char_escaped = 1;
        }
        break;

      /*
        Set the termination flags on end-of-line unless it is quoted.
      */
      case '\r':
      case '\n':
        if (in_quote)
        {
          field_buf.append(c);
        }
        else
        {
          end_of_line = 1;
          end_of_field = 1;
        }
        break;

      /* Comma signifies end-of-field unless quoted. */
      case ',':
        if (in_quote)
        {
          field_buf.append(c);
        }
        else
          end_of_field = 1;
        break;

      /*
        Regular characters just get appended to the field
        value buffer.
      */
      default:
        field_buf.append(c);
        break;
    }

    /*
      If at the end a field, and a matching field exists in the table
      (it may not if the CSV file has extra fields), transfer the field
      value buffer contents into the corresponding Field object. This
      actually takes care of initializing the correct parts of the buffer
      argument passed to us by the caller. The internal convention of the
```

Example 7-4. The ha_csv.cc storage engine implementation for MySQL 5.1 (continued)

```
        optimizer dictates that the buffer pointers of the Field objects
        must already be set up to point at the correct areas of the buffer
        argument prior to calls to the data-retrieval methods of the handler
        class.
      */
      if (end_of_field && *field)
      {
        (*field)->store(field_buf.ptr(),field_buf.length(),
          system_charset_info);
        field++;
        field_buf.length(0);
      }

      /*
        Special case - a character that was escaped itself should not be
        regarded as an escape character.
      */
      if (char_escaped)
        last_c = 256;
      else
        last_c = c;
      p++;

      /* Prepare for loop exit on end-of-line. */
      if (end_of_line)
      {
        if (c == '\r')
          p++;
        line_read_done = 1;
        in_quote = 0;
        break;
      }
    }

    /* Block read/parse cycle is complete - update the counters. */
    bytes_parsed += (p - buf);
    cur_pos += bytes_read;
  }

  /*
    Now we are done with the line read/parsing. We still have a number
    of small tasks left to complete the job.
  */

  /* Initialize the NULL indicator flags in the record. */
  memset(buf,0,table->s->null_bytes);

  /*
    The parsed line may not have had the values of all of the fields.
    Set the remaining fields to their default values.
  */
```

```
  for (;*field;field++)
  {
    (*field)->set_default( );
  }

  /* Move the cursor to the next record. */
  pos += bytes_parsed;

  /* Report success. */
  return 0;
}

/* Called once for each record during a sequential table scan. */
int ha_csv::rnd_next(byte *buf)
{
  /*
    Increment the global statistics counter displayed by SHOW STATUS
    under Handler_read_rnd_next.
  */
  ha_statistic_increment(&SSV::ha_read_rnd_next_count);

  /* fetch_line( ) does the actual work. */
  int error = fetch_line(buf);

  /*
    On success, update our estimate for the total number of records in the
    table.
  */
  if (!error)
    records++;

  /* Return whatever code we got from fetch_line( ) to the caller. */
  return error;
}

/*
  Positions the scan cursor at the position specified by set_pos and
  read the record at that position. Used in GROUP BY and ORDER BY
  optimization when the "filesort" technique is applied.
*/
int ha_csv::rnd_pos(byte * buf, byte *set_pos)
{
  ha_statistic_increment(&SSV::ha_read_rnd_count);
  pos = my_get_ptr(set_pos,ref_length);
  return fetch_line(buf);
}

/*
  Stores the "position" reference to the current record in the ref
  variable. At this point, this method is called in situations that are
  impossible for this storage engine, but this could change in the future.
*/
```

Example 7-4. The ha_csv.cc storage engine implementation for MySQL 5.1 (continued)

```
void ha_csv::position(const byte *record)
{
  my_store_ptr(ref,ref_length,pos);
}

/* Updates the statistical variables in the handler object */
void ha_csv::info(uint flags)
{
  /*
    The optimizer must never think that the table has fewer than
    two records unless this is indeed the case. Reporting a smaller number
    makes the optimizer assume it needs to read no more than one record from
    the table. Our storage engine doesn't always know the number of records,
    and in many cases cannot even make a good guess. To be safe and to keep
    things simple, we always report that we have at least 2 records.
  */
  if (records < 2)
    records = 2;

  /*
    The rest of the variables merely appear in SHOW TABLE STATUS output and
    do not affect the optimizer. For the purpose of this example they can
    be set to 0.
  */

  deleted = 0;
  errkey = 0;
  mean_rec_length = 0;
  data_file_length = 0;
  index_file_length = 0;
  max_data_file_length = 0;
  delete_length = 0;
  if (flags & HA_STATUS_AUTO)
    auto_increment_value = 1;
}

/*
  This is essentially a callback for the table lock manager saying:
  "I am locking this table internally; please take care of the things
  specific to the storage engine that need to be done in conjunction with
  this lock." MyISAM needed to lock the files in this case in some
  configurations, thus the name external_lock(). In our case, there is
  nothing to do - we just report success.
*/
int ha_csv::external_lock(THD *thd, int lock_type)
{
  return 0;
}

/*
  Returns an array of all possible file extensions used by the storage
  engine.
*/
```

Example 7-4. The ha_csv.cc storage engine implementation for MySQL 5.1 (continued)

```
const char ** ha_csv::bas_ext( ) const
{
  return csv_ext;
}

/*
   We need this function to report that the records member cannot be used
   to optimize SELECT COUNT(*) without a WHERE clause. Note that the value
   records actually shows the correct count after a full scan, and can
   indeed be used to optimize SELECT COUNT(*). This is left as an exercise
   for the reader.
 */
ulong ha_csv::table_flags(void) const
{
  return HA_NOT_EXACT_COUNT;
}

/*
   Our storage engine does not support keys, so we report no special
   key capabilities.
*/
ulong ha_csv::index_flags(uint idx, uint part, bool all_parts) const
{
  return 0;
}

/* Nothing special to do on the storage engine level when the table
   is created. The .CSV file is placed externally into the data directory.
*/
int ha_csv::create(const char *name, TABLE *form, HA_CREATE_INFO *info)
{
  return 0;
}

/* This method is needed for the table lock manager to work right. */
THR_LOCK_DATA ** ha_csv::store_lock(THD *thd,
             THR_LOCK_DATA **to,
             enum thr_lock_type lock_type)
{
  if (lock_type != TL_IGNORE && lock.type == TL_UNLOCK)
    lock.type=lock_type;

  *to++ = &lock;
  return to;
}

/* Defines the global structure for the plug-in. */
mysql_declare_plugin(oreilly_csv)
{
  MYSQL_STORAGE_ENGINE_PLUGIN,
  &csv_hton,
  csv_hton_name,
```

Example 7-4. The ha_csv.cc storage engine implementation for MySQL 5.1 (continued)

```
    "Sasha Pachev",
    csv_hton_comment,
    NULL, /* Plugin init function */
    NULL, /* Plugin end function */
    0x0100,
    0
}
mysql_declare_plugin_end;
```

Example 7-5. Makefile.am for MySQL version 5.1

```
MYSQLDATAdir =          $(localstatedir)
MYSQLSHAREdir =         $(pkgdatadir)
MYSQLBASEdir=           $(prefix)
MYSQLLIBdir=            $(pkglibdir)
INCLUDES =              -I$(top_srcdir)/include -I$(top_builddir)/include \
                        -I$(top_srcdir)/regex \
                        -I$(top_srcdir)/sql \
                        -I$(srcdir)

WRAPLIBS=

LDADD =

DEFS =                  @DEFS@

noinst_HEADERS =        ha_csv.h


EXTRA_LIBRARIES =       liboreillycsv.a
noinst_LIBRARIES =      @plugin_oreilly_csv_static_target@
liboreillycsv_a_CXXFLAGS =    $(AM_CFLAGS)
liboreillycsv_a_CFLAGS =      $(AM_CFLAGS)
liboreillycsv_a_SOURCES=      ha_csv.cc


# Don't update the files from bitkeeper
%::SCCS/s.%
```

There are a number of ways to deploy your new binary. If you plan to extend it, review the information in Chapter 3 on how to write a test case and execute it in a debugger. If you just want to run the binary and see what happens, assuming you already have a regular MySQL installation from the same version as your source, you can just back up your regular *mysqld* binary, replace it with the newly built one, and restart the server.

To see the new storage engine in action, create a comma-delimited file with the base name matching the name of the table and the extension *.csv* (e.g., *t1.csv*), and place it in the directory corresponding to the database you plan to work in. For example, if your datadir is set to */var/lib/mysql* and you want the table to be created in the database test, place the file in the directory */var/lib/mysql/test*. After creating the file, create a table of type OREILLY_CSV with the fields corresponding to those in the file in the appropriate database. You are now ready to run SELECT queries on the table.

The comments in the long examples contain detailed explanations of the finer points of the code. I will add a few comments here on the issues you would need to deal with were you to extend the engine.

To simplify the example, we have made our storage engine read-only; there is no support for updates or delete operations. To add the ability to write, we would need to address the issue of having multiple instances of the handler object for the same table. In our example, this does not present a big problem other than wasting file descriptors. Write access will require us to keep track of the current write position, which could catch us by surprise if another instance of the handler object was used to perform a write. Other storage engines solve this problem by maintaining a cache of shared, low-level table descriptor structures. This also has a nice side effect of using fewer file descriptors. For an example of a CSV storage engine that has write capabilities, take a look at *sql/examples/ha_tina.h* and *sql/examples/ha_tina.cc*.

Our storage engine does not support keys. If you want to add key support, it is highly recommended that you implement the write capability first. Afterward, you can have a lot of fun creating your own B-trees, hashes, and other forms of indexing.

Our engine reads blocks from a file descriptor using calls to my_pread( ), and then parses them. This is not as efficient and convenient as using mmap( ), but it is more robust in case of an I/O error. The example in *sql/examples/ha_tina.cc* uses mmap( ). InnoDB uses regular file I/O. MyISAM uses mmap( ) for compressed tables. In version 5.1, MyISAM has the option to use mmap( ) for regular tables as well.

## CHAPTER 8

Concurrent Access and Locking

A proper locking mechanism is necessary to ensure data consistency when there is a possibility of multiple clients accessing and possibly modifying the same data at the same time. There are three main approaches to solving this problem: table-level locks, page-level locks, and row-level locks. Each approach has its own advantages and disadvantages.

Table-level locks have the simplest logic, which results in fewer bugs and better performance in the area of lock acquisition. Deadlocks can be fairly easily avoided. On the other hand, locking the entire table results in poor performance for applications that do a large number of concurrent reads and writes.

Row-level locks allow high performance at a very high level of concurrency at the cost of greater complexity in the implementation. This results in slower performance for applications that have a low probability of lock contention as well as higher probability of bugs. It is also very difficult to completely avoid deadlocks, and many implementations do deadlock detection instead.

As the granularity of a lock decreases, the amount of memory required to lock the same amount of data generally increases. So does the complexity of the algorithm, and the potential for a deadlock. However, the decrease in the granularity of the lock increases the potential for concurrent access, which can delay the unfortunate application that has to wait for the lock.

The row-level lock has the smallest granularity; the table-level lock has the greatest; and the page-level lock comes in between, offering a compromise.

MyISAM and MEMORY storage engines can only work with table-level locks. InnoDB supports row-level locks, and Berkeley DB supports page-level locks.

When a parser processes a query, it determines somewhat simplistically what type of table locks need to be acquired based on the query type. Once the execution reaches the lock manager, it gives each associated storage engine an opportunity to update the type of lock for each table. Then the table locks are acquired according to a generic storage-engine-independent algorithm. The storage engines that support finer granularity locks request a lock that permits concurrent reads and writes, and then handle the locking issues internally.

The architecture of locking in MySQL is largely a result of its development history. MySQL was originally built with a storage-engine-independent table lock manager and the original storage engines (MyISAM and MEMORY) performed all of the operations under the assumption that the table would not be modified concurrently. In the early days of 3.23, a feature was introduced that changed this assumption. It became possible in MyISAM to concurrently read from a table and insert a new row into it as long as that row was being placed at the end of the datafile. This feature became known as *concurrent insert*.

The introduction of concurrent insert required some changes to the table lock manager but did not alter its basic architecture. Prior to that, the locking algorithm was entirely determined by the query. The newly introduced complication was solved by adding a callback function pointer to the lock structure to check for the availability of concurrent insert. If the pointer is set to 0, or if the callback reports that concurrent insert is not available, the lock gets upgraded to a regular write lock.

Things changed with the arrival of BDB, which supports page-level locks. It introduced the challenge of making sure that the table lock manager would not try to lock the entire table when only one or several rows needed to be locked. Now a simple callback was not enough. Somewhere down the call hierarchy the storage engine now needed to examine the nature of the query and communicate to the table lock manager which tables it did not want locked. The problem was solved by adding the new method handler::store_lock( ), which permits the storage engine to change the types of the locks originally requested by the query parser.

Table Lock Manager

As explained earlier, all queries involving tables of all storage engines go through the table lock manager regardless of the granularity levels of the locks supported by the storage engine. For example, even if row-level locks are supported, a special table lock is acquired that permits concurrent write access. In the source code, all possible lock types are defined in the enum thr_lock_type from *include/thr_lock.h*. Table 8-1 lists and discusses the supported lock types.

Table 8-1. Types of locks in MySQL

Lock type	Description
TL_IGNORE	A special value used in locking requests to communicate that nothing should be done in the lock descriptor structures.
TL_UNLOCK	A special value used in locking requests to communicate that a lock should be released.

Table 8-1. Types of locks in MySQL (continued)

Lock type	Description
TL_READ	A regular read lock.
TL_READ_WITH_SHARED_LOCKS	A higher priority lock used by InnoDB for SELECT ... LOCK IN SHARE MODE.
TL_READ_HIGH_PRIORITY	A high priority read lock used by SELECT HIGH_PRIORITY....
TL_READ_NO_INSERT	A special read lock that does not allow concurrent inserts.
TL_WRITE_ALLOW_WRITE	A special lock used by storage engines that take care of locking on their own. Other threads are allowed to acquire read and write locks while this lock is being held.
TL_WRITE_ALLOW_READ	A special lock for ALTER TABLE. Altering a table involves creating a temporary table with the new structure, populating it with new rows, and then renaming it to the original name. Thus a table can be read while being altered during most of the operation.
TL_WRITE_CONCURRENT_INSERT	The write lock used by concurrent inserts. If this type of lock is already placed on the table, read locks are granted to other threads immediately unless TL_READ_NO_INSERT is requested.
TL_WRITE_DELAYED	A special lock used by INSERT DELAYED....
TL_WRITE_LOW_PRIORITY	A low-priority lock used in UPDATE LOW_PRIORITY... and other queries with the LOW_PRIORITY attribute.
TL_WRITE	A regular write lock.
TL_WRITE_ONLY	An internal value used when aborting old locks during operations that require closing tables.

Table locks are divided into two groups: read locks and write locks. The table lock manager maintains four queues for each table:

- Current read-lock queue (lock->read)
- Pending read-lock queue (lock->read_wait)
- Current write-lock queue (lock->write)
- Pending write-lock queue (lock->write_wait)

Threads that currently hold a read lock are found in the current read-lock queue in the order of lock acquisition. Threads currently waiting for a read lock are found in the pending read-lock queue. The same paradigm applies to the current and pending write-lock queues.

Lock acquisition logic can be found in thr_lock( ) in *mysys/thr_lock.c*.

Read Lock Request

A read lock is always granted as long as there are no current write locks on the table and no higher-priority write locks in the pending write-lock queue. If the lock request can be granted immediately, the corresponding lock descriptor is placed in the current read-lock queue. Otherwise, the lock request enters the pending read-lock queue, and the requesting thread suspends itself to wait for the lock (see wait_for_lock( ) in *mysys/thr_lock.c*).

The requested read and pending write locks are prioritized according to the following rules:

- A TL_WRITE lock in the pending write-lock queue has precedence over all read locks except for TL_READ_HIGH_PRIORITY.
- A request for TL_READ_HIGH_PRIORITY has precedence over any pending write lock.
- All write locks in the pending write-lock queue that are not a TL_WRITE have a lower priority than a read lock.

The presence of a current write lock causes the requesting thread to suspend itself and wait for the lock to become available except in the cases below:

- With the approval of the storage engine, accomplished through the check_status( ) function pointer call in the THR_LOCK descriptor, all read locks except TL_READ_NO_INSERT permit one TL_WRITE_CONCURRENT_INSERT lock.
- TL_WRITE_ALLOW_WRITE permits all read and write locks except TL_WRITE_ONLY.
- TL_WRITE_ALLOW_READ permits all read locks except TL_READ_NO_INSERT.
- TL_WRITE_DELAYED permits all read locks except TL_READ_NO_INSERT.
- TL_WRITE_CONCURRENT_INSERT permits all read locks except TL_READ_NO_INSERT.
- The conflicting write lock belongs to the requesting thread.

Write Lock Request

When a write lock is requested, the table lock manager first checks whether there are any write locks already in the current write-lock queue. If there are none, the pending write-lock queue is checked. If the pending write-lock queue is not empty, the request is placed in the write-lock queue and the thread suspends itself to wait for the lock. Otherwise, with the empty pending write-lock queue, the current read-lock queue is checked. The presence of a current read lock causes the write lock request to wait except in the following cases:

- The requested lock is TL_WRITE_DELAYED.
- The requested lock is TL_WRITE_CONCURRENT_INSERT or TL_WRITE_ALLOW_WRITE and there are no TL_READ_NO_INSERT locks in the current read-lock queue.

If the exceptional requirements are met, the lock request is granted and placed in the current write-lock queue.

If there are locks in the current write queue, the exceptional case of TL_WRITE_ONLY request is handled first. TL_WRITE_ONLY is granted only if there are no current write locks. Otherwise, the request is aborted and an error code is returned to the caller.

With the exceptional case out of the way, the table lock manager can now examine the possibility of coexistence for the requested and the current write lock at the head of the current write-lock queue. The request can be granted without a wait under one of the following circumstances:

- The conflicting write lock in the current write-lock queue is `TL_WRITE_ALLOW_WRITE`; the request is also `TL_WRITE_ALLOW_WRITE`; and the pending write-lock queue is empty.
- The conflicting write lock is being held by the requesting thread.

Storage engine interaction with the table lock manager

The locking mechanism provided by the table lock manager is insufficient for a number of storage engines. MyISAM, InnoDB, NDB, and Berkeley DB storage engines provide some form of an internal locking mechanism.

MyISAM. MyISAM mostly depends on the table lock manager to ensure proper concurrent access. However, there is one exception: a concurrent insert. If the insert operation results in writing the record at the end of the datafile, reading can be done without a lock. In this case, the table lock manager permits one concurrent insert lock and many read locks. The storage engine ensures consistency by remembering the old end of file prior to the start of the concurrent insert, and by not permitting the reads to read past the old end of file until the concurrent insert is complete.

InnoDB. InnoDB asks the table lock manager to defer locking to the storage engine by changing the lock type to `TL_WRITE_ALLOW_WRITE` for write locks. Internally, it implements a complex row-level locking system that includes deadlock detection.

NDB. NDB is a distributed storage engine that also supports row-level locks. It deals with the table locks in a manner similar to InnoDB.

Berkeley DB. Berkeley DB internally supports page-level locks, and thus needs the write locks to become `TL_WRITE_ALLOW_WRITE` just like NDB and InnoDB.

InnoDB Locking

Although InnoDB is not the only storage engine that supports some internal locking mechanism, it is perhaps the most interesting. Being the most stable and mature of all the transactional storage engines in MySQL, it is usually the engine of choice for mission-critical, high-load environments. This section provides a brief overview of InnoDB locking.

Lock types

There are two types of row-level locks: *shared* and *exclusive*. InnoDB supports both.

To support the coexistence of row- and table-level locks, InnoDB also uses so-called intention locks on a table. There are also two types of intention table locks, shared and exclusive.

As the name *intention locks* suggests, it is possible for another transaction to acquire another shared lock if one is holding a shared lock already. However, only one transaction can hold an exclusive lock at any one time.

It is necessary for a transaction to acquire the appropriate intention lock on the table before locking a row in it. Shared row locks are possible after acquiring an exclusive intention lock. However, only an exclusive intention lock allows a transaction to acquire an exclusive row lock.

Record locking

Record or row locking occurs as InnoDB is searching for records requested by the optimizer. What InnoDB actually locks is the index entry, the space before it, and the space after the last record. This method is called *next-key locking*.

The next-key locking is necessary to avoid the *phantom row problem* in transactions. If we did not lock the space before the record, it would be possible for another transaction to insert another record in between. Thus, if we were to run the same query again, we would see the record that was not there the first time we ran the query. This would make it impossible to meet the requirement of the serializable read transaction isolation level.

Dealing with deadlocks

What happens if transaction A locks record R1, and then tries R2, while transaction B simultaneously locks record R2 first, and then tries to lock R1? Row-level locking naturally introduces the problem of deadlocks.

InnoDB has an automatic deadlock detection algorithm. It will usually roll back the last transaction involved in a deadlock. The deadlock detection algorithm fails in some cases; for example, if tables from other storage engines are used, or if some tables were locked with LOCK TABLES. Additionally, some transactions may be considered to be in a virtual deadlock. For example, if a query is written is such a way that it examines several billion records, it may not release its locks for weeks, although from a theoretical point of view it eventually will. For such situations InnoDB uses a lock timeout, which is controlled by the configuration variable innodb_lock_wait_timeout.

Any transaction can potentially be caught in a deadlock. It is important for the application programmer to write code that deals with this possibility. Usually, retrying a rolled-back transaction is sufficient. It is also possible to minimize the chance of a deadlock by careful programming. Accessing records always in the same index order, writing properly optimized queries, and committing transactions frequently are some of the techniques that help prevent potential deadlocks.

## CHAPTER 9

Parser and Optimizer

The MySQL server receives queries in the SQL format. Once a query is received, it first needs to be parsed, which involves translating it from what is essentially a textual format into a combination of internal binary structures that can be easily manipulated by the optimizer.

In this context, when we say *optimizer*, we refer to the server module responsible for creating and executing the plan to retrieve the records requested by the query. The optimizer picks the order in which the tables are joined, the method to read the records (e.g., read from an index or scan the table), as well as which keys to use. Its goal is to deliver the query result in the least amount of time possible.

In this chapter, we'll examine the parser and optimizer in detail.

Parser

MySQL's parser, like many others, consists of two parts: the *lexical scanner* and the *grammar rule module*. The lexical scanner breaks the entire query into tokens (elements that are indivisible, such as column names), while the grammar rule module finds a combination of SQL grammar rules that produce this sequence, and executes the code associated with those rules. In the end, a parse tree is produced, which can now be used by the optimizer.

Unlike some parsers, which translate the textual representation of the query into byte code, MySQL's parser converts it directly into internal interlinked C/C++ structures in the program memory.

For example, imagine the server receives the following query:

```
SELECT count(*),state FROM customer GROUP BY state
```

The lexical scanner examines the stream of query characters, breaks it into tokens, and identifies each token. It finds the following tokens:

- SELECT
- count
- (
- *
-)
- ,
- state
- FROM
- customer
- GROUP
- BY
- state

Each token is given a type—for example, a keyword, a string literal, a number, an operator, or a function name. The grammar rules module matches the stream of tokens against a set of rules, and finds the correct rule, which in this case is the select rule (see *sql/sql_yacc.yy*). It initializes the parse tree structure accordingly, which later leads to the execution of `mysql_select()` from *sql/sql_select.cc*.

The parser has two main objectives, not necessarily listed in the order of importance. First, it must be lightning fast. Many installations of MySQL have to support the load of thousands of queries per second. This would not be possible if parsing alone took even one millisecond. Second, the generated parse tree must provide the information to the optimizer in a way that permits it to access the data efficiently. The optimizer needs quick access to various parts of the `WHERE` clause, table, field, and key lists, `ORDER BY` and `GROUP BY` expressions, subquery structuring, and other data. As difficult as it is to reach those two objectives, the MySQL development team has largely succeeded at the task so far.

Lexical Scanner

Many open source projects use the very popular utility GNU Flex to generate lexical scanners. The programmer only provides a set of guidelines for classifying characters, and Flex produces the C code to do the scanning that can be integrated with the rest of the code.

Unlike them, MySQL has its own lexical scanner to gain both performance and flexibility. A handwritten token identifier can be fine-tuned with optimizations that are not possible with generated code. Additionally, it can also be coded to identify the tokens with context sensitivity.

A very efficient keyword lookup hash is generated by a special utility called *gen_lex_hash* (see *sql/gen_lex_hash.cc*) prior to the compilation of the server, and then compiled with the rest of the code. The generated hash is perfect, meaning there are no collisions. The scanner (see *sql/sql_lex.cc*) tags each token as a keyword, a function name, a number of a particular type, or some other special symbol that has a meaning in the grammar rules.

The list of keywords is found in the array `symbols[]` in *sql/lex.h*. The list of functions is contained in the array `sql_functions[]` in the same file.

Note that there was a change in later releases of 5.1. Most of the built-in functions were moved out of the `sql_functions[]` array into `native_functions_hash`. Now the built-in functions are looked up by the grammar rules module instead of the lexical scanner.

The entry point to the Lexical Scanner is yylex( ) in *sql/sql_lex.cc*. The name of the function has special significance: it needs to be compatible with GNU Bison, the grammar rules module generator, which expects to retrieve the tokens by calling a function with this name.

Grammar Rules Module

This module is often called the parser, but I refer to it as the *grammar rules module* to separate it from the lexical scanner part of the server. Just like in many other open-source projects, the grammar rules module is generated using the parser generator utility GNU Bison. It is recommended that you become familiar with Bison if you plan on modifying MySQL syntax, or just want to understand the parsing process better. You can learn more about it from the Bison manual (published by the Free Software Foundation), also available online at *http://www.gnu.org/software/bison/manual*.

The grammar rules are defined in *sql/sql_yacc.yy*. Bison processes this file to generate *sql/sql_yacc.cc*. The entry point to the grammar rules module is yyparse( ).

Parse Tree

The end result of the parser execution is the parse tree. As you can imagine, the complexity of the SQL syntax requires an equally complex structure that efficiently stores the information needed for executing every possible SQL statement. While it would not be possible within the scope of this chapter, or perhaps even one book, to comprehensively describe all of the elements of the parse tree, I will attempt to provide a brief overview of the essentials.

The parse tree is represented by an object of type LEX, which is a typedef for the structure st_lex from *sql/sql_lex.h*. LEX has many members. We will focus our attention on two of them: enum_sql_command sql_command and SELECT_LEX select_lex.

The sql_command shows what type of SQL query we are executing, whether it is a select, an update, an insert, a delete, or some other query type. The value of this field is used in mysql_execute_command( ) (see *sql/sql_parse.cc*) to direct the execution flow to the function associated with this particular query type.

The select_lex member belongs to the type SELECT_LEX, which is a typedef alias for the class st_select_lex, also defined in *sql/sql_lex.h*. The class has many members containing the information about various query particulars such as the WHERE clause; the table list; the field list; information about optimizer hints; cross-references to other instances of SELECT_LEX for subqueries; the ORDER BY, GROUP BY, and HAVING expressions; and many other details. We will focus on the Item* where member, which is the root node of the WHERE clause tree, because most of the information needed by the optimizer is extracted from the WHERE clause.

The Item class defined in *sql/item.h* is the base class for all other Item_ classes, which represent the nodes of an expression tree. This family of classes covers arithmetic operations (e.g., addition, subtraction, multiplication, division), various SQL functions, logical operators such as AND and OR, references to table fields, subqueries returning one row, and every other element of an SQL expression found in WHERE, HAVING, GROUP BY, ORDER BY, or the field list of a select query.

Item has several methods whose names begin with val_. The rest of the name depends on the type of the return value. For example, if the return value is an integer, the method name is val_int( ). The optimizer later uses the Item contained in the where member of LEX_SELECT to build a filter expression for record combinations it examines. The filter expressions are evaluated via a call to Item::val_int( ). If it returns 1, the record is considered to have met the constraint and is included in the result set; otherwise, it is discarded.

The filter expression is identical to the original WHERE clause if the optimizer is not able to make any improvements to it. Otherwise, it may be rewritten to eliminate unnecessary computations, and permit better use of keys. It may also contain parts of the HAVING clause.

An example of an expression tree for the WHERE clause is shown in Figure 9-1. The expression in the example may have come from the following query:

```
SELECT count(*) FROM customer WHERE lname='Jones' AND age BETWEEN 25 AND 30
```

Optimizer

To help you understand the role of the optimizer, consider the following query:

```
SELECT c.first_name,c.last_name,c.phone,p.name,p.price
FROM customer c,orders o, product p
WHERE c.id = o.
customer_id AND o.product_id = p.id AND o.payment_status = 'FAILED'
ORDER BY c.last_name,c.first_name
```

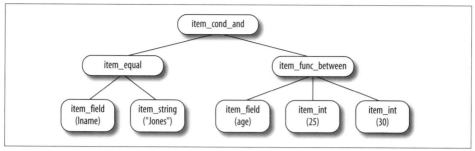

Figure 9-1. Parse tree for typical WHERE clause

We want to retrieve the first name, the last name, the phone number, and the product name and price for all the orders where payment has failed for one reason or another.

A naïve approach would loop through all of the records of customer, and for each record of customer loop through all of the records of order, and then for each combination of the two records loop through each record of product. For each three-record combination, the retrieval process would examine whether the combination matches the WHERE clause, and keep only the combinations that do. Afterward, the retrieval process would sort the matched records and deliver them to the client.

You can see that this approach is not very efficient. Suppose each table has 10,000 records. The optimizer would have to examine 10,000×10,000×10,000 combinations, which is equal to 1 trillion. With a processor capable of examining 1 million records per second, the query would take 1 million seconds, or more than 11 days.

On the other hand, suppose we have keys on customer.id, orders.payment_status, and product.id, and that the keys customer.id and product.id are unique. Since we have a potentially restrictive constraint that could eliminate a lot of records on orders.payment_status, it makes sense to start by finding all of the matching records from orders using the payment_status key. For each of those records we retrieve a matching record out of customer using the key on its id column, and also a matching record out of product using the key on its id column. We now have to examine as many record combinations as there are records in orders that have the payment_status value set to 'FAILED'. Even if it happens to be every record in our 10,000 record table, we are now examining only 10,000 record combinations.

Although the use of keys did increase the amount of time needed to create each combination, this overhead in the end was worthwhile. According to the standard MySQL optimizer cost estimate model, each key access takes three times as long for the same table as the scan access. Therefore, while in the naïve approach our cost of creating a record combination was 1+1+1=3, the improved approach for the same operation costs 3+3+3=9. Neglecting the time for examining the combination, we can now process only 333,333 combinations per second, instead of 1 million. However, we now need to process no more than 10,000 of them, and our query should take less than 0.03 seconds, down from 11 days.

Thus it becomes apparent that the optimizer must not only figure out a way to deliver the records requested by a query but also do it in a way that is optimal—or at least be able to deliver satisfactory performance. This is a much bigger challenge than just delivering the results, which therefore justifies the name of *optimizer* for this module.

MySQL's optimizer has several important tasks:

- Determine which keys can be used to retrieve the records from tables, and choose the best one for each table.
- For each table, decide whether a table scan is better than reading on a key. If there are a lot of records that match the key value, the advantages of the key are reduced and the table scan becomes faster.
- Determine the order in which tables should be joined when more than one table is present in the query.
- Rewrite the WHERE clause to eliminate dead code, reducing the unnecessary computations and changing the constraints whenever possible to open the way for using keys.
- Eliminate unused tables from the join.
- Determine whether keys can be used for ORDER BY and GROUP BY.
- Attempt to replace an outer join with an inner join.
- Attempt to simplify subqueries, as well as determine to what extent their results can be cached.
- Merge views (expand the view reference as a macro).

Basics of the Optimizer Algorithm

In MySQL optimizer terminology, every query is a set of joins. The term *join* is used here more broadly than in SQL commands. A query on only one table is a degenerate join. While we normally do not think of reading records from one table as a join, the same structures and algorithms used with conventional joins work perfectly to resolve the query with only one table.

Simple queries without subqueries or UNION consist of only one join. Queries with subqueries that cannot be optimized, as well as UNION queries, will involve more than one join. Some subqueries may require what can be called a recursive join: while one join is being performed, the optimizer needs to execute a subquery for each row of the join, which results in its own join. Nevertheless, a join is the basic unit of the optimizer's work. In the source code, a join is connected to the join descriptor class JOIN defined in *sql/sql_select.h*. Each join is started by calling mysql_select() from *sql/sql_select.cc*.

The procedure described in this section thus falls into two parts: first the optimizer determines the best join order, then it does a nested loop to accomplish the join.

A join is essentially a Cartesian product of table subsets. Each subset is obtained by reading records from the table based on a single key value, a key range (or a set of key ranges), a full index scan, or a full table scan. The records are then eliminated, if necessary, using the constraints from the WHERE clause.

The optimizer selects the record access methods and puts the tables in an order it believes would minimize the cost, which is more often than not in proportion to the total number of record combinations it would have to examine. The problem of query optimization can be broken down into two parts: first, for a given join order, find the best access paths for each table, and second, once you have that ability, find the best join order, or at least a reasonably good one, in a short amount of time.

The first problem is solved by best_access_path( ) in *sql/sql_select.cc*. The access path defines whether the optimizer is going to read on a key, scan the table (ALL), or scan the key (index). If a key read is performed, it defines how that key is going to be used—for example, reading one record based on one value (eq_ref), possibly more than one record based on one value (ref), or a range of values (range). best_access_ path( ) is called with the precomputed access path for a partial plan (join order). Therefore, the best access path has already been computed for the old partial plan, and the optimizer only needs to compute it for the newly added table. The selection and order of the tables in the old partial plan greatly affect the best access path for the new table. For example, in one case, the old tables may contain a column whose value can be used to perform a key read, while in another case that possibility may not exist, necessitating a full scan for the new table.

The remaining problem of finding the best join order can be solved in two ways: the exhaustive search (find_best( ) in *sql/sql_select.cc*), and the greedy search (greedy_ search( ) in *sql/sql_select.cc*). The exhaustive search examines all of the possible combinations of tables and finds the best plan. However, it may take a very long time. The greedy search works as follows: first try all possible combinations of optimizer_ search_depth tables (optimizer_search_depth is a server configuration variable) out of n tables in the query, and find the best one. Take the first table out of the resulting set, and place it first in the partial join order. Then examine all possible combinations of optimizer_search_depth tables out of the remaining $n-1$ tables. For each tested combination, append it to the existing partial plan and evaluate the cost. Pick the combination with the lowest cost, and place the first table in that combination next in the partial plan. Repeat until the cardinality of the set of the remaining tables reaches optimizer_search_depth.

Both the exhaustive and the greedy search have the optimization to discontinue the pursuit of the path if the current partial combination has a cost that exceeds the best cost found so far. Therefore, while in theory the exhaustive search can examine as many as $n!$ combinations, and the greedy search as many as optimizer_search_depth! * (n - optimizer_search_depth) combinations, in practice those numbers are very often substantially reduced.

Thus while the greedy search may not always find the best plan, it has a controlled complexity, and will have the performance advantage over the exhaustive search. Indeed, it does not matter if the optimizer finds the best plan if the gain in the execution time is offset by the loss in the discovery time.

For more details, see make_join_statistics( ), choose_plan( ), optimize_key_use( ), best_access_path( ), get_best_combination( ), create_ref_for_key( ), find_best( ), and greedy_search( ) in *sql/sql_select.cc*.

 Prior to version 5.0, only the exhaustive search was available. Version 5.0 implemented the greedy search.

After the join order has been determined, the optimizer begins to execute the join. The join is performed via a sequence of nested loops, starting from the first table. For each record of the first table, the optimizer loops through the second to create combinations. For each record in the second table, in turn, the optimizer loops through each record of the third, and so on and so forth, creating a record combination for each iteration of the innermost loop.

The combination is then compared against the WHERE clause of the query—or more precisely, the optimized filter expression generated from the original WHERE clause. For example, if the WHERE clause is lname='Johnson' and age=31+1, the filter expression becomes lname='Johnson' and age=32. You may wonder why anybody would ever write such a constraint in its unoptimized form. In many applications queries are frequently generated via complex business logic algorithms, which often produce unoptimized queries a human would never write. Additionally, query rewriting may produce such a query when a column reference gets replaced with a constant. Thus, trivial optimizations like the one discussed here often lead to significant speed gains.

Note that expressions in WHERE are evaluated as early as possible; e.g., if some condition in WHERE refers only to the first table, it is evaluated after reading a row from the first table and before joining it to the second table (see make_cond_for_table( ) in *sql_select.cc*).

The matched records are passed to the send_data( ) method of the result processing object associated with the join. The resultant processing object may send the records to the client, write them to a file or a temporary table, or pass them on somewhere else for further processing. The result processing object type is a derivative of the select_result class (see *sql/sql_class.h* and *sql/sql_class.cc*).

Using EXPLAIN to Understand the Optimizer

The MySQL EXPLAIN command tells the optimizer to show its *query plan*. A query plan describes what the optimizer is going to do to solve the query. For example, start with the table orders; read records on key payment_status; for each record of orders look up a record in customer on key id; for each (order,customer) combination look up a corresponding record in product using key id; use the produced (order, customer, product) combination to update a temporary summary table; and when finished, iterate through the temporary table retrieving the results of GROUP BY.

Much can be learned by studying the output of EXPLAIN on a query. EXPLAIN shows the order of the tables in a join, which keys can in theory be used, which keys are actually used and in what way, whether some records are excluded early using the WHERE clause constraints, the estimated size of each join subset, whether temporary tables are used, whether the records are read in the key order already or additional sorting is required for ORDER BY, and other information relevant to the optimization of the query.

Let's begin by looking at an example of EXPLAIN. Suppose we have the following query:

```
SELECT count(*) FROM orders o, customer c
WHERE o.customer_id = c.id AND c.state = 'UT'
```

To understand the query plan, execute the following in the MySQL command-line client:

```
EXPLAIN SELECT count(*) FROM orders o, customer c
WHERE o.customer_id = c.id AND c.state = 'UT' \G
```

The purpose of the \G switch at the end of the query is to request that the result set be displayed vertically. The output of EXPLAIN contains a lot of columns, which often makes the default mode of horizontal output unreadable.

The EXPLAIN produces the following output:

```
 1 *************************** 1. row ***********************
 2             id: 1
 3    select_type: SIMPLE
 4          table: c
 5           type: ref
 6  possible_keys: PRIMARY,state
 7            key: state
 8        key_len: 2
 9            ref: const
10           rows: 12
11          Extra: Using where
12 *************************** 2. row ***********************
13             id: 1
14    select_type: SIMPLE
15          table: o
16           type: ref
17  possible_keys: customer_id
18            key: customer_id
19        key_len: 4
20            ref: book.c.id
21           rows: 5
22          Extra: Using index
```

The output on line 4 tells us that the optimizer will first examine the customer table. It has the option to read either on the PRIMARY or the state key (line 6), and chooses state (line 7). The state key will be queried by supplying one key value, but the result may contain more than one record (line 5). The optimizer will use the first 2 bytes of the key, which in this case is the entire key (line 8). The key value used is a constant supplied directly in the WHERE clause or obtained some other way as opposed to the value of some other column, which may vary (line 9). The optimizer estimates that the key lookup will match 12 records (line 10). The records retrieved from this table will be checked to see whether they match the WHERE clause (line 11).

Line 15 reveals that the second table in the join is orders. Only one key can be used: customer_id (line 17), and that key does get used (line 18). The first 4 bytes of the key are used (line 19), which in this case is the entire key. Similar to the key access method in the customer table for the state key, the customer_id key will be queried by supplying one key value, and the result may contain more than one record (line 16). However, the value of the key this time is not a constant anymore. It is taken from the field id of the currently processed record of customer (line 20). It will vary as the optimizer retrieves different records of customer. Note that this optimization strategy is possible only if customer is placed before orders in the join order. Thus we say that orders depends on customer.

The optimizer estimates that on average for every record combination of the tables preceding the join order (in this case it is just one table, customer), it will have to examine five records in the orders table (line 21). Because the optimizer needs only the value of customer_id, it is sufficient to read only the value of the key without also retrieving the whole record (line 22).

Why did the optimizer choose to do what it did in this example? To help you understand, we'll force it to choose a different query plan:

```
EXPLAIN  SELECT count(*) FROM orders o STRAIGHT_JOIN customer c
WHERE o.customer_id = c.id AND c.state = 'UT' \G
```

The STRAIGHT_JOIN directive tells the optimizer that the orders table must come before the customer table in all of the possible join orders it may consider. In this case the STRAIGHT_JOIN instruction leaves only one possible combination: first orders, then customer. EXPLAIN produces the following:

```
1  *********************** 1. row ***********************
2             id: 1
3    select_type: SIMPLE
4          table: o
5           type: index
6  possible_keys: customer_id
7            key: customer_id
8        key_len: 4
9            ref: NULL
10          rows: 19566
11         Extra: Using index
```

```
12 ************************ 2. row ************************
13            id: 1
14   select_type: SIMPLE
15         table: c
16          type: eq_ref
17 possible_keys: PRIMARY,state
18           key: PRIMARY
19       key_len: 4
20           ref: book.o.customer_id
21          rows: 1
22         Extra: Using where
```

The optimizer scans the customer_id index in the orders table (lines 5 and 7) and estimates it will match 19,566 records (line 10). For each matched record in the orders table, a corresponding record in the customer table is looked up using the primary key (line 18), in which case only one match per given value is possible (line 16). Only one match should indeed be expected since a primary key by definition has to be unique. The value of the customer_id read previously from the orders table is used for the key lookup (line 20).

Why was the first plan better than this one? The optimizer chooses the plan that has the minimum cost, which it estimates (to a great extent) in proportion to the total number of record combinations it would have to examine. The estimate of the total number of record combinations is computed as a product of the estimates of the average number of records that would be retrieved from each table (the rows field of the EXPLAIN output). Thus, according to the estimates, the original plan would examine $12 \times 4 = 48$ combinations, while the alternative examines many more: $19,566 \times 1 = 19,566$!

What else could the optimizer have done differently? Due to the nature of the WHERE clause, there are two possible keys to use in the customer table: the primary key and the state key. Let us try to make the optimizer use the original join order but use the primary key instead:

```
EXPLAIN  SELECT count(*) FROM customer c FORCE KEY(PRIMARY) STRAIGHT_JOIN orders o
WHERE o.customer_id = c.id AND c.state = 'UT' \G
```

The EXPLAIN produces:

```
1 ************************ 1. row ************************
2            id: 1
3   select_type: SIMPLE
4         table: c
5          type: ALL
6 possible_keys: PRIMARY
7           key: NULL
8       key_len: NULL
9           ref: NULL
10         rows: 3913
11        Extra: Using where
12 ************************ 2. row ************************
13            id: 1
14   select_type: SIMPLE
15         table: o
```

```
16          type: ref
17 possible_keys: customer_id
18           key: customer_id
19       key_len: 4
20           ref: book.c.id
21          rows: 5
22         Extra: Using index
```

The optimizer, forced to use only the primary key, decided it was not worth it and preferred to scan the whole table (line 5). Indeed, not having a reference value for the primary key required a full key traversal. Had it been possible to get everything needed for
the join and the WHERE clause to match from the key without accessing the datafile, the
optimizer would have used the key. However, in order to check the state='UT' constraint the optimizer needs to read the value of the state field, which is not a part of
the primary key. Therefore, the entire record has to be fetched, which makes reading
on a key slower than scanning the whole table. The total number of record combinations is $3,913 \times 5 = 19,565$, which is much greater than the 48 in the original plan!

Understanding the output of EXPLAIN

As you have seen in the previous examples, EXPLAIN produces a set of rows. Each row
describes a table participating in a join and shows how the records are going to be
retrieved from that table. The order of rows corresponds to the join order in the algorithm. It also shows the order of the queries, which is meaningful only if there is
more than one query involved (for example, in a query with subqueries).

The output of EXPLAIN is in essence a human-readable dump of the JOIN class (see *sql/
sql_select.h*), which serves as the query plan descriptor. Table 9-1 defines the relationships between the EXPLAIN fields and corresponding elements of the source code.

Table 9-1. Relationship between EXPLAIN and elements of the source code

EXPLAIN field	Description	Source code element
id	Query ID. Meaningful only when subqueries are used.	select_lex->select_number
select_type	Indicates what happens with the result set retrieved from the table. A join not involving subqueries or UNION will have this value set to simple. See the upcoming section "Select types" for details.	select_lex->type
table	The alias the table is referenced by in the query. If no alias is used, the real name of this table.	For regular (nonderived) tables, join_tab[k-1].table->alias, where k is the number of the table in the join order. For derived tables, join_tab[k-1].table-> derived_select_number.
type	The method used for retrieving the records from the table. See the upcoming section "Record access types" for details.	join_tab[k-1].type, where k is the number of the table in the join order.
possible_keys	A list of keys that can be used in conjunction with the WHERE clause to retrieve the records from this table.	join_tab[k-1].keys, where k is the number of the table in the join order.

Table 9-1. Relationship between EXPLAIN and elements of the source code (continued)

EXPLAIN field	Description	Source code element
key	The name of the key used for retrieving the records. When `index_merge` optimization is used, contains a list of keys.	If the key is used to look up one or more records based on one value of the key or its prefix, the zero-based index number of the key is contained in `join_tab[k-1]. ref.key`. If the index is being scanned, the key number is found in `join_ tab[k-1].index`. If a range optimization is performed, the key number is found in `join_tab[k-1].select-> quick->index`. The key definitions are stored in an array of KEY structures starting at `join_tab[k-1].table-> key_info`. The name of the key is stored in the name member of the KEY structure.
key_len	The length of the key used in a query. This does not have to be the full length of the key—it is possible to use only a key prefix.	See the explanation for the key field on how to locate the key definition structure. The length of the key being used is the `key_ length` member of the KEY structure.
ref	A list of fields from other tables whose values are involved in an index lookup in this table.	`join_tab[k-1].ref.key_copy`
rows	Average estimated number of records in this table to be retrieved on each join iteration.	`join_tab[k-1].best_positions. records_read`
Extra	Additional comments on the optimization strategy. See the section "Extra field" for details.	Collected from a number of the join descriptor data members.

Select types

This section describes the types of selects that can be indicated by the `select_type` field in the output of the EXPLAIN command.

SIMPLE

Select that does not use UNION or subqueries. Example:

```
SELECT count(*) FROM customer c, orders o WHERE c.id = o.customer_id AND c.state =
'CA'
```

PRIMARY

The outermost select or the first select of a union. In the following example, the select from the orders table is labeled PRIMARY. Example:

```
SELECT * FROM orders WHERE customer_id IN (SELECT id FROM customer WHERE state =
'CA')
```

UNION

Select that is a part of a union and does not come first in the query. In the following example, SELECT id FROM customer WHERE state = 'AZ' is labeled UNION, while SELECT id FROM customer WHERE state = 'NV' is PRIMARY.

```
SELECT id FROM customer WHERE state = 'NV' UNION SELECT id FROM customer WHERE
state = 'AZ'
```

DEPENDENT UNION

Same as the UNION, except in a dependent subquery. A subquery is considered dependent on the outer select if the optimizer thinks it could possibly use the information that will change for each row of the outer select. This, unfortunately, means that the optimizer will rerun the subquery for each row of the outer select. Example:

```
SELECT * FROM orders WHERE customer_id IN (SELECT id FROM customer WHERE state =
'NV' UNION SELECT id FROM customer WHERE state = 'AZ')
```

UNION RESULT

Result of a union. Example:

```
SELECT id FROM customer WHERE state = 'NV' UNION SELECT id FROM customer WHERE
state = 'AZ'
```

SUBQUERY

A nondependent subquery. The optimizer sees that it only needs to run it once. Example:

```
SELECT * FROM orders WHERE customer_id = (SELECT id FROM customer WHERE
fname='Paul' AND lname='Jones')
```

DEPENDENT SUBQUERY

A dependent subquery. The optimizer thinks it needs to run it once for every row of the outer query. Note that even though it may not be necessary to do so, the optimizer may merely fail to notice the independence of the subquery. This happens in the following example:

```
SELECT * FROM orders WHERE customer_id IN (SELECT id FROM customer WHERE state =
'NV')
```

DERIVED

A select to create a derived table. A table is called *derived* if it is generated from the result set of another query. In the SQL standard such tables are called "subquery in the FROM clause." In the following example, the wy table is derived:

```
SELECT count(*) FROM orders,(SELECT id FROM customer WHERE state='WY') wy WHERE
wy.id = orders.customer_id
```

Record access types

This section describes the types of selects that can be indicated by the select_type field in the output of the EXPLAIN command.

system

A special case when the table has only one record.

const

The table has at most one matching row, which is read only once at the start of the query. This happens when the table has a unique key and the WHERE clause supplies a value for it. In the following example, we assume that id is a unique key in customer:

```
SELECT * FROM customer WHERE id = 32
```

eq_ref

Similar to const, except the value is not a fixed constant but instead is taken from another table. Only one record is retrieved. Therefore, the key has to be unique. In the following example, eq_ref is used to look up the values of customer.id on the primary key using the values of order.customer_id:

```
SELECT DISTINCT customer.id FROM customer,orders WHERE customer.id =
orders.customer_id AND orders.payment_status = 'FAILED'
```

ref

Similar to eq_ref and const in that only one value is used for key lookup. However, it is possible to retrieve more than one record. This happens either when the key is not unique, or when only the prefix of the key is available. For example:

```
SELECT count(*) FROM customer WHERE last_name = 'Johnson'
```

ALL

Full table scan. Happens when no key constraint can be used, and the optimizer needs to read columns that are not covered by an index. In the following example, we assume that customer does not have a key that spans first_name, last_name, and state:

```
SELECT first_name,last_name,state WHERE first_name='James' AND
last_name='Johnson' AND state='IN'
```

range

The records will be read via an index using one or more range constraints. This record access method is possible only for range-capable keys. B-tree keys are range capable, while hash keys are not. In the following example, we assume customer has a range-capable key on last_name:

```
SELECT last_name,first_name FROM customer WHERE last_name > 'B' AND last_name < 'P'
```

index

The whole index will be scanned. This is not an efficient use of the index and means the user did not employ the index well. Nevertheless, it is the best the optimizer can do with the query the user provided. There were no constraints on the index values, which would have reduced the number of values to read. While using the whole index, the scan will access only the parts of the record covered by the index. This kind of index scan can be more efficient than the full table scan if the index covers only a small part of the entire record. In the following example, we assume that customer has a key spanning last_name:

```
SELECT last_name FROM customer
```

fulltext

The optimizer uses a full-text matching method to retrieve records. This is possible only for full-text capable keys, which are currently implemented only in the MyISAM storage engine. In the following example, we assume that customer has a full-text key on description:

```
SELECT * FROM customer WHERE MATCH(description) AGAINST ('pays bills')
```

`ref_or_null`

Similar to `ref` except that a search for `NULL` values is additionally performed. In the following example,we assume that `last_name` is a key that can contain `NULL` values:

```
SELECT * FROM customer WHERE last_name = 'Johnson' OR last_name IS NULL
```

`unique_subquery`

Used to optimize `IN` with a subquery when the subquery selects unique key values. In the following example, we assume that `id` is a unique key in `customer`:

```
SELECT * FROM orders WHERE customer_id IN (SELECT id FROM customer WHERE
lname='Johnson')
```

`index_subquery`

Similar to `unique_subquery`, except that the index is not unique. In the following example, we assume that `customer_id` is a non-unique key in `orders`:

```
SELECT * FROM customer WHERE id IN (SELECT customer_id FROM orders WHERE
product_id = 3)
```

`index_merge`

Two keys are being used separately, and the results are being merged. In the following example, we assume that the `product` table has a key on `price` and another key on `name`:

```
SELECT * FROM product WHERE name='AMD Laptop' OR price=1300.00
```

Extra field

This section describes the strings that can appear in the `Extra` field in the output of the `EXPLAIN` command.

`Using where`

The `WHERE` clause was evaluated to eliminate some records. This is necessary unless the optimizer can detect that all of the records it is going to read on a key will automatically satisfy the `WHERE` clause. In the following example, we assume that `price` is not a key in `product` and we see `Using where`:

```
SELECT * FROM product WHERE price=1300.00
```

Note that if we were to add a key on `price`, `Using where` disappears. The optimizer has requested a read on the price key of all the records with the price equal to 1300.00. This automatically satisfies the `WHERE` clause.

`Using index`

The optimizer noticed that all of the columns it needed are contained in a key. Therefore, it decided to scan just the key instead of the entire data. In the following example, we assume that `name` is a key in `product`:

```
SELECT name FROM product WHERE name LIKE '%laptop%'
```

Using index for group-by

The optimizer is able to optimize GROUP BY or DISTINCT by reading only the first and/or the last record on a key for each distinct value. With GROUP BY this is possible only if there are no aggregate functions except MIN( ) and MAX( ); the query involves one table; all of the needed columns are covered by the index the optimizer has chosen; and the order of the columns in the GROUP BY works with the WHERE clause and/or the columns of MIN( )/MAX( ) in such a way that the answer can be given without having to look at all of the records of each distinct key value. In the following example, we assume that product has a key on (name,price):

```
SELECT name,MAX(price),MIN(price) FROM product GROUP BY name
```

Note that if we replace MAX(price) with COUNT(*), the same index is used, but the Extra column now says Using index. The query is optimized in a different way because COUNT(*) cannot be done without looking at all of the values in the index. It needs to know how many there are, and the storage engine interface currently does not provide a way for the optimizer to ask or for the storage engine to communicate even if the value is being stored by the storage engine.

Using filesort

The optimizer was asked to retrieve the records in sorted order (ORDER BY), but its record access method does not guarantee it. Therefore, post-sorting is required. The term *filesort* refers to the MySQL sorting algorithm, which performs a radix or quick sort on small chunks in the memory. If the entire record set to be sorted does not fit into the sort buffer, the temporary results get stored in a file. Then the merge step is performed on all chunks. In the following example, we assume that product does not have a key on price:

```
SELECT * FROM product WHERE price < 1000.00 AND name LIKE 'AMD%' ORDER BY price
```

Note that if we add a key on price, the Using filesort message disappears. The optimizer is able to use the key, and it will routinely retrieve the records in the key order, thus eliminating the need for post-sorting.

Using temporary

The optimizer needs to create a temporary table to store an intermediate result. For example, if a GROUP BY is done on a nonkey column, the optimizer creates a temporary table with a unique key consisting of the GROUP BY expression. For each record of the regular result set (omitting GROUP BY), an attempt is made to insert it into the temporary table. If the insert fails due to the unique constraint violation, the existing record is updated appropriately. Once the temporary table has been populated, the result set is sorted and returned to the client. In the following example, we assume that product does not have a key on name:

```
SELECT name,COUNT(*) FROM product GROUP BY name
```

If we add a key on name, the need for using the temporary table disappears. GROUP BY can now be done by traversing the key.

Distinct

The optimizer is able to eliminate records in a join, which is made possible by the use of the DISTINCT keyword in the query. In the example, we assume that orders has a key on product_id, that id is a unique key in product, and that the optimizer puts orders first in the join order:

```
SELECT DISTINCT orders.product_id FROM orders,product WHERE orders.product_id =
product.id AND product.name LIKE '%AMD%' AND orders.customer_id = 1
```

Indeed, while there might be a number of records in orders that match the orders part of the WHERE clause, it is sufficient to check the product part of the WHERE clause only for each distinct value of product_id. Due to the nature of the query, any two records with the same product_id in orders will have identical product parts. Therefore, since the query asked only for distinct values of the product_id, once the optimizer finds a unique value of product_id in orders that matches the WHERE clause, it does not have to examine the rest of the records with the similar value of the key, and it can move on to the next unique value in the index instead.

Not exists

A special optimization is used during a left join to eliminate record combinations. If a join is done on a column that is defined with the NOT NULL attribute in the second table, and the WHERE clause requires that the column be NULL, the only way this is possible is if the matching value of the first table column does not exist in the second table. In the following example, we assume that orders.product_id is defined as NOT NULL:

```
SELECT product.id FROM product LEFT JOIN orders ON product.id = orders.product_id
WHERE orders.product_id IS NULL
```

Indeed, it is not possible for orders.product_id to be NULL unless it is the special record inserted into the left join product to mark that the ON clause failed to match. Thus, even if only one ON clause match is discovered for a record in product, the optimizer can safely move on to the next record in product without examining all the other combinations of that record with the records in orders.

range checked for each record: (index map: N)

The optimizer did not find an index it is going to use all the time for the given table. However, as the join progresses, certain record combinations in the preceding tables (in the join order) may permit either a range or index merge optimization on some keys. Thus, the optimizer for each record combination in the preceding tables checks to determine which index is best to use. In the example, we assume that w2 has two indexes, one on s and one on s1:

```
SELECT count(*) FROM w1,w2 WHERE  w2.s > w1.s AND w2.s1 < w1.s
```

In some cases, the optimizer may choose to use the index on s, while other times it may choose to use the one on s1. If the range is not very restrictive, the optimizer may even choose to scan w2 instead. The choice depends on the value of w1.s. The value of N in index map: N is a hexadecimal (in version 5.0) expression of the bitmap of the keys that are being considered in this optimization.

This optimization is expensive and fairly uncommon. It is more of an attempt to rescue a sinking ship: a query that, without it, would be a complete performance disaster. If the optimizer chooses it, it should be considered an invitation to write a better query.

Using union( )

This comment appears in the case of the index_merge access method. Two or more keys are being used to retrieve the records, and the correct result can be obtained via a sorted list merge of the results. In other words, the constraints for each key are such that there is no need to sort the records from each index by row ID: each key naturally produces a sorted list. Natural sorted order by row ID is guaranteed when all of the parts of a key are known, or when the key is a clustered primary key (in InnoDB and BDB tables).

In the following example, we assume that customer has a key on state and a key on (lname,fname):

```
SELECT COUNT(state) FROM customer WHERE (lname = 'Jones' AND fname='John') OR
(state = 'UT')
```

Using sort_union( )

This comment appears in the case of the index_merge access method. Two or more keys are being used to retrieve the records, but the optimizer is not sure that each key will naturally produce a sorted list. Thus, to eliminate the duplicate rows, additional processing is required.

In the example, customer table has a key on state and on (lname,fname). It does not have a key on lname:

```
SELECT COUNT(*) FROM customer WHERE (lname = 'Jones') OR (state = 'UT')
```

Since there is no key on lname, the (lname,fname) key has to be used. The optimizer does not have a constraint that covers all of its parts, and the records therefore are not necessarily ordered by row ID.

Using intersect( )

This comment appears in the case of the index_merge access method. Two or more keys are being used to retrieve the records, and the correct result can be obtained via a sorted list intersection of the results. This optimization is very similar to Using union( ) except that the result sets are intersected (AND operation) instead of combined (OR operation).

In the following example, we assume that customer has a key on state and a key on (lname,fname):

```
SELECT COUNT(state) FROM customer WHERE (lname = 'Jones' AND fname='John') AND
(state = 'UT')
```

Using where with pushed condition

Prior to the introduction of NDB tables, the optimizer operated under the assumption that reading a record from a table either on a key or via a scan would, in the worst case scenario, have to access a local disk. Even if this was not the case, there was not much else it could do; none of the existing storage engines had the ability to prefilter the records. With the introduction of NDB, the ability to prefilter became a necessity. NDB table access often results in network I/O. Thus, the performance could be optimized a great deal if the storage engine was smart enough to communicate a filtering constraint to a remote node.

If the storage engine supports it (currently only NDB does), the optimizer can push a filtering constraint onto the condition stack of the storage engine instance. In turn, the storage engine can use this additional information to optimize record retrieval. In the example, table t is of type NDB and does not have a key on column n:

```
SELECT * FROM t WHERE n=5
```

Range Optimizer

MySQL developers have put a lot of effort into optimizing queries with constraints restricting the values of a key to a particular range. There is a module that is dedicated to this particular purpose, which is called the *range optimizer*. The source code of the range optimizer is found in *sql/opt_range.h* and *sql/opt_range.cc* with the entry point in SQL_SELECT::test_quick_select().

The range optimizer supports the following optimizations.

Range

Regular range optimization occurs when the range of the key values is known for only one key in the ascending key order. Example:

```
SELECT * FROM t WHERE key1 > 'a' AND key1 < 'b'
```

Regular range optimization can handle various key value combinations used in combination with Boolean operators. It can also handle a variety of range constraint operators. In the following example, table t1 has a key on (c1,c2):

```
SELECT * FROM t1 WHERE (c1 IN(5,6) AND c2 IN(1,2)) OR
(c1 = 15 AND c2 BETWEEN 1 AND 2) OR (c1 BETWEEN 20 AND 30)
```

The range optimizer will search the following set of intervals for the key (c1,c2):

$(1,2)–(1,2)$; $(1,6)–(1,6)$; $(2,2)–(2,2)$; $(2,6)–(2,6)$; $(15,1)–(15,2)$; $(20,-inf)–(30,+inf)$

Note the capability to convert a constant into a degenerate interval.

This type of optimization is done by the class QUICK_RANGE_SELECT.

There is a special case of the range optimization when spatial keys are used. Those are handled by a QUICK_RANGE_SELECT_GEOM, which is a superclass of QUICK_RANGE_SELECT.

Index_merge

This is used when range constraints are available for more than one key, but the result does not come in a sorted order, thus requiring additional processing. See the explanation of Using sort_union( ) in the earlier section, "Extra field," for more details.

Handled by the class QUICK_INDEX_MERGE_SELECT.

Range_desc

Similar to Range, except the records are read in the descending key order. Handled by the class QUICK_SELECT_DESC.

Fulltext

Implements full-text key matching constraints. Handled by the class FT_SELECT. Although there are no ranges in the full-text search, the code organization made the range optimizer the most natural fit for the full-text optimization code.

ROR_intersect

Used when range constraints are available for more than one key, the result set comes naturally in a sorted order in each key, and the final result is obtained via the intersection of the results on each key. See the explanation of Using intersect( ) in the earlier section, "Extra field." Handled by the class QUICK_ROR_INTERSECT_SELECT.

ROR_union

Used when range constraints are available for more than one key, the result set naturally comes in a sorted order in each key, and the final result is obtained via the union of the results on each key. See the explanation of Using union( ) in the earlier section, "Extra field." Handled by the class QUICK_ROR_UNION_SELECT.

Group_min_max

Handles some special cases of MIN( )/MAX( ) functions with a GROUP BY when several keys have range constraints. Handled by the class QUICK_GROUP_MIN_MAX_SELECT.

Subquery Optimization

Currently, MySQL performs relatively few optimizations of subqueries. If it notices that a subquery would return only one record for each evaluation, it evaluates the query and replaces the whole subquery with a constant. It also attempts some rather minor rewriting of subqueries in special cases. Other important optimizations are still on the to-do list and are so far scheduled for version 5.2:

- Ability to cache the results of a subquery returning multiple records, and use them instead of executing the subquery for each record combination.
- Ability to create and use appropriate keys in the temporary tables that store the result of the FROM clause subqueries.
- Ability to create and use appropriate keys in the temporary tables storing the result of subqueries from the WHERE clause.
- Support for dependent FROM clause subqueries.
- Ability to rewrite the join order during subquery optimization.
- Ability to modify the table with UPDATE/INSERT/DELETE using a subquery involving the same table.

The MySQL subquery optimizer at this point is very much a work in progress.

Core Optimizer Classes and Structures

The key structures and classes used by the optimizer are defined in *sql/sql_select.h*. If you are interested in getting to know the optimizer internals, you should also become familiar with the structures and classes from *sql/opt_range.h*. We will discuss the ones of the most critical importance.

JOIN

As we have mentioned already, every SELECT query in MySQL is considered a join. If only one table is referenced, it is treated as a special case of one-table join. Thus, the key class that describes the query plan for a SELECT query is called JOIN. You can find its definition in *sql/sql_select.h*. Table 9-2 describes its most significant data members and methods.

Table 9-2. Most significant members of JOIN class

Definition	Description
JOIN_TAB* join_tab	An array of JOIN_TAB descriptors for this query plan. See the section "JOIN_TAB" that follows.
TABLE** table	An array of table descriptors for this join.
uint tables	Number of tables participating in the join. Also the cardinality of the join_tab array.
uint const_tables	Number of constant tables. A table is considered constant if it contains at most one record, or if at most one record match is possible during a key lookup (the key is either primary or unique).
bool do_send_rows	A flag indicating whether the results of this SELECT should be sent to the client.
table_map const_table_map	A bit mask showing which tables are constant.
ha_rows examined_rows	Total number of records examined so far.

Table 9-2. Most significant members of JOIN class (continued)

Definition	Description
`POSITION positions[MAX_TABLES+1]`	Temporary storage array of table positions used for calculating the best join order.
`POSITION best_positions [MAX_TABLES+1]`	Keeps track of the currently known best join order during the computation of best join order.
`double best_read`	A relative cost metric of the join operation defined by `best_ positions`.
`List<Item> *fields`	A list of columns in the `SELECT` statement.
`THD *thd`	MySQL thread descriptor.
`Item *having`	The `HAVING` expression tree.
`SELECT_LEX_UNIT *unit`	Points to the current select lex unit. A select lex unit is either a single `SELECT` or a union of `SELECT` statements.
`select_result *result`	Result processing handler. Depending on its type, the result could be sent to a client, to a file, written to another table, or be stored in memory for further processing.
`ORDER *order`	The `ORDER BY` expression tree.
`ORDER *group_list`	The `GROUP BY` expression tree.
`bool optimized`	A flag to avoid executing the optimizer twice.
`JOIN(THD *thd_arg, List<Item> &fields_arg, ulonglong select_options_ arg, select_result *result_arg)`	Constructor. The arguments are the thread descriptor, a `SELECT` column list, a bit mask of `SELECT` options, and a result set object that handles the processing of the output rows. Really a wrapper around `init( )`.
`void init(THD *thd_arg, List<Item> &fields_arg, ulonglong select_options_ arg, select_result *result_arg)`	Pseudoconstructor. Its arguments are the same as the constructor's. It does the real work of initialization.
`int prepare(Item ***rref_pointer_array, TABLE_LIST *tables, uint wind_num,COND *conds, uint og_num, ORDER *order, ORDER *group, Item *having, ORDER *proc_param, SELECT_LEX *select, SELECT_LEX_UNIT *unit)`	Post-initialization of some internal structures. Necessary to call before `optimize( )`. Most of the arguments correspond to members of the JOIN that require initialization.
`int optimize( )`	Determines the query plan. May create the first temporary table if the query requires the use of temporary tables.
`void exec( )`	Executes the query plan and sends resulting rows to the client or some other place determined by the logic of the query (see the later section "select_result").
`int reinit( )`	Prepares the structures for another call to `exec( )`.
`void cleanup(bool full)`	Releases resources allocated during optimization and execution.

JOIN_TAB

`JOIN_TAB` contains the information relevant to the optimization about each table instance participating in a join. It is defined in *sql/sql_select.h*. Table 9-3 describes its most significant data members.

Table 9-3. Most significant members of JOIN_TAB

Definition		Description
TABLE	*table	Table descriptor.
KEYUSE	*keyuse	Descriptor containing the information about which key is used to retrieve records for this table instance, and in what way.
SQL_SELECT	*select	Optimization data for the range optimizer. The type is defined in *sql/opt_range.h*.
COND	*select_cond	Parts of the expression tree from the WHERE clause involving this table. The type is an alias of Item.
Read_record_func	read_first_record	A pointer to a function that reads the first record from the associated table in the join.
Next_select_func	next_select	A pointer to a function that executes the next SELECT query in a chain of subselects.
READ_RECORD	read_record	Record reading descriptor. The type is defined in *sql/structs.h*.
double	worst_seeks	The worst possible cost of reading records from the table on a key. Measured in comparison with the cost of reading a record via table scan.
ha_rows	records	An estimate of the average number of records to examine in this table per iteration of a join.
ha_rows	found_records	An estimate of the average number of records in this table per iteration of a join that will match the query constraints.
ha_rows	read_time	The average cost per iteration of a join for this table in the current query plan.
table_map	dependent	Bit mask of dependent tables. Table B is dependent on table A if table A must precede table A in the join order of any possible query plan.
enum join_type	type	Indicates the record access method (path) used in the query plan for this table.
TABLE_REF	ref	An auxiliary descriptor mostly containing the information about the key being used for this table.
JOIN_CACHE	cache	Record cache used in full joins.
JOIN	*join	Main (parent) execution plan descriptor.

select_result

select_result is a base class in the hierarchy of classes that deal with the output of a SELECT query. It is defined in *sql/sql_class.h*. Its most important methods are shown in Table 9-4. select_result has a number of derived classes, which are listed in Table 9-5.

Table 9-4. *Most signficant methods of select_result class*

Definition	Description
`virtual int prepare(List<Item> &list, SELECT_LEX_UNIT *u)`	Performs preliminary intialization.
`virtual bool send_fields (List<Item> &list, uint flags)=0`	Called by the optimizer when the list of the fields in the result set becomes available.
`virtual bool send_data (List<Item> &items)=0`	Called by the optimizer once for each row of data in the result set.
`virtual void send_error (uint errcode,const char *err)`	Called by the optimizer when an error occurs during the generation of the result set.
`virtual bool send_eof( )=0`	Called by the optimizer when the result set has been fully generated to report that there will be no more rows.
`virtual void cleanup( )`	Releases allocated resources.

Table 9-5. *Descendants of select_result*

Class name	Class description
`select_send`	Sends the result set to a regular client connected either through the network or a local socket.
`select_export`	Used by `SELECT INTO OUTFILE`. The results of the `SELECT` are written to a local file.
`multi_delete`	Used by multi-table `DELETE` statements, such as `DELETE t1.*,t2.* FROM t1,t2 WHERE t1.id = 3 AND t2.t1_id = t1.id`. In order to execute this delete, a corresponding `SELECT` is performed with the result being handled in a special way to make it a `DELETE`.
`multi_update`	Used by multi-table `UPDATE` statements, such as `UPDATE t1,t2 SET t1.flag=1 WHERE t1.id = 3 AND t2.t1_id = t1.id`. In order to execute this update a corresponding `SELECT` is performed with the result being handled in a special way to make it an `UPDATE`.
`select_singlerow_subselect`	Used for handling subqueries returning only one record.
`select_exists_subselect`	Used for handling subqueries using `ANY`, `EXISTS`, `IN`, `ALL`, or `SOME`.
`select_max_min_finder_subselect`	Used for `ANY` and `ALL` subquery optimization.
`select_insert`	Used for handling `INSERT INTO...SELECT` statements.

SELECT Parse Tree

Prior to the introduction of subqueries, the `SELECT` parse tree was trivial. There was no hierarchy to speak of since there could only be one `SELECT`. The introduction of subqueries brought in this tree structure.

The base building block of a `SELECT` parse tree is the class `st_select_lex_node` defined in *sql/sql_lex.h*. It serves as the base class for `st_select_lex_unit` and `st_select_lex`. The former serves as a descriptor of a `UNION`, while the latter describes a single `SELECT`.

Execution of a SELECT on the code level

The execution of a SELECT is dispatched to handle_select( ) from *sql/sql_select.cc* by the parser after a number of initializations and checks. Unions are dispatched to mysql_union( ) from *sql/sql_union.cc*, while single selects go to mysql_select( ).

The essence of executing a single SELECT consists of the following steps:

1. JOIN::prepare( )
2. JOIN::optimize( )
3. JOIN::exec( )
4. JOIN::cleanup( )

If a JOIN has already been executed with JOIN::exec( ), and it needs to be executed again, a call to JOIN::reinit( ) is necessary.

JOIN::prepare( ) performs numerous initializations, some of which are:

- A call to setup_tables( ) from *sql/sql_base.cc* to add additional information to table lists needed by the optimizer.
- A call to setup_wild( ) from *sql/sql_base.cc* to expand wild cards (*) in field names of queries such as SELECT * FROM t1.
- A call to setup_fields( ) from *sql/sql_base.cc* to resolve the field names and initialize the field lists with appropriate field descriptors.
- A call to setup_conds( ) from *sql/sql_base.cc* to process and reorganize the WHERE, HAVING, and ON clause trees.
- A call to setup_order( ) and setup_group( ) to process and reorganize the trees of ORDER BY and GROUP BY, respectively.
- Performs some transformations of subselects.

The purpose of JOIN::optimize( ) is to restructure the query in a more optimal way, and determine the execution plan. Here are its highlights:

- A call to simplify_joins( ) from *sql/sql_select.cc* to convert outer joins to inner joins whenever possible.
- A call to optimize_cond( ) to eliminate redundancies from the WHERE clause and rewrite it to be more efficient.
- A call to opt_sum_query( ) from *sql/opt_sum.cc* to attempt to short-circuit the execution of queries with aggregate functions (e.g., MIN( ), MAX( ),COUNT( ), SUM( )) and no GROUP BY.
- A call to make_join_statistics( ) to create the execution plan.
- A call to substitute_for_best_equal_field( ) to prune the ON expressions in the joins.

- A call to `remove_const()` to remove constants from ORDER BY and GROUP BY expressions.

- A call to `make_join_readinfo()` to set up structures for reading records during the query execution.

- An attempt to replace simple subqueries with constants.

- A call to `create_tmp_table()` to create a temporary table if needed.

The `make_join_statistics()` function performs the following operations:

- Initializes a number of members of the JOIN class, allocating memory as needed.

- Detects dependency relationships between tables, and initializes dependency bitmaps.

- Calls `update_ref_and_keys()` to mark which keys can be used for record retrieval.

- Detects constant tables (where no more than one record match is possible), and sets up the constant table bitmap.

- Initializes statistical information on the number of records in each table, and key cardinalities. May call `get_quick_record_count()`.

- Calls `choose_plan()`, unless the join has been reduced to trivial (all constant tables). `choose_plan()` tries all possible join order combinations to the pre-defined depth level, and picks the most optimal one.

`JOIN::exec()` performs the actual execution of the query. Depending on the type of `select_result`, the results may be sent to a client, a temporary table, a file, or an internal processor (e.g., in the case of optimized subqueries). Here are some of its highlights:

- A call to `select_result::prepare2()` for appropriate initializations.

- A call to `select_describe()` if the query is an EXPLAIN.

- Special handling of a SELECT with no tables.

- Special handling of a result set with no records via a call to `return_zero_rows()`.

- For DISTINCT, GROUP BY, and ORDER BY queries that were not possible to optimize in another way, a call to *create_tmp_table()* to create a post-processing temporary table.

- A call to `do_select()` to perform the nested loop logic of a join.

`JOIN::cleanup()` releases all or some of the resources allocated in the initialization or during the execution, depending on the value of the argument.

CHAPTER 10

Storage Engines

In this chapter we will discuss the most prominent storage engines within MySQL in more detail. Unfortunately, due to the large number of different storage engines and the complexity that some possess, we are not able to examine each one in sufficient detail on the code level. Indeed, storage engines like MyISAM and InnoDB each deserve their own thousand-page book. However, I will provide pointers to the source for those who would like to learn more.

Different storage engines have different capabilities. Table 10-1 contains a comparison of different storage engines.

Table 10-1. MySQL storage engine comparison

	MyISAM	InnoDB	Memory	Merge	NDB	Archive	Federated
Transactions	No	Yes	No	No	Yes	No	No
Indexing	B-tree, R-tree, full text	B-tree	Hash, B-tree	B-tree, R-tree	Hash, B-tree	None	Depends on the remote table engine
Storage	Local disk	Local disk	RAM	Local disk	Remote and local cluster nodes	Local disk	Remote MySQLserver instance
Caching	Key cache	Key and data cache	N/A	Same as MyISAM	Key and data cache	None	Depends on the remote table engine
Locking	Table	Row	Table	Table	Row	Row	Relies on the remote table engine
Foreign keys	No	Yes	No	No	No	No	Depends on the remote table engine

Shared Aspects of Architecture

While there is a great degree of freedom in the implementation of a storage engine, all storage engines must integrate with the main MySQL server code. As a result they have a few things in common. Aside from having to support the basic concepts of tables residing in a database, records, columns, keys, read and write operations, and other aspects stipulated by the storage engine interface requirements, each storage engine also inherits the features and properties from the core table manipulation code. In other words, they get some functionality and architecture regardless of whether they need it.

Regardless of the storage engine, all tables have one *.frm* file per table containing the table definition with the column names, their types and sizes, key information, and other table properties. A *.frm* file in essence gathers and stores the information from CREATE TABLE. Up until version 5.1 the filename was always the same as the name of the table, and it resided in a directory corresponding to the database name. Version 5.1 introduced a change. The table and database name are now encoded in build_table_filename( ) in *sql/sql_table.cc*. Code reads and parses the files using openfrm( ) from *sql/table.cc*, and writes to them using *create_frm( )* from the same source file.

Regardless of the storage engine, the server reads the table definition from the *.frm* file, and stores it in what is called a *table cache*. This way, the next time the table needs to be accessed, the server does not have to reread and reparse the *.frm* file, but rather can use the cached information.

MySQL server utilizes the mechanism of table locking. Thus, each storage engine can either take advantage of this feature, or politely ask the table lock manager to always grant a write lock, which bypasses the core code table locking. In that case, the storage engine itself becomes responsible for ensuring consistency during concurrent access.

MyISAM

The MyISAM storage engine has roots very far back in the history of MySQL. When MySQL was first released, the original storage engine was ISAM. However, at that time there was no abstraction of storage engines in the code that would be easily visible to a user or a developer trying to extend MySQL. When that abstraction was introduced, ISAM was refactored and enhanced to become MyISAM.

MyISAM Architecture

MyISAM stores its data on a local disk. In addition to the *.frm* file common to all storage engines, it uses two additional files: a datafile (*.MYD*), and an index file (*.MYI*).

Datafile

The datafile has a fairly simple format. It is essentially a concatenation of table records with some necessary meta information. There are two record formats: fixed length and variable length.

A fixed length record begins with a record header. If the table does not have fields of type BIT, the length of the header can be computed using the formula len = $(8 + n)/8$, where n is the number of columns in the table that could possibly contain a NULL value. The first bit in the record header indicates whether this record is valid or has been deleted. If the bit is set (1), the record is valid; deleted records will have that bit cleared (0). For a valid record, the subsequent bits indicate whether their corresponding columns that could be NULL are actually NULL. After that, the remaining bits of the header act merely as padding bits and have no meaning.

Having fields of type BIT (in MySQL 5.0.3 and higher) complicates the situation, because in some cases bit values might be stored in the header as well. Thus, to compute the length of the header, the n in the formula from the previous paragraph should be increased by the number of bits being stored in the header. If a field is defined as BIT(K), meaning that it stores k bits, the number of bits to be stored in the header is k mod 8. For example, if the field is BIT(19), 3 out of those 19 bits are stored in the header.

If the first bit of the header indicates the record has been deleted, the subsequent bits serve as a pointer to the next deleted record in the deleted record chain. The deleted record chain allows inserts to overwrite the old deleted records instead of appending the new record to the end of file.

Immediately after the header, we find a concatenation of column values for the record in the column order of the table. Integers and floating point numbers in the record are stored in the little-endian (low byte first) order.

You can find the details of the fixed-length record storage in *storage/myisam/mi_statrec.c*.

For records with variable length, the format is more complicated. The first byte contains a special code describing the subtype of the record. The meaning of the subsequent bytes varies with each subtype, but the common theme is that there is a sequence of bytes that contains the length of the record, the number of unused bytes in the block, NULL value indicator flags, and possibly a pointer to the continuation of the record if the record did not fit into the previously created space and had to be split up. This can happen when one record gets deleted, and the new one to be inserted in its place exceeds the original one in size. You can get the details of the meanings of different codes by studying the switch statement in _mi_get_block_info( ) in *storage/myisam/mi_dynrec.c*.

Index file

MyISAM index files are much more complex than the datafiles. In short, they consist of a detailed header describing the various key and column properties, and containing a large amount of meta information, followed by the actual key pages. The basic structure is shown in Figure 10-1.

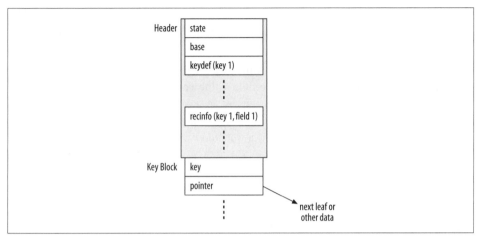

Figure 10-1. Structure of index (.MYI) file in MyISAM

The header consists of the following section types: state, base, keydef, and recinfo. The state and base sections occur only once, the keydef section is present once for each key, and the recinfo section is present once for each field of each key. Note that each record in the table starts with a special field that is used to mark deleted records and NULL fields, and this additional field will also have its own recinfo section.

The state section gets written by mi_state_info_write( ) and is read by mi_state_info_read( ) in *storage/myisam/mi_open.c*. It contains such information as key and datafile length, timestamps, number of times the table was opened, number of keys, number of deleted and actual records, pointers to the root key block for each key, as well as many other parameters. In the code, the state section information is stored in a MI_STATE_INFO structure, defined in *storage/myisam/myisamdef.h*.

The base section follows the state section. In many ways it is conceptually similar to the state section. It stores the number of records in the table, total number of fields (including the extra ones for dealing with NULL values and deleted records), various limit values (such as maximum key length and maximum key block) length, and a number of other items. The base section is shared among all threads accessing the table, while each thread has its own copy of the state section. The base section is written by mi_base_info_write( ) and read by my_n_base_info_read( ) in *storage/myisam/mi_open.c*. The internal structure storing the data from the base section is MI_BASE_INFO, defined in *storage/myisam/myisamdef.h*.

Following the base section, you may find one or more keydef sections—one per key. Each keydef section begins with a relatively short header containing the number of key parts, the type of key algorithm (B-tree or R-tree), special option flags, the block length used for this key, and key length limits. Following that there are one or more keyseg sections, one per column in the key. Each keyseg section contains the information about the corresponding key part (or column). Keydef sections are written by mi_keydef_write( ) and read by mi_keydef_read( ) in *storage/myisam/mi_open.c*. The internal structure storing the data from the base section is MI_KEYDEF, defined in *storage/myisam/myisamdef.h*.

Recinfo sections follow the keydef sections. Each recinfo consists of a field type code, the field length, a flag indicating if the field value can be NULL, and the offset of the NULL marker. keydef sections are written by mi_recinfo_write( ) and read by mi_recinfo_read( ) in *myisam/mi_open.c*. The internal structure storing the data from the base section is MI_COLUMNDEF defined in *include/myisam.h*.

Recinfo sections are followed by key blocks (pages). MyISAM supports two types of storage structures, B-tree and R-tree. Thus, each block is a leaf of a B-tree or an R-tree containing key values along with pointers to other blocks or offsets into the datafile for the leaf nodes. Each block has a 2-byte header. The first bit is used to indicate whether this is a leaf node (it is a leaf if the bit is cleared). The remaining bits contain the size of the used portion of the block.

MyISAM Key Types

MyISAM supports three types of keys: regular B-tree, full-text (which uses a B-tree), and spatial (which uses an R-tree).

B-tree keys

The B-tree is a very common storage structure, and the subject has been treated in great detail in many other publications; therefore, we will only briefly visit the MyISAM B-tree. Those interested in more detail should refer to *mi_key.c*, *mi_search.c*, *mi_write.c*, and *mi_delete.c* in the *storage/myisam* directory.

A MyISAM B-tree consists of leaf and nonleaf nodes, or *pages*. By default, each page is 1,024 bytes. It can be changed by testing the myisam_block_size variable. You can distinguish a nonleaf node from a leaf node by looking at the highest bit of the first byte of the page. It will be set for a nonleaf node.

Both leaf and nonleaf nodes contain key values and pointers to the record positions in the datafile. Nonleaf nodes additionally contain pointers to child nodes. Key values in a node may be compressed by replacing a common prefix with a referencing pointer.

Full-text keys

A full-text key is essentially a B-tree that stores a pointer to the record and the relevancy weight for each word in each indexed column or set of columns. A full-text key can be created with syntax similar to this:

```
CREATE FULLTEXT INDEX ft_ind ON t1(col1);
```

or any other variation of the standard index creation syntax adding the FULLTEXT modifier. Once you have created a full-text index, you may use the *myisam_ftdump* utility to view the details of the index with a command similar to:

```
$ myisam_ftdump -d /var/lib/mysql/test/t1 1
```

The first non-option argument is the full table path (datadir, database name, and table name). The second is the number of the key. One way to get the key number is to execute SHOW CREATE TABLE. Count the keys. The ordinal number of the index minus 1 is the key number to be used with the utility. If the table has a primary key, a full-text key, and no other keys, that number will be 1.

myisam_ftdump produces output similar to this:

```
188         0.6668773 argument
310         0.7772509 column
310         0.7772509 columns
188         0.6668773 count
188         0.6668773 create
310         0.7772509 created
188         0.6668773 database
188         0.6668773 datadir
310         0.7772509 essentially
188         0.6668773 execute
188         1.1291214 full
310         1.3160002 full
188         0.6668773 index
310         0.7772509 indexed
188         1.1291214 keys
188         0.6668773 minus
188         1.7401749 number
188         0.6668773 option
188         0.6668773 ordinal
188         0.6668773 path
310         0.7772509 pointer
188         0.6668773 primary
310         0.7772509 record
310         0.7772509 relevancy
188         0.6668773 show
310         0.7772509 similar
310         0.7772509 stores
310         0.7772509 syntax
188         1.5913655 table
188         0.6668773 text
```

```
310            1.3160002 text
310            0.7772509 tree
188            0.6668773 utility
310            0.7772509 weight
310            0.7772509 word
```

The first column shows the position (in bytes) of the start of the record containing the search keyword in the datafile. The second column is a specially computed relevancy rating. (Details are in walk_and_match( ) in *storage/myisam/ft_nlq_search.c*; make sure to look up the GWS_IN_USE, GWS_PROB, and GWS_IDF macros in *storage/myisam/ft_defs.h*.) The third argument is the search term.

Full-text SELECT. A full-text lookup essentially consists of performing a B-tree search in the full-text index, finding the appropriate record positions, computing the relevancy rankings of each record for the search with the help of the individual key word relevancy values stored in the tree, and then ordering the records by the computed record relevancy ratings. On the SQL level, the full-text functionality is available via MATCH( ) ... AGAINST( ) syntax. In the following example, we assume that the table documents has a full-text key on (title,body). We can use a query similar to this to retrieve the results:

```
SELECT title,body FROM documents WHERE MATCH(title,body) AGAINST ('mysql internals')
```

Full-text INSERT. A full-text insert parses the appropriate columns of the record (see *storage/myisam/ft_parser.c*), breaking it into a sequence of words. The stop words (such as a, and, the) are ignored (see *storage/myisam/ft_stopwords.c* and *storage/myisam/ft_static.c*). Word frequencies are computed, and eventually the relative weight of each keyword in the record is obtained. Then the keywords with the weights and the record position are inserted into the full-text index. See *storage/myisam/ft_update.c* for details.

Spatial keys

The idea of a spatial key comes from the following type of problem. Suppose you have the latitude and the longitude for every point of interest, and you would like to determine which ones lie within a given bounding rectangle. In a practical application, the points of interest could be restaurants, and the bounding rectangle could be the zip code boundary.

With a traditional B-tree approach you could store the latitude and the longitude in a table, and have a key on one or the other, or even a compound key containing both. While this is better than a full scan, it is impossible to avoid the problem of not using the ranges for both coordinates efficiently. You retrieve all the values for a range on one, but the range of the other does not get used very well. Even with the introduction of index_merge optimization in MySQL 5.0, which permits the use of more than one key in the same table during query optimization, a B-tree key remains less than ideal for this type of problem.

In 1984, Antonin Gutman proposed an extension to a traditional B-tree to address this challenge. The extended B-tree was given the name of *R-tree*, with *R* standing for *region*. While a traditional B-tree node contains key values and pointers to child nodes and/or actual records or pointers to actual records, the R-tree replaces the key values with bounding boxes that contain all of the descendant nodes under the given element of the node.

Due to the nature of an R-tree, a key value is a geometric object in an n-dimensional space. In MySQL, in order to have an R-tree index, the column must be of the type GEOMETRY, or there must be a way for MySQL to convert it to the GEOMETRY type. Thus, to create an index on a column in table stores named gps_coord of the type GEOMETRY, use the following syntax:

```
CREATE SPATIAL INDEX sp_ind ON stores(gps_coord)
```

To insert a record with the gps_coord of (–110.5, 40.5), use the following syntax:

```
INSERT INTO stores (id,gps_coord) VALUES (1,GeomFromText('POINT(-110.5 40.5)')
```

To retrieve all records in a rectangular region with the vertices (–111,40), (–111,41), (–110,41), (–110,40), you can use the following syntax:

```
SELECT  id, AsText(gps_coord)  FROM stores WHERE
MBRContains(GeomFromText('POLYGON((-111 40,-111 41,-110 41,-110 40,-111 40))'),
gps_coord)
```

Note that the bounding polygon does not have to be rectangular, nor do the GEOMETRY column values have to be points. In fact, the same column can contain points, lines, polygons, and other geometric objects.

The insertion algorithm (see rtree_insert_req( ) in *storage/myisam/rt_index.c*) searches through a node (starting at the root) for the bounding box that would be extended the least if it were combined with the search key (see rtree_pick_key( ) in *storage/myisam/rt_index.c*). The measure of extension can be defined in two ways: by area (in the n-dimensional sense) or by perimeter. By default, the extension by area is used. However, it is possible to compile MySQL to use the extension by perimeter by adding *-DPICK_BY_PERIMETER* to the compiler flags.

Once the right bounding box is found in the node, the child node is examined the same way until a leaf node is reached. The insertion is performed (see rtree_add_key( ) in *storage/myisam/rt_key.c*). The upper-level bounding boxes are appropriately updated (see rtree_set_key_mbr( ) in *storage/myisam/rt_key.c*). If the node is full, it needs to be split.

The split is done in rtree_split_page( ) from *storge/myisam/rt_split.c*. First, all pairs of keys (bounding boxes) are examined to find the pair that will waste the most area (in the n-dimensional sense) if joined. The wasted area is calculated as the area of the minimum bounding box of the union minus the sum of the areas of each key in the pair (see pick_seeds( ) in *storage/myisam/rt_split.c*). Each is put in a separate group.

Then the remaining keys are assigned. Each key that has not yet been selected is hypothetically added to both groups. The algorithm then calculates the increase in the area of the minimum bounding box for each group that results from the addition, and compares the increases. The difference of increases serves as a measure of the preference of this key for one group or the other. The one with the greatest measure of preference is chosen to join the group for which it produces the smaller increase in the minimum bounding box area. The process is repeated until all keys are assigned (see pick_next( ) in *storage/myisam/rt_split.c*).

This split algorithm is called *quadratic-cost split* because its complexity is $O(N^2)$ with respect to the number of keys in the node. There exist faster split algorithms (*linear-cost*), and slower (*exhaustive split*). A slower algorithm produces more balanced trees. The quadratic cost algorithm is a nice trade-off between keeping a balanced tree and maintaining a good insertion speed.

The R-tree search is very similar to the B-tree search. Start at the root node. Although the match is not found, we scan the current node until we find a bounding rectangle of interest, which in the simplest case will contain the search rectangle. Descend into the matching node unless we are at a leaf. If at a leaf, follow the record pointer to retrieve the record. See rtree_find_first( ), rtree_find_next( ), and rtree_find_req( ) in *storage/myisam/rt_index.c*, as well as rtree_key_cmp( ) in *storage/myisam/rt_mbr.c*.

To delete a record, the search key is found and removed from the leaf node. Then, if that makes the node less than one-third full, the whole node is removed and placed into the reinsert list along with its descendants. The matching key is also deleted from the parent node, and the deletion is propagated in this manner upward. When the deletion is complete, the reinsert list is processed to restore the removed key values into the tree. See rtree_delete( ), rtree_delete_req( ), rtree_fill_reinsert_list( ), and rtree_insert_level( ) in *storage/myisam/rt_index.c* for details.

InnoDB

InnoDB is one of the most complex storage engines currently present in MySQL. It supports transactions, multi-versioning, row-level locks, and foreign keys. It has an extensive system for managing I/O and memory. It has internal mechanisms for deadlock detection, and performs a quick and reliable crash recovery. It implements a number of algorithms to overcome the performance limitations of traditional databases that support transactions.

Unlike MyISAM, which always stores its data in files, InnoDB uses tablespaces. A tablespace can be stored in a file or on a raw partition. All tables may be stored in one common tablespace, or every table may have its own tablespace.

The data is stored in a special structure called a *clustered index*, which is a B-tree with the primary key acting as the key value, and the actual record (rather than a pointer) in the data part. Thus, each InnoDB table must have a primary key. If one is not supplied, a special row ID column not normally visible to the user is added to act as a primary key. A secondary key will store the value of the primary key that identifies the record. The B-tree code can be found in *innobase/btr/btr0btr.c*.

Both primary and secondary keys are stored in a B-tree on disk. However, when buffering the index page, InnoDB will build an adaptive hash index in memory to speed up the index lookups for the cached page. The code that deals with InnoDB adaptive hashing can be found in *storage/innobase/ha/ha0ha.c*.

While MyISAM buffers only the key pages, InnoDB buffers both keys and data. This approach has both advantages and disadvantages. On one hand, the buffering of the data does not have to depend on the operating system's file cache, and good performance is achieved even when there is something wrong with the operating system's file caching. Additionally, in comparison with the operating system's file cache, accessing the data avoids an extra system call. On the other hand, with the operating system's file cache still enabled, *double caching* (the same data being cached in the operating system's file cache and in the data buffer) is possible, which only wastes memory. However, the operating system's file caching can be disabled by starting InnoDB with `innodb_flush_method` set to `O_DIRECT`. The code that deals with the data and key buffering is found in *storage/innobase/buf/buf0buf.c*.

The InnoDB engine keeps two types of logs: an undo log and a redo log. The purpose of an *undo log* is to roll back transactions, as well as to display the older versions of the data for queries running in the transaction isolation level that requires it. The code that handles the undo log can be found in *storage/innobase/log/log0log.c*.

The purpose of a *redo log* is to store the information to be used in crash recovery. It permits the recovery process to re-execute the transactions that may or may not have completed before the crash. After re-executing those transactions, the database is brought to a consistent state. The code dealing with the redo log can be found in *storage/innobase/log/log0recv.c*.

An InnoDB data row can come in two different formats: an old, less compact one (pre 5.0.3), and a new, more compact one (version 5.0.3 and later). Both formats store mostly the same information, but the new one uses less space. The record begins with a list of field data offsets in the record. Next come 4 bits used for marking the record as deleted and for other purposes; 4 bits to show the number of records owned by this record; and 13 bits for the heap number of the record. The old format has 10 bits containing the number of fields in the record, followed by a bit showing whether the field offsets use 1 byte or 2. The new format has 3 bits with the record type. Both formats follow with a 2-byte next-key pointer. The remainder of the record contains the actual field data. The code that deals with the record format and operations can be found in *storage/innobase/rem/rem0rec.c*.

The complexity of the record format is necessary to optimize the insert operation. A conventional B-tree would require moving half of the records on average when a new record is inserted. InnoDB tries to avoid that with a very creative approach. The records are inserted into a page in the natural order. The heap number indicates the sequential order of the record in the page. The next key pointer indicates the position of the next record in the primary key order.

To locate keys in a page efficiently, InnoDB maintains an additional structure known as the *page directory*. It is a sparse sorted array of pointers to keys within the page. A given record is located via a binary search. Afterward, since the index is sparse, it may still be necessary to examine a few more keys in the linked list of records. The number of records owned indicates how much further to go before the next record that has a pointer to it from the page directory is reached, and thus contains the information when the search for a given key stops. The code dealing with InnoDB pages can be found in *storage/innobase/page/page0page.c*.

Each InnoDB data row has two additional internal fields storing the information to be used in transactions, recovery, and multi-versioning. One field is 6 bytes long and contains the ID of the last transaction that modified the record. It also contains a 7-byte field known as a *roll pointer*. The roll pointer points to the record in the rollback segment in the undo log. This pointer can be used to roll back a transaction, or to show the older version of the data if the current transaction isolation level requires it.

Memory (Heap)

The MEMORY storage engine, formerly known as HEAP, stores its data in memory. The original purpose of the code was for the optimizer to be able to create and use temporary tables when performing a SELECT that could be done in one pass. After the introduction of the storage engine architecture in version 3.23, it became fairly easy to give users access to this in-memory table engine that was being used for temporary tables.

This simple addition has provided numerous benefits to MySQL users. An in-memory table can be used to store temporary results when executing a complex set of queries; as a fast data accumulator that gets periodically flushed to disk; as a fast cache for a portion of the data from some large disk-based table; and in many other ways.

The MEMORY engine supports two types of keys: hash and B-tree. The definition of the table is stored if the server is restarted. However, the data rows are present only for as long as the server is running, and they are lost after a restart.

A hash index lookup is faster than a B-tree one if the exact value of the key is known. However, if only the prefix of the key value is known, or only the limit values of a range are known, a hash index is of no help. A B-tree, however, can answer such requests via the index.

A MEMORY table is generally faster than a similar MyISAM table on most operations. However, if the MyISAM table is small enough to fit into the file cache of the operating system, the difference is not as big as you might expect: perhaps a factor of

1.5 or so. MEMORY table speed gains come from two sources: a simpler algorithm and the absence of I/O syscalls.

Those interested in learning more about the MEMORY tables should refer to *sql/ha_heap.h*, *sql/ha_heap.cc*, and the *.c* and *.h* files in the *storage/heap* directory.

MyISAM Merge

The MERGE storage engine combines a group of identically structured MyISAM tables into one logical unit. Reads and writes can still happen to and from one of the MyISAM tables, or to and from the MERGE table.

The MERGE engine was created to solve a very common problem. Suppose your system collects some historical data over time. Most of the queries are restricted to a fairly narrow and easily predictable time range. However, once in a while you need to query the whole table. If you had all of the data in one MyISAM table, you would not get very good performance for a number of reasons: lock contention, increased unnecessary I/O, or long repair times in case of a crash. Having all of the data in separate tables based on the time makes those queries that need to see more than one table unnecessarily complex.

A MERGE table provides a good solution. You can now query individual tables when the time range is sufficiently narrow, and the MERGE table when it is not. For more information on MERGE, refer to *sql/ha_myisammrg.h*, *sql/ha_myisammrg.cc*, and the *.c* files in the *storage/myisammrg* directory.

NDB

The NDB acronym stands for *Network DataBase*. This storage engine is capable of storing the data on a fail-safe cluster of database servers. In 2003, MySQL AB acquired the division of Ericsson (a Swedish telecom company) that had developed the NDB code to handle Ericsson's phone system, and started the work on integrating it into MySQL.

A running MySQL server provides a central point of access to the NDB cluster. The queries are parsed by the MySQL parser, and passed on to the optimizer. Then, if the table storage engine is NDB the appropriate methods of the NDB handler class are invoked as the query is being executed (see *sql/ha_ndbcluster.h* and *sql/ha_ndbcluster.cc*). At that time, the calls to the handler class method are translated into NDB, API calls (see the *.hpp* and *.cpp* files in the *ndb/src/ndbapi* directory), which in turn communicate with the cluster nodes.

The cluster nodes are divided into two types: *management nodes* (ndb_mgmd), and *data nodes* (ndbd). The management node is responsible for controlling the cluster. The data node stores and replicates the data.

NDB supports transactions, row-level locking, B-tree and hash keys, internal synchronous replication two-phase commit (separate from MySQL server replication), and data partitioning based on the primary key. Each data node loads its entire dataset into memory on startup, and writes it to disk on shutdown. There are periodic asynchronous writes to disk to ensure that not much gets lost in case of a catastrophic failure of the entire cluster (e.g., the power goes down on all nodes at the same time). The idea is that if you have a large dataset, you can set up enough data nodes to have enough combined memory to operate the cluster this way. There is some work in progress to support operating the cluster from disk.

As one would expect, the performance of NDB greatly depends on the speed of the network that connects the cluster nodes. The NDB cluster can use TCP/IP over Ethernet, or be connected via SCI bus and use SCI sockets. If the nodes are on the same computer, shared memory can also be used. Although using SCI can provide significant speed gains, TCP/IP over Ethernet is by far the simpler and the better tested method.

It is important to remember that NDB was created for a particular purpose (to meet the needs of a large telephone database application), which it has fulfilled very well. It is well suited for similar applications that follow a similar design philosophy. However, it has a fairly extensive list of limitations and still has a long way to go before you could set up a cluster, run ALTER TABLE ...ENGINE=NDB for all of the tables, and expect any application to just work.

Archive

The purpose of the ARCHIVE storage engine is to provide the functionality to store large amounts of data using the minimum amount of space. The idea is to compress and archive away the data but still be able to query or append to it on occasion with minimum hassle. This engine was created during several inspired coding sessions by Brian Aker, the Director of Architecture at MySQL AB. Brian has an amazing ability to code up something very useful in a very short amount of time in between his other responsibilities.

Compared to MyISAM, InnoDB, or NDB, this is a very simple storage engine. It supports only two operations: SELECT and INSERT. This simplification has great benefits. Deleting or updating a record in a compressed datafile is a very costly operation. Not having to worry about updating and deleting data permits you to keep the records in a compressed format. Additionally, such a limitation makes tampering with the existing data difficult: the only way to delete or update a record is to change it to another storage engine, run the modification query, and then change it back to the ARCHIVE storage engine. With no need to worry about updates and deletes, solving the issue of high-performance concurrent access is easy. Since the datafile can have no holes from record deletions, INSERT and SELECT operations can proceed concurrently unless the SELECT tries to read the record that is currently being written at the end of file. Thus, the ARCHIVE engine provides the effect of having row-level locks as far as performance is concerned.

The ARCHIVE storage engine currently does not support keys. There is some discussion among MySQL developers that they might be supported in the future.

The source code of the ARCHIVE storage engine is found in *storage/archive* directory. A reader interested in implementing his own storage engine is well advised to study this code. It is simple enough to be fairly easily understood, and yet accomplishes enough to be useful as a next step for the examples we've covered thus far.

Federated

This is another simple storage engine, and again the fruit of Brian Aker's coding inspiration. Its purpose is to allow access to tables stored on a remote MySQL server as if they were local.

The FEDERATED storage engine stores the information about how to access the remote server, and which table to map to in the comments field of the CREATE TABLE statement. This information is stored in the *.frm* file. There are no other datafiles created or used by this storage engine. When the optimizer requests the data from the storage engine, the storage engine in turn issues an SQL query to the remote server using the regular MySQL client/server communication protocol, and retrieves the data from the remote table. When processing queries that update the table, the storage engine translates them into corresponding update queries on the remote server, and also sends them via the standard client/server protocol.

This storage engine also serves as a very good learning example. You can find its implementation in *storage/federated/ha_federated.h* and *storage/fedrated/ha_federated.cc*.

CHAPTER 11

Transactions

In the MySQL architecture, the majority of the burden for implementing transactions is placed on the storage engine. The details of transaction logging, row or page locks, implementing the isolation levels, commits and rollbacks, and other critical components of transaction implementations vary greatly from storage engine to storage engine. However, every storage engine has to use the same interface to communicate with the upper SQL layer. Thus the focus of this chapter will be to outline how to integrate an already existing transactional storage engine into MySQL.

InnoDB is the most robust transactional storage engine in MySQL. Therefore I will use it as an example and analyze why things are done a certain way.

Overview of Transactional Storage Engine Implementation

Chapter 7 discussed the basics of implementing a storage engine. As you may recall, there are two parts to integrating a custom storage engine into MySQL: defining and implementing the `handler` subclass, and defining and implementing the `handlerton`. We discussed these in a fair amount of detail.

While the proper implementation of transactions definitely requires a great attention to detail in implementing the virtual methods of the handler subclass, the core of the transaction-specific work happens in a few `handlerton` functions. This is understandable: the `handler` subclass methods are conceptually associated with a particular table instance, while the `handlerton` functions are associated only with the thread or connection. Thus, operations such as COMMIT, ROLLBACK, and SAVEPOINT naturally fit into the `handlerton` mode of integration.

It is important to understand that the task of the actual implementation of transactions essentials is left completely to the discretion of the storage engine. It is possible to have a full-fledged transactional storage engine such as InnoDB, or you could just write a prototype that reports that it committed or rolled back a transaction but in essence did nothing. The core SQL layer will not know the difference as long as you follow the proper interface/communication protocol.

Even if you already have a fully functional transactional storage engine, the process of integration is not trivial. There are a number of issues to deal with. How do you work with nontransactional or even transactional tables belonging to another storage engine? How do you handle the possible caching of queries? How do you handle replication logging? How do you avoid deadlocks?

If you look at the source code of InnoDB (starting in *sql/ha_innodb.cc*), you will notice many of the struggles that such an integration involved. You will also see solutions to the various challenges that you can try to understand and apply to your situation.

Implementing the handler Subclass

The first simple but very important method to implement is `handler::has_transactions()`. It is used to report to the upper SQL layer that the storage engine has transactional support. The return value of 1 (`TRUE`) is interpreted as the positive answer.

The next two methods of importance are `handler::start_stmt()` and `handler::external_lock()`. They both can be used by a transactional storage engine to start a transaction.

`handler::external_lock()` is invoked at least once per table instance during parsing. Originally, the purpose of this method was to prevent a table that could have been used by some application outside of MySQL server from being modified. This use of `handler::external_lock()` is now rather obsolete. However, its strategic position in the hierarchy of calls makes it very useful for transactional storage engines to perform per-table-instance initializations to start a transaction.

The one exceptional condition when a transaction can be started by passing a call to `handler::external_lock()` is the LOCK TABLES statement, which places a manual table-level lock on a list of tables to be used in the current connection session. To deal with this problem, the `handler::start_stmt()` method was added to the `handler` class, which is invoked once per table instance during LOCK TABLES.

A transactional storage engine will usually need a data structure to keep track of the state of the current transaction. The MySQL storage engine architecture meets this need by allocating memory for a pointer to the transaction descriptor in the THD class. That memory is found in the `ha_data` array under THD. Each storage engine gets a location at a fixed offset in that array, specified by an autogenerated value that is placed in the slot member of the `handlerton`.

That memory location can be initialized when a transaction is started by handler::
external_lock( ) or handler::start_stmt( ). As an example, this is how InnoDB initializes it:

```
trx = trx_allocate_for_mysql( );
...
thd->ha_data[innobase_hton.slot] = trx;
```

When a transaction is started, the storage engine needs to register it in the core SQL
layer via a call to trans_register_ha( ). In the case of InnoDB, this requirement is
met via two functions: innobase_register_stmt( ) and innobase_register_trx_and_
stmt( ). innobase_register_stmt( ) calls trans_register_ha( ) as follows:

```
trans_register_ha(thd,FALSE,&innobase_hton);
```

whereas innobase_register_trx_and_stmt( ) first calls innobase_register_stmt( ) and
then invokes trans_register_ha( ) as follows:

```
trans_register_ha(thd,TRUE,&innobase_hton);
```

As you can see, the difference is in the value of the second argument. If it is FALSE,
only the current statement of the transaction is registered. Otherwise, the entire
transaction is registered.

The purpose of registering transactions and statements is to facilitate the COMMIT and
ROLLBACK operations. While the operation is in progress, the core server code needs to
locate the handlertons to be able to invoke the storage-engine-specific code.

A transaction may be started in two ways, externally or internally. A transaction is
started externally when the client issues a statement BEGIN or START TRANSACTION.
Alternatively, merely issuing a query that uses a transaction-capable storage engine
table starts a transaction internally. When a transaction starts externally, the upper
SQL layer has control and can record the current state of the storage engine if
needed. However, when the transaction starts internally, the upper SQL layer does
not have control. Thus, the transaction registration process serves to notify the upper
SQL layer of times when transactions start internally.

A transactional storage engine may also implement handler::try_semi_consistent_
read( ), handler::was_semi_consistent_read( ), and handler::unlock_row( ) to help
avoid extra lock waits in UPDATE and DELETE queries.

For the most part, however, the implementation of the handler subclass is very much
storage-engine-dependent. The core of the work to implement the handler is defining what it means to read a record via various methods (on a key, read next row in a
scan, read from a range, etc.), and to write, update, and delete a record. So the handler methods themselves normally would not do much related specifically to transaction support. Rather, they serve as wrappers for the lower-level engine API calls that
take care of transactional integrity as they store and retrieve the records.

Let us briefly examine how InnoDB implements the handler (see *sql/ha_innodb.cc*).
There is a lot of work—mostly not related to transactions—required to bridge the

gap between the native InnoDB structures and the data that comes from the MySQL upper SQL layer in its native format, which was originally designed with MyISAM in mind. We see calls to core InnoDB API functions such as `row_search_for_mysql()`, `row_unlock_for_mysql()`, `row_insert_for_mysql()`, `row_update_for_mysql()`, and a number of others. As their names suggest, those functions have a common theme: they take a record in MySQL upper SQL layer format, perform the necessary format conversions, and then perform their respective operations such as searching for a record, updating a record, or inserting a record. These and other format bridging functions can be found in *storage/innobase/row/row0mysql.c*.

One of the key data members of ha_innobase (the InnoDB handler) that is heavily involved in the operations to bridge the formats (as well as just about any other operation done inside the InnoDB handler) is innobase_prebuilt, which has the type struct row_prebuilt_struct*. This is a pointer to a structure that organizes InnoDB table data in a way to be able to perform operations using records in the MySQL upper SQL layer format most efficiently. It is initialized in ha_innodb::open() via a call to row_create_prebuilt().To study the internals of InnoDB, which can give you ideas for how to integrate transactional engines, refer to the definition of row_prebuilt_ struct in *storage/innobase/include/row0mysql.h*, as well as the initialization in row_ create_prebuilt() in *storage/innobase/row/row0mysql.c*. There is one member in this structure that deserves more detailed attention, though: trx of type stuct trx_struct*.

trx is a pointer to a transaction descriptor that includes data such as transaction ID; transaction isolation level; whether the transaction created or dropped a table or an index; log serial number of the transaction at the last commit; log name and offset in the binary replication log corresponding to the transaction; and a variety of other flags, count holders, and descriptor pointers relevant to processing a transaction. InnoDB places the trx pointer into the memory slot under THD that is provided for the main transaction descriptor (thd->ha_data[innobase_hton.slot]).

This structure may be of particular interest to those trying to integrate their own transactional storage engine. The definition of trx_struct can be found in *storage/ innobase/include/trx0trx.h*. It is initialized via trx_create() in *storage/innobase/trx/ trx0trx.c*. However, when it is called from within the handler, InnoDB uses the trx_ allocate_for_mysql() wrapper rather than calling trx_create() directly.

Most of the record manipulation methods (rnd_next(), index_first(), index_next(), index_prev(), and so on) of ha_innobase follow a pattern. They start with some usually simple initialization, followed by a call to ha_innobase::general_fetch(), which in turn dispatches the execution into the depths of the InnoDB API, usually entering via one of the functions in *storage/innobase/row/row0mysql.c*. Transactional issues are dealt with in stride as they arise. Other operations, such as opening or creating a table, also follow a pattern. There is usually a lengthy initialization followed by a call to a core InnoDB API function, which in turn is followed by some cleanup.

Overall, studying the implementation of the InnoDB handler reveals the complexity involved in integrating a powerful transactional storage engine into MySQL.

Defining the handlerton

As you may recall from Chapter 7, a handlerton is a structure with data members and callback function pointers specific to a storage engine. Unlike the handler class, a handlerton is not specific to a table instance. A *singleton* is a well-known design pattern that applies when a class is created is such a way that only one instance of it can exist through the whole application. A handlerton is in essence a singleton that is connected to a table handler, hence the name.

If you look at the listing of the handlerton function callbacks in Chapter 7 (Table 7-3), you'll see that most of them have something to do with transactions. The introduction of the handlerton initiated from the need to support XA transactions, which have caused a major refactoring of the transaction handling within MySQL. Thus, the handlerton became a crucial hub of transaction capability integration for storage engines.

The transaction-specific callbacks of a handlerton are:

```
savepoint_set( )
savepoint_rollback( )
savepoint_release( )
commit( )
rollback( )
prepare(
recover( )
commit_by_xid( )
rollback_by_xid( )
```

These functions are invoked in direct response to their corresponding SQL commands. Other callbacks are also utilized by transactional storage engines:

```
close_connection( )
panic( )
flush_logs( )
start_consistent_snapshot( ),
binlog_func( )
release_latches( )
```

Let's briefly examine the InnoDB handlerton in *sql/ha_innodb.cc*. The naming convention for the callbacks is fairly straightforward. Each handlerton member is prefixed with innobase_ to form the name of the actual InnoDB callback. There are a few exceptions:

- prepare( ) and recover( ) are called innobase_xa_prepare( ) and innobase_xa_recover( ), respectively, for greater clarity and to emphasize that they are dealing with XA transactions.
- panic( ) corresponds to innobase_end( ).
- start_consistent_snapshot( ) points to innobase_start_trx_and_assign_read_view( ).

Some `handlerton` callbacks follow a simple pattern. They have some initialization, a call to a core InnoDB API function to actually do the job, and then possibly some cleanup afterward. Other callbacks require several calls to the core InnoDB API. But in both cases, a `handlerton` callback serves mainly as glue between the core MySQL code and the core InnoDB API, to allow transactions to happen as they are supposed to.

Note that the complexity of the `handlerton` callbacks is much lower than that of the `handler` methods. The reason for this might be that InnoDB has a streamlined transactional system, and therefore, when asked to do a standard transactional operation such as commit, rollback, or savepoint, it doesn't require much glue to make it work from inside the core MySQL code. However, things are different when records are being accessed individually via the `handler` methods. The expectations of the MySQL upper SQL layer might not always be in line with the native capabilities of InnoDB. Thus, a lot of glue work is required, and the code is more complex.

Working with the Query Cache

MySQL has a unique feature for a database: a query cache. The server can be configured to cache the results of every `SELECT`. Then, if another `SELECT` arrives that is identical to one that is cached, and the tables involved in the query have not changed, the cached result is returned immediately instead of MySQL actually going to the tables and pulling out the matching records.

This feature provides a great performance boost for a number of applications, especially web applications that heavily rely on a database and are frequently accessed by a large number of users in a way that makes them send identical queries to the MySQL server. Since the introduction of the query cache, many MySQL users have reported two- to threefold improvements in performance. Thus, any storage engine, transactional or not, needs to be able to work correctly with the query cache.

The main issue of working with the query cache is being able to easily tell if the table has changed or not. While it is not difficult for a nontransactional storage engine to answer that question, things are not as easy for a multiversioned transactional storage engine that supports various isolation levels. Thus, the `handler` interface provides a method `handler::register_query_cache_table()` to give transactional storage engines a chance to answer the question of whether it is safe to cache the query. This method is optional. If a handler does not support it, the query cache will use the pessimistic approach: on every commit it will invalidate all queries that refer to tables used in the committed transaction.

`register_query_cache_table()` gets a chance to set a callback, along with the argument to pass to it that the query cache will invoke to decide whether the queries involving that table are safe to cache.

InnoDB uses `innobase_query_caching_of_table_permitted( )` for the callback. It performs a fairly complex analysis to make the decision. Care must be taken to avoid a deadlock. The function handles all the issues and returns `TRUE` if the query involving the given table is safe to cache, and `FALSE` otherwise.

Working with the Replication Binary Log

MySQL replication works by having the master maintain a binary log of updates (called the *binlog*), and having the slave read and apply them. Thus, it becomes critical for a transactional storage engine to make sure that the contents of the binary log are consistent with the state of the database.

The core MySQL code already provides a lot of help. The SQL statements are not written into the binary log until the transaction commits, and they are not written at all if the transaction gets rolled back. However, there are a couple of critical issues a transactional storage engine might need to address:

- To guarantee consistency of binlog and table data in case of a crash, the storage engine must implement XA transactions.
- In a statement-based replication, slaves execute binlog updates sequentially and in one thread. Thus, all of the updates on the master must happen under the `SERIALIZABLE` transaction isolation level in order to guarantee the same results on the slave.

Avoiding Deadlocks

A transactional storage engine with row-level locking, especially one integrated with an SQL server, is naturally prone to deadlocks. Thus, it is important to have a plan for avoiding or resolving deadlocks.

InnoDB has a deadlock detection algorithm. When placing a new lock, InnoDB makes sure that it doesn't cause deadlocks. It will roll back a problematic transaction when a deadlock is discovered. However, the deadlock detection algorithm is aware only of InnoDB locks, and cannot detect deadlocks when some of the problem locks do not belong to InnoDB. To solve this problem, InnoDB has also timeout-based deadlock detection that rolls back transactions that are taking a long time. The limit is controlled by the server variable `innodb_lock_wait_timeout`. Thus, the application programmer should be prepared to reissue a transaction if it gets rolled back due to a timeout or risk of deadlock. While this may appear to be a major setback in the area of performance, in practice, properly optimized queries in a well-designed application almost never cause a deadlock.

Another issue that working with the MySQL server adds to the deadlock dilemma is the need to be aware of MySQL table locks. MySQL allows a user to lock a table directly at the start of a transaction via the LOCK TABLES command. InnoDB is being made aware of table locks via the server variable innodb_table_locks, which is set to 1 by default. When set to 1, InnoDB acquires an internal storage-engine-level table lock when LOCK TABLES is issued.

With the increasing number of storage engines being added to MySQL, a possibility that existed mostly on the theoretical level is becoming more and more of a reality. A storage engine developer now needs to be concerned about cross-storage-engine deadlocks. The InnoDB method of lock timeout can be used to address this problem.

CHAPTER 12

Replication

MySQL implements asynchronous master-slave replication. The master keeps a log of updates, while the slave reads it and executes it in sequence. This chapter discusses some details of MySQL replication.

Overview

MySQL replication is relatively simple and straightforward. A server may act as a master or a slave. The master maintains a log of updates that is called the binary log for historical reasons. The binary log records events. Each event contains some information that is relevant for the slave to be able to execute the update exactly the same way the master did it. The majority of events are merely SQL queries that update the database in one way or another. However, it is also necessary to store some metadata that the slave must use to recreate the context of the update in order for the update query to yield the same results.

The slave connects to the master and starts executing updates as it reads them from the master's binary log. There are two threads on the slave to perform this work: the *I/O thread* and the *SQL thread*. The I/O thread downloads the contents of the master binary log and stores them locally in temporary files called *relay logs*. The relay logs are processed by the SQL thread, which re-creates the original execution context and executes the updates.

The slave keeps track of where it is in the replication process via two parameters: current log name and current log position. If the slave ever disconnects from the master and then reconnects, the slave will request a feed of updates starting from its current position in the current log. The master keeps track of the log sequence order and will automatically switch to the next log once the end of the last one is reached during the binary log feed process. During the initial connection, the slave requests a read from the first log known to the master. It is possible to tell the slave to start replication from an arbitrary position using the CHANGE MASTER TO command.

The replication is asynchronous. This means that at some point in the future the slave will catch up to the current state of the master, but the master does not normally wait for the slave to catch up. The lag between the slave and the master depends on a number of factors: the speed of the network connecting the two servers, the types of update queries being run, the processing capabilities of the master and the slave, and the load on both servers.

It is possible to synchronize the master and the slave programatically using a combination of FLUSH TABLES WITH READ LOCK, SHOW MASTER STATUS, and SELECT MASTER_POS_WAIT( ) queries. While this technique may be useful in a number of situations, it is frequently impractical. Network delays and outages, load spikes on the master or the slave, and possibly other circumstances may create unacceptable delays of the application user.

Statement-Based Versus Row-Based Replication

Replicating the data between two SQL databases can take place on the SQL level or on the row level. In the statement-based approach, every SQL statement that could modify the data gets logged on the master. Then those statements are re-executed on the slave against the same initial dataset and in the same context. In the row-based approach, every row modification gets logged on the master and then applied on the slave. Both approaches have their advantages and disadvantages. Statement-based replication generally requires less data to be transferred between the master and the slave, as well as taking up less space in the update logs. It does not have to deal with the format of the row. The compactness of the data transfer will generally allow it to perform better. On the other hand, it is necessary to log a lot of execution context information in order for the update to produce the same results on the slave as it did originally on the master. In some cases it is not possible to provide such a context. Statement-based replication is also more difficult to maintain, as the addition of new SQL functionality frequently requires extensive code updates for it to replicate properly.

Row-based replication is more straightforward. No context information is required. It is only necessary to know which record is being updated, and what is being written to that record. Given a good code base, the maintenance of a row-based replication is also fairly simple. Since the logging happens at a lower level, the new code will naturally execute the necessary low-level routines that modify the database, which will do the logging with no additional code changes. However, on a system that frequently executes queries such as UPDATE customer SET status='Current' WHERE id BETWEEN 10000 and 20000, row-based replication produces unnecessarily large update logs and generates a lot of unnecessary network traffic between the master and the slave. It requires a lot of awareness of the internal physical format of the record, and still has to deal with the schema modifications. In some situations the performance overhead associated with the increased I/O could become unacceptable.

MySQL initially began with statement-based replication. Up to version 5.0, the developers managed to deal with the drawbacks of this approach. Creative techniques were invented to properly replicate the execution context in difficult situations. However, with the introduction of stored procedures it became impossible to keep up. A stored procedure has the ability to branch on a number of conditions and in a number of different ways. MySQL replication developers addressed the problem by adding an option to replicate row by row, starting in version 5.1.5.

As of version 5.1.8, MySQL can take advantage of three *replication modes*: row, statement, and mixed. The mode is controlled by the configuration variable binlog_ format. In *row mode*, the replication is physical whenever it can be: when actual rows are updated, the entire updated row is written to the binary log. However, when a new table is created, dropped, or altered, the actual SQL statement is recorded.

In *statement mode*, the replication works the same as it did in the earlier versions: SQL statements are logged for every update. In *mixed mode*, the master decides on a per-query basis which logging to use, statement-based or row-based.

Two-Threaded Slave

The original implementation of the slave (version 3.23) used only one thread, which was responsible for reading the binary log feed from the master and applying it to the slave data. This approach was fine for reliable masters and slaves that did not lag too far behind. However, there were situations in which this was not adequate. Suppose the slave somehow ends up lagging a day behind a master, while the master somehow becomes completely unusable. This would result in the loss of a day's worth of data.

At the suggestion of Jeremy Zawodny from Yahoo!, the slave code was rewritten in version 4.0 to use two threads. The I/O thread is responsible for reading the binary log feed from the master and storing it in temporary relay logs. The SQL thread then reads the relay logs and applies the updates to the slave data.

To a great extent, this eliminated the risk of losing large amounts of data when the slave lags behind and the master becomes unusable. The majority of the time, the reason the slave lags behind is not in the I/O but in the slow execution of the updates. For example, slaves are often used to perform the reads that are not time-critical so that the master can be relieved. Thus, a slave may experience a spike in the load, which will delay the application of the updates arriving from the master.

Another possibility is that an update query is encountered in the binary log feed that takes a long time to execute—let's say three hours. Assuming the master and the slave are equally capable hardware-wise and are equally loaded, we can have the following scenario. The master executes a three-hour update, and it is written to the binary log once it is completed. Then the slave reads that update and starts executing it. In the meantime, the master had three hours to perform possibly a very large number of updates. By the time the slave is done with the long update query, it is three hours' worth of updates behind the master.

In both scenarios, the two-threaded slave architecture permits the additional updates to be transferred from the master in the binary log feed while the slave is applying the long three-hour update. If the master happens to become unusable beyond repair during that window, the update feed in the relay logs will contain a very recent update. It is still possible to miss a couple of updates prior to the crash due to the network delays, but it is much better than losing several hours of data.

Multi-Master

MySQL replication was not originally written with multi-master support in mind. A slave is natively capable of replicating only one master. A fairly simple patch can be created to allow one slave to collect updates from multiple masters without conflict resolution. This was done at one time, but for a number of reasons did not make it into the main branch of the source tree. A more complex patch to allow some conflict resolution was planned at one point, but for a number of reasons did not make it to development. It may still be implemented in the near future.

In the mean time, there exists a very popular configuration that in essence serves as a multi-master. Two servers are bound in a *mutual master-slave relationship*. Specifically, server A is configured with the binlog enabled and as a slave of server B, while server B has its binlog also enabled and acts as a slave of server A. Thus it becomes possible to write to either of the servers and have the updates appear on both. This configuration, however, will maintain a consistent data snapshot as long the stream of updates is guaranteed to produce the same results regardless of their order, or as long as the updates are serialized. Consider the following example:

```
Server A executes: UPDATE customer SET balance = 50 WHERE id = 9
Server B executes: UPDATE customer SET balance = 100 WHERE id = 9
```

It is possible that server B will get the update event from server A before server B executes its update. In that case, server B will end up with the balance set to 100 for id 9. However, it is also possible that server B will take a while to get the update from server A, and will execute its update first. In that case, server B ends up with the balance of 50 instead of 100. The logic of the application would anticipate it to be 100 since that is the query that was executed last.

However, if all updates are order-independent, then the mutual master-slave relationship configuration will produce consistent results.

It is also possible to use this configuration for a hot failover. The application always writes to one selected server. It that server goes down, the application switches to the other server. When the original server comes back up, it will catch up automatically (barring a drastic crash with the loss of data), and can serve as a standby.

SQL Commands to Help Understand Replication

A good way to explore and understand how MySQL replication works is to look at the output of some replication monitoring commands. Let us first configure one server as a master by enabling the `log-bin` option and setting a server ID with the `server-id` option to some unique number, e.g., the last byte of the IP address. Then we run:

```
SHOW MASTER STATUS\G
```

in the command-line client. We use the \G option to enable vertical display of columns, which makes the output more readable. The command produces an output similar to this:

```
*************************** 1. row ***************************
            File: laforge-bin.011
        Position: 566920603
    Binlog_do_db:
Binlog_ignore_db:
```

The `File` field is the name of the current binary log to which the master is writing. The `Position` field shows the offset in the current binary log where the next event is going to be written, or in other words, the size of the current binary log.

The `Binlog_do_db` and `Binlog_ignore_db` fields show the values of the corresponding options in the configuration of the master. The master can be instructed to either log updates that were done with only certain default databases selected (`Binlog_do_db`, the inclusive rule), or to exclude all of the updates that were done in a specified database list (`Binlog_ignore_db`, the exclusive rule). Note that those rules apply to the default database of the thread (selected via the USE command, or a call to `mysql_select_db( )` in the client API), rather than the actual database where the update occurred.

The combination of the `File` and the `Position` fields is sometimes referred to as the *replication coordinates*. The replication coordinates allow a slave to tell the master where to start the binary log feed when the slave connects to the master. They also make it possible to track the progress of a slave as it applies the updates, and can be used to synchronize the master and the slave.

Now let us configure a slave. First, create a replication user on the master:

```
GRANT REPLICATION SLAVE ON *.* TO 'rpl_user@slave-host' IDENTIFIED BY 'rpl_pass';
```

In this example, *slave-host* should be replaced with the host name or the IP address of the slave.

Then we configure the slave. We choose a unique server ID (the last byte of the IP address works well), load the current dataset from the master, and instruct the slave of the location of the master with the following command:

```
CHANGE MASTER TO MASTER_HOST='master-host', MASTER_USER='rpl_user',
MASTER_PASSWORD='rpl_pass';
```

master-host should be replaced with the host name or the IP address of the master.

Then the slave threads can be started:

```
START SLAVE;
```

Next run:

```
SHOW SLAVE STATUS\G
```

If we did not encounter any problems, we will see an output similar to this:

```
        Slave_IO_State: Waiting for master to send event
            Master_Host: www1.internal
            Master_User: repl
            Master_Port: 3306
          Connect_Retry: 60
        Master_Log_File: www1-bin.107
    Read_Master_Log_Pos: 403398225
         Relay_Log_File: slave-relay-bin.000894
          Relay_Log_Pos: 92576794
  Relay_Master_Log_File: www1-bin.107
       Slave_IO_Running: Yes
      Slave_SQL_Running: Yes
        Replicate_Do_DB:
    Replicate_Ignore_DB:
     Replicate_Do_Table:
 Replicate_Ignore_Table:
Replicate_Wild_Do_Table:
Replicate_Wild_Ignore_Table:
             Last_Errno: 0
             Last_Error:
           Skip_Counter: 0
    Exec_Master_Log_Pos: 403398225
        Relay_Log_Space: 92576794
        Until_Condition: None
         Until_Log_File:
          Until_Log_Pos: 0
      Master_SSL_Allowed: No
      Master_SSL_CA_File:
      Master_SSL_CA_Path:
        Master_SSL_Cert:
      Master_SSL_Cipher:
         Master_SSL_Key:
  Seconds_Behind_Master: 0
```

Table 12-1 contains a brief explanation of each field.

Table 12-1. Output of SHOW SLAVE STATUS

Field name	Description
Slave_IO_State	Textual description of what the I/O thread on the slave is doing.
Master_User	The slave I/O thread connects to the master as this user.
Master_Port	The TCP/IP port on which the slave IO thread connects to the master.
Connect_Retry	If the slave IO thread loses the connection to the master, it will retry after the timeout specified by this parameter.

Table 12-1. Output of SHOW SLAVE STATUS (continued)

Field name	Description
Master_Log_File	The logfile name on the master corresponding to the event that the SQL thread is currently processing.
Read_Master_Log_Pos	The position in the log on the master that the I/O thread is currently on.
Relay_Log_File	The name of the relay log that the SQL thread is on.
Relay_Log_Pos	The position in the relay log that the SQL thread is on.
Relay_Master_Log_File	The logfile currently being written to by the I/O thread.
Slave_IO_Running	Shows whether the I/O thread is running.
Slave_SQL_Running	Shows whether the SQL thread is running.
Replicate_Do_DB	Shows which databases are replicated according to the replicate-do-db rules.
Replicate_Ignore_DB	Shows which databases are ignored according to the replicate-ignore-db rules.
Replicate_Do_Table	Shows which tables are replicated according to the replicate-do-table rules.
Replicate_Ignore_Table	Shows which tables are ignored according to the replicate-ignore-table rules.
Replicate_Wild_Do_Table	Shows which tables are replicated according to the replicate-wild-do-table rules.
Replicate_Wild_Ignore_Table	Shows which databases are ignored according to the replicate-wild-ignore-table rules.
Last_Errno	The error code of the last error that caused the replication to stop.
Last_Error	The text of the error message of the last error that caused the replication to stop.
Skip_Counter	The number of subsequent events that the SQL thread is going to skip. This is used mostly when replication breaks due to some problem or possibly an oversight on the part of the database administrator, and there is a query that needs to be skipped for the replication to continue as planned.
Exec_Master_Pos	The position in the master log corresponding to the current position of the SQL thread.
Relay_Log_Space	The amount of disk space (in bytes) occupied by the relay logs.
Until_Condition	Sometimes a slave can be instructed to replicate until a certain position in the master or relay log is reached. This parameter tells whether there is an UNTIL condition, and whether it is in the context of the master or the relay log.
Until_Log_File	The name of the logfile in the UNTIL condition.
Until_Log_Pos	The position in the logfile in the UNTIL condition.
Master_SSL_Allowed	Indicates whether the slave I/O thread should connect to the master via SSL.
Master_SSL_CA_File	Pathname to the certificate authority file the slave will use to connect to the master.
Master_SSL_CA_Path	Pathname to a directory containing trusted SSL CA certificates in *pem* format.

Table 12-1. Output of SHOW SLAVE STATUS (continued)

Field name	Description
Master_SSL_Cert	Pathname to the certificate file.
Master_SSL_Cipher	The cipher to be used in the SSL connection.
Master_SSL_Key	Pathname to the SSL key file.
Seconds_Behind_Master	Shows the difference in seconds between the current time and the master time-stamp of the last executed event, adjusting for a possible clock difference between the master and the slave if the SQL thread is behind the I/O thread. Otherwise, it will show 0, which may not always be accurate because the I/O thread may take some time to read an event from the master.

To an observant reader, the status variables in Table 12-1 tell a story about how replication works. For example, the Master_ connect parameters indicate that the slave connects to the master and acts as a regular MySQL client. The presence of the Connect_retry parameter explains that a slave is capable of dealing with disruptions in the connectivity. The Slave_IO_Running and Slave_SQL_Running parameters tell us about the two-threaded slave replication model. The Relay_ parameters explain how the slave stores data temporarily in relay logs. The SSL parameters tell us the I/O between the master and the slave can be encrypted via SSL. The Replicate_ options tell us about the ability of the slave to replicate selectively.

Binary Log Format

Learning some details of the binary log format can reveal a lot about the replication internals. The code that deals with the binary logging is found in *sql/log_event.h* and *sql/log_event.cc*.

The binary log starts with a 4-byte magic number, which is set in the following line of *sql/log_event.h*:

```
#define BINLOG_MAGIC        "\xfe\x62\x69\x6e"
```

The magic number is used by the code that reads the binary log for a quick sanity check to make sure a valid binary log is being used. It is also used by the Unix *file* utility, which identifies file types.

The magic number is followed by a sequence of event entries. All events have a common header with the fields listed in Table 12-2 in sequential order. The second field represents the type code of the event, and is explained in Table 12-3. All of the integers in the header are stored in the little-endian format (low byte first). The header is written out by Log_event::write_header( ) in *sql/log_event.cc*.

Table 12-2. Binary log event header

Size (bytes)	Description
4	Timestamp of the event. Number of seconds since the start of the year 1970 as returned by the *libc* call `time( )`.
1	The type code of the event. The values and the meaning of the code are explained in Table 12-3.
4	Server ID. Uniquely identifies the server among its replication peers. Mainly used for avoiding infinite update loops.
4	The length of the whole event, including the header, in bytes.
4	Offset of the event in the log in bytes.
2	Event flags. For details see *sql/log_event.h*; search for macros matching the pattern `LOG_EVENT_*_F`.

Table 12-3. Binary log event type codes

Numeric value	Name	Description
1	Start	Written at the start of the binary log in earlier versions of MySQL. Now replaced by the Format Description event.
2	Query	Contains a query that updated the master.
3	Stop	Written on server shutdown.
4	Rotate	Written when the logs are rotated.
5	Intvar	Contains the value of the auto-increment field to be used in the next query.
6	Load	Used in 3.23. Registers a `LOAD DATA INFILE` operation. In the newer version of MySQL, the `New Load` event is used instead.
7	Slave	Not used.
8	Create File	Tells the slave to create a file with the given ID for the purpose of replicating `LOAD DATA INFILE`.
9	Append Block	Tells the slave to append a block to the file specified by the ID. Used for replicating `LOAD DATA INFILE`.
10	Exec Load	Tells the slave to execute the `LOAD DATA INFILE` associated with the file ID.
11	Delete File	Delete the file created with Create File.
12	New Load	Records `LOAD DATA INFILE` in the newer format.
13	Rand	Records the information necessary to reseed the random-number generator used by the `RAND( )` function so that it will produce the same results on the slave as it did on the master.

14	User Var	Records the value stored in a user variable that was used in an update. This is necessary to replicate something like this:
		
		`SELECT (@n:=count(*)) FROM customers;`
		
		`UPDATE growth_history SET customer_count = @n WHERE ts = NOW( );`

Table 12-3. *Binary log event type codes (continued)*

Numeric value	Name	Description
15	Format Description	Starting in version 5.0.2 of MySQL, written as the first event in the binary log to specify which format version it is using.
16	XID	Logs the transaction ID of the transaction to be committed and serves as the commit mark in the two-phase commit protocol.
17	Begin Load Query	Combines Create File and Append Block into one event.
18	Execute Load Query	Works like the Query event, except the name of the file in LOAD DATA INFILE is first substituted with the name of the temporary file created earlier.
19	Table Map	Contains a mapping between database/table names and their numeric IDs. Used in row-based replication.
20	Write Rows	Contains a list of rows to write to a table. Used in row-based replication.
21	Update Rows	Contains a list of rows to update in a table. Used in row-based replication.
22	Delete Rows	Contains a list of rows to delete from a table. Used in row-based replication.

The header of an event is followed by the body. The structure of the body greatly varies by the event type.

Again, the study of the binlog format reveals a lot of hidden details and challenges associated with replication. Although the basic conceptual idea of a master-slave replication with the master keeping an update log and the slave re-executing it is nearly trivial, the devil is in the details, and the complexity of the binary log format and the variety of event types are a witness to it. How do we handle log rotation? How do we deal with the slave disconnecting, and reconnecting again? How do we handle auto-increment fields? How do we replicate timestamp-sensitive queries? How do we replicate LOAD DATA INFILE? How do we replicate an update that uses a random number? How do we avoid infinite replication loops when a master is doubling as a slave of another server in a complex replication topology, and it is possible for an update event originating on this server to come back to it through its slave?

Those interested in the specifics should refer to the source code in *sql/log_event.cc*. The body is written out via a call to Log_event::write_data_header() for the fixed-length event-type-specific info, followed by a call to Log_event::write_data_body() for the variable length event type specific info. Log_event is the base class for a family of classes responsible for each event. write_data_body() and write_data_header() are virtual methods that each class implements in its own way to handle the specifics of the event-type data storage. The names of the classes begin with the name of the event, and end with _log_event. Thus, if you would like to explore how the query events are stored, you should look at Query_log_event::write_data_header() and Query_log_event::write_data_body().

mysqlbinlog is a very helpful tool for analyzing and understanding the replication binary logs. It accepts the name of the log as an argument and dumps it out in the SQL format with some comments about the log details. For example:

```
$ mysqlbinlog /var/lib/mysql/www1-bin.001
```

produces output similar to this:

```
/*!40019 SET @@session.max_insert_delayed_threads=0*/;
/*!50003 SET @OLD_COMPLETION_TYPE=@@COMPLETION_TYPE,COMPLETION_TYPE=0*/;
# at 4
#060809 21:03:48 server id 1  end_log_pos 102
Start: binlog v 4, server v 5.1.11-beta-log created 060809 21:03:48 at startup
ROLLBACK;
# at 102
#060809 21:03:48 server id 1  end_log_pos 197   Query   thread_id=2
    exec_time=0    error_code=0
use test;
SET TIMESTAMP=1155179028;
SET @@session.foreign_key_checks=1,
@@session.sql_auto_is_null=1, @@session.unique_checks=1;
SET @@session.sql_mode=0;
/*!\C latin1 */;
SET @@session.character_set_client=8,
@@session.collation_connection=8,@@session.collation_server=8;
drop table if exists t1,t2,t3,t4;
# at 197
#060809 21:03:48 server id 1  end_log_pos 306   Query   thread_id=2
    exec_time=0    error_code=0
SET TIMESTAMP=1155179028;
create table t1(n int, m int) type=oreilly_csv;
# at 306
#060809 21:03:48 server id 1  end_log_pos 439
Query   thread_id=2    exec_time=0    error_code=0
SET TIMESTAMP=1155179028;
create table t2(name char(20), age int, comment text) type=oreilly_csv;
# at 439
#060809 21:03:48 server id 1  end_log_pos 548
   Query   thread_id=2    exec_time=0    error_code=0
SET TIMESTAMP=1155179028;
create table t3(s text,n int) type=oreilly_csv;
# at 548
#060809 21:03:48 server id 1  end_log_pos 660
   Query   thread_id=2    exec_time=0    error_code=0
SET TIMESTAMP=1155179028;
create table t4(s1 text,s2 text) type=oreilly_csv;
# at 660
#060809 21:03:48 server id 1  end_log_pos 755
Query   thread_id=2    exec_time=0    error_code=0
SET TIMESTAMP=1155179028;
drop table if exists t1,t2,t3,t4;
# at 755
#060809 21:03:48 server id 1  end_log_pos 774   Stop
# End of log file
ROLLBACK /* added by mysqlbinlog */;
/*!50003 SET COMPLETION_TYPE=@OLD_COMPLETION_TYPE*/;
```

Each event in the output starts with a comment line indicating its offset in the binary log. The next line, also a comment, shows the timestamp of the event, the server ID originating the event, the position of the next event, and the type of the event. Following that is a set of SQL queries that will produce the same change in the database on the slave as the original event produced on the master. It is possible to examine only portions of a binary log using the arguments *--start-position*, *--stop-position*, *--start-datetime*, and *--stop-datetime*.

Creating a Custom Replication Utility

Usually replication can be successfully managed via SQL commands alone. This is the recommended approach and should be used to its fullest extent whenever possible. Occasionally a situation arises when SQL commands alone are not enough. For example, you may want to replicate only a certain subset of events that are not easily defined with the standard replication table matching rules. Or perhaps you need to rewrite certain queries before replicating them. In this case, the open source nature of MySQL comes handy. There are two approaches.

The approach that yields the best performance and also provides a more robust solution when done right is to modify the loop in the code of the SQL thread in *sql/slave.cc* or somewhere down the calling hierarchy. That code is found in handle_slave_sql( ), which in turn calls exec_relay_log_event( ). However, this task is for a brave programmer. One simple mistake can not only break replication, but crash the entire slave server. Keeping up with the new releases of MySQL may become a hassle. And, overall, a deeper understanding of MySQL source code is required to accomplish the task.

The simpler approach is to create a custom client using the source of *mysqlbinlog* (found in *client/mysqlbinlog.cc*) as a base, and add a few custom features as necessary. *mysqlbinlog* can already read a remote log. One can modify the output loop found in *dump_remote_log_entries()* as needed to execute custom event filtering.

On the positive side, this approach requires less knowledge of MySQL source code and is less intrusive. On the negative side, you do not get to tap into the proven robustness of the native slave event management and processing code, and a fair amount of unnecessary I/O will happen due to the presence of a mediator.

Index

Numbers

3-byte field, compressed packets, 63

A

Abstracted Storage Engine Interface, 15
Abstracted Storage Engine Module, 6
Access Control Module, 6, 11
API calls, utility calls, 54–57
ARCHIVE storage engine, 206
authenticating handshake, 64–66
authentication, protocol security, 66
autoconf, 22
automake, 22

B

BerkeleyDB, table lock manager and, 165
big-tables configuration variable, 88
binary log (binlog), 113
binary log format, replication and, 223–227
binlog (see binary log)
bison, 22
bit masks, protocol capabilities, 67
BitKeeper, 19–22
   MySQL versions, 21
   patches, 40
   repository
      cloning, 21
      updates, 39
   tree
      BUILD directory, 24
      building MySQL, 24, 25

breakpoints, debuggers, 34
B-tree keys, 198
BUILD directory, BitKeeper tree, 24
building MySQL
   from BitKeeper tree, 24
   from source distribution, 25

C

C library, threads, 113
caches
   double caching, 203
   query, 222
   query cache, 213
   table, 120
   thread, 112
classes
   Field, 51–53
   handler, 119, 120–134
   THD, 41–45
Client/Server Protocol API, 17
Client/Server Protocol Module, 7
clustered indexes, 202
coding guidelines
   ease of integration, 39
   performance, 38
   portability, 38
   stability, 37
   style, 39
Command Dispatcher, 5, 12
command packets, 69–73
command-line
   arguments, processing, 82
   configuration variables, 81–83

We'd like to hear your suggestions for improving our indexes. Send email to *index@oreilly.com*.

F

FEDERATED storage engine, 207
Field class, 51–53
forked processes
    advantages, 108
    disadvantages, 109
ft_stopword_file configuration variable, 91
full table scan, 123
full-text keys, 199
functions, utility, 54–57

G

gcc, 22
gdb, 30
    common commands, 32
global variables, 59–61
GNU make, 22
Grammar Rules Module, 167, 169
greedy search, 173

H

handler class, 119, 120–134
handler subclass implementation, 209
handler::external_lock( ) method, 209
handler::start_stmt( ) method, 209
handlerton, 134–136
    defining, 212
    transactions and, 212
handshake (see authenticating handshake)
headers, 24
    definitions, 24
history of MySQL, 1

I

index files, 197
indexes (see keys)
init-file configuration variable, 95
Initialization Module, 5
in-memory tables, 99
InnoDB, 202
    buffers, 92
    table lock manager and, 165
InnoDB locking, 165
innodb_buffer_pool_size configuration
        variable, 92
innodb_file_per_table configuration
        variable, 93
innodb_flush_log_at_trx_commit
        configuration variable, 92

innodb_lock_wait_timeout configuration
        variable, 94
installation to system directory, 26
intention locks, 166

J

joins, 172
    optimizer, 173–178
    subsets, 173

K

key_buffer_size configuration variable, 96
keys
    delay-key-write configuration variable, 91
    full-text, 199
    MyISAM, 198
    represented in fields (columns), 51
    represented in tables, 48
    R-tree, 201
    spatial, 200

L

language configuration variable, 96
lexical scanner, 167, 168
libtool, 22
locks
    deadlocks, 94, 166
    InnoDB locking, 165
    intention locks, 166
    mutexes, 114
    read locks, 163
    read-write, 116
    record locking, 166
    row-level, 90, 161
    table-level, 161
    write locks, 164
log configuration variable, 97
log-bin configuration variable, 97
Logging Module, 7, 16
log-isam configuration variable, 98
logs
    InnoDB transaction, 92
    MyISAM, 98
    redo, 203
    slow query, 98
    undo, 203
log-slow-queries configuration variable, 98
Low-Level Network I/O API, 18
Low-Level Network I/O module, 7

M

m4, 22
macros, preprocessor, 57, 58
make files, generating, 24
max_allowed_packet configuration
        variable, 99
max_connections configuration variable, 99
max_heap_table_size configuration
        variable, 99
max_join_size configuration variable, 100
max_sort_length configuration variable, 100
MEMORY storage engine, 204
memory, threads and, 107
MERGE storage engine, 205
methods
    handler::external_lock( ), 209
    handler::start_stmt( ), 209
modules
    Abstracted Storage Engine Interface, 15
    Access Control Module, 11
    Client/Server Protocol API, 17
    Command Dispatcher, 12
    Connection Manager, 9
    Connection Thread, 10
    Core API, 18
    core modules, 4
        interaction, 5
    definition, 4
    Logging Module, 16
    Low-Level Network I/O API, 18
    Optimizer, 12
    Parser, 11
    QueryCache Module, 12
    Replication Master Module, 16
    Replication Slave Module, 17
    Server Initialization Module, 9
    Status Reporting Module, 14
    Storage Engine Implementations, 15
    Table Handler, 15
    Table Maintenance Module, 14
    Table Manager, 13
    Table Modification Modules, 13
    Thread Manager, 10
    User Authentication Module, 10
multi-master support, replication, 219
mutexes, 114
    variables, 114

MyISAM, 165
    architecture, 195
    B-tree keys
        full-text, 199
        spatial keys, 200
    data files, 196
    index files, 197
    key types, 198
        B-tree keys, 198
    storage engine, 195
myisam-recover configuration variable, 100
MySQL
    1.0 release, 2
    3.22, 2
    4.0, 3
    5.0, 3
    5.1, 3
    building, readiness, 23
    history of, 1
MySQL AB, 2
MySQL/InnoDB, 3

N

NDB storage engine, 205
    table lock manager and, 165
NET class, 46–48
noncompressed packets, 62

O

OK packets, 75
optimizer, 12, 170
    algorithm, 172
    core classes, 188
    joins, 174
    query plan, 174–186
    range optimizer, 186
    structures, 188
    subquery optimization, 187
options (see configuration variables)

P

packets
    command packets, 69–73
    compressed, 62
        fields, 63
        ZLIB, 63
    data packets, 62

end-of-data-stream packets, 62
EOF packets, 77
error message, 62
error packets, 76
NET, 46
noncompressed, 62
OK packets, 75
result set packets, 77
server response, 62
success report packets, 62
parse tree, 169
    SELECT, 191
Parser, 11
    lexical scanner, 167
passwords
    hackers and, 66
    protocol security and, 66
patches, BitKeeper, 40
portability, 38
preemption, threads, 118
preprocessor macros, 57, 58
protocol packets, OS layer and, 63, 64
protocols
    authentication, 66
    capabilities bitmask, 67

Q

queries
    debuggers, 29
    subquery optimization, 187
query cache, 213
Query Cache Module, 12
query plan, optimizer, 174–186
query_cache_type configuration
        variable, 101

R

range optimizer, 186, 187
read locks, 163
read_buffer_size configuration variable, 101
read-write locks, 116
record locking, 166
redo log, InnoDB, 203
relay_log configuration variable, 102
replication
    binary log, 97, 214
    binary log format, 223–227
    coordinates, 220

custom utility, 227
    multi-master support, 219
    overview, 216
    row-based, 217
    server ID, 103
    SQL commands, 220–223
    statement-based, 217
    threads, 216
    two-threaded slaves, 218
replication coordinates, 220
Replication Master Module, 16
Replication Slave Module, 7, 17
repository, BitKeeper, 21
request handling, implementation, 109–113
result set packets, 77
row-based replication, 217
row-level locks, 90, 161
R-tree keys, 201

S

scan, full table, 123
searches
    debuggers, 33
    source code, 33
security, authentication, 66
SELECT parse tree, 191
Server Initialization Module, 9
server response packets, 62
server responses
    data fields, 74–75
    EOF packets, 77
    error packets, 76
    OK packets, 75
    result set packets, 77
server-id configuration variable, 103
singleton, 212
skip-grant-tables configuration variable, 103
skip-stack-trace configuration variable, 104
slave-skip-errors configuration variable, 104
slow query log, 98
sort_buffer_size configuration variable, 105
source code
    directory layout, 27
    modifying, 36
    searching, 33
source distribution, building MySQL
        from, 25
spatial keys, 200

6875

About the Author

Sasha Pachev graduated from Brigham Young University in 1998 with a degree in Computer Science. He worked on the MySQL development team from 2000–2002 and was the original developer of replication in MySQL. In 2003, he wrote his first book, *MySQL Enterprise Solutions* (Wiley). He currently lives in Provo, Utah, with his wife, Sarah, and his five children, and works as an independent consultant with an emphasis on MySQL.

In addition to his great interest in computers, Sasha is equally passionate about distance running. He has won a number of marathons, has a personal best time of 2:24:47, and is attempting to qualify for the U.S. Olympic Trials. He feels it is important to help other runners reach their potential, and he operates a web site dedicated to that purpose, FastRunningBlog.com.

Colophon

The animal on the cover of *Understanding MySQL Internals* is a banded broadbill (*Eurylaimus javanicus*). Broadbills are a family of small- to medium-size passerine (perching) birds marked by their bright colors and a whitish dorsal patch. They have large heads, rounded wings, and short to long tails. Their name originates from their large, flattened, hooked bill (often covered by a short crest), which they use to snap up insects in a kingfisher-like fashion. They also feed on fruit, seeds, and small vertebrates.

Broadbills live in the subcanopies of tropical forests: 11 species can be found in southeast Asia, the Philippines, Borneo, and Sumatra; and 4 others are native to central African rainforests. Because of their dense habitats, they are often incredibly difficult to observe despite their bright coloring. Broadbills build elaborate, pear-shaped nests, which are suspended on tree limbs over quiet forest backwaters and streams. Biologists believe this may be an adaptive behavior to deter mammalian and reptilian predators. Adult broadbills will also sometimes feign injury to draw predators away from their nests.

Broadbills are gregarious creatures and are often found in small feeding flocks. They communicate using a variety of mating and territorial displays. Male green broadbills, for instance, have a spinning display, while other species of broadbills may employ head bobbing, wing flapping, and feather fluffing. Some have display flights in which their primary wing feathers "buzz" during times of courtship or territorial defense. The sound can be heard from as far as 60 meters away. In addition, broadbills have a variety of calls—often described as a cacophony of whistles, rattles, or screams—which they use during courtship rituals, as an alarm signal, and for contact between mates.

The cover image is from Wood's *Animate Creation*. The cover font is Adobe ITC Garamond. The text font is Linotype Birka; the heading font is Adobe Myriad Condensed; and the code font is LucasFont's TheSans Mono Condensed.

Better than e-books

Buy *Understanding MySQL Internals* and access
the digital edition FREE on Safari for 45 days.

Go to www.oreilly.com/go/safarienabled
and type in coupon code FSKGZCB

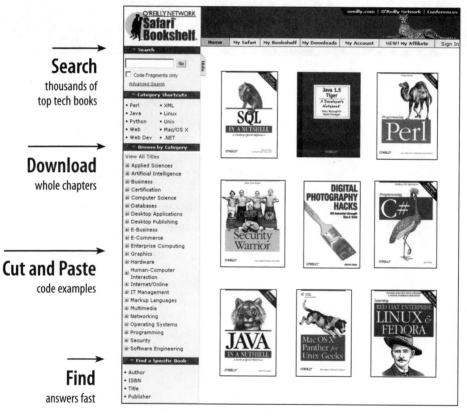

Search
thousands of
top tech books

Download
whole chapters

Cut and Paste
code examples

Find
answers fast

Search Safari! The premier electronic reference
library for programmers and IT professionals.